Anonymus

South-Sea bubbles

Anonymus

South-Sea bubbles

ISBN/EAN: 9783741166365

Manufactured in Europe, USA, Canada, Australia, Japa

Cover: Foto ©Andreas Hilbeck / pixelio.de

Manufactured and distributed by brebook publishing software (www.brebook.com)

Anonymus

South-Sea bubbles

SOUTH-SEA BUBBLES.

BY THE EARL AND THE

DOCTOR.

NEW YORK:
D. APPLETON AND COMPANY,
549 & 551 BROADWAY.
1872.

PREFACE.

This little work was composed originally of different sketches taken from my logs and put into shape, the aforesaid logs having been saved in a moist and pithy state from the wreck; they were then put into a rough kind of order, to serve as a memorial of the cruise; but after our arrival home we were persuaded to publish them.

These excuses are tendered to any readers who may be driven into a mild exasperation at the occasional confusion of persons, the incongruous jumps from the highest subjects to the most solemn philosophy, or any other such slight characteristics, which make it, as Mark Twain said of his map of Paris, quite unlike any thing of the kind that was ever seen.

THE EARL.

CONTENTS.

Chap. I.—Tahiti,	7
II.—Eimeo, or Morea,	51
III.—Huahine,	64
IV.—Raiatea and Tara,	92
V.—Bora-Bora,	119
VI.—Tubai Tropical Birds and the Labor Question,	133
VII.—Rarotonga,	149
VIII.—Samoa,	184
IX.—Shipwreck,	219
X.—Missionaries,	250
Note,	295

SOUTH-SEA BUBBLES.

CHAPTER I.

TAHITI.

"HAVE you never had a bad bilious fever?" says Tom Cringle; "then you have never known what it is to be in heaven or in the other place." I have had a bad fever, and can testify to the truth of the remark. Physical, and, worse still, mental agonies of indescribable horror, followed by visions of perfect peace, happiness, and beauty. There are certain places and scenes that are always blended in my mind with those glorious, strange, delirious dreams, filling me with a luxurious feeling of poetry and pleasure; yet utterly indescribable, because half their charm lies in the remembrance of the happiness they brought me. And so it is that, urged by my fellow-laborer in this work, I sit down with a certain reluctance to write what I fear will be but a commonplace and colorless description of a place and time that will live forever in my thoughts as some splendid dream of beauty and pleasure.

Such things will seldom stand the magic test of pen and ink, even when they are used by a master of the art of writing. I—and I believe I am not the only sinner in the world—sneakingly shirk descriptions of beautiful scenery in novels, except those in "Westward Ho!" "Geoffry Hamlyn," and, above all, "Tom Cringle's Log." What glorious masterpieces of word-painting they are, showing new beauties each time they are read—free and unconstrained, yet quaint and fanciful, filled with little points and touches seemingly minute and almost unnecessary in themselves, which, however, constitute the charm and perfection of the picture!

But this is above my hand. All I can do is to scribble down my dreams as they float before my brain, and please myself if not my readers.

I can never forget the scene that burst upon my astonished and half-opened eyes as I turned out of bed one morning and found myself entering the port of Papiete. Great mountains, of every shade of blue, pink, gray, and purple, torn and broken into every conceivable fantastic shape, with deep, dark, mysterious gorges, showing almost black by contrast with the surrounding brightness; precipitous peaks and pinnacles rising one above the other like giant sentinels, until they were lost in the heavy masses of cloud they had impaled; while below, stretching from the base of the mountains to the shore, a forest of tropical trees, with the huts and houses of the town peeping out between them.

The finest islands of the West Indies idealized, with a dash of Ceylon, is all I can compare it to. And

the natives! How well they match the scene! The
women, with their voluptuous figures, their unique,
free, graceful walk, their night-gowns (for their dress is
nothing but a long chemise, white, pale, green, red, or
red and white, according to the taste of the wearer,
which is invariably good) floating loosely about in a
cool, refreshing manner—their luxuriant black tresses,
crowned with a gracefully-plaited araroot chaplet, and
further ornamented by a great flowing bunch of white
"reva-reva"—their delicious perfume of cocoa-nut oil
(it is worth going to Tahiti for the smell alone), and,
above all, their smiling, handsome faces, and singing,
bubbling voices, full of soft cadences—all this set off by
the broken, scattered rays of green light shining through
the shady avenues. Oh, that I were the artist that could
paint it! What pleasant places those avenues are for a
stroll in the evening, when the heat of the sun is beginning to die away! To meet the great, strapping,
pleasant-looking men, in their clean white shirts and
party-colored waist-cloths, each greeting you, especially
if you are English, with a ready smile and a hearty
"Ya rana!" which means all kinds of salutations and
blessings; sometimes, even, if they like the look of
you, stopping to shake hands, with no earthly object
but kindly good-fellowship. I have seen even small
pickaninnies stop in their infantine gambols, and tod-
dling up with their little faces puckered into dimples,
and their little puds held up to reach your fingers, pipe
up a shrill "How do you do?" And as for the young
ladies! the most bashful and coy will never pass you
without a greeting, a glance of the eyes, and a slight
gathering in of her dress with her elbows to exhibit

her buxom figure to full perfection. Or else, perhaps, she will come up coquettishly, and ask you for the loan of your cigar, take a few puffs at it, and hand it back again gracefully to the rather astonished owner; and then, with a parting compliment, which you most likely don't understand, let you go your way in peace —or *not!* I suppose it is a fault on the right side, but they are a trifle too amiable sometimes. The conduct of Mrs. Potiphar would scarcely have excited a passing comment if she had been lucky enough to have lived in Tahiti.

The streets of Papiete, at night, are very pleasant and merry. The first night we arrived, the doctor and I went for a stroll; and, following the run of the crowd, soon found ourselves in the principal grog-shop street. There all was reckless jollity and good-nature. Gangs of French sailors careering wildly to and fro, singing part-songs at the top of their voices, in capital time and tune, all the natives within hearing joining in; native men and girls sitting about the door-steps of the shops, or strolling up and down together, some romping, some spooney. By-the-by, the proper way to walk with your lady-love in Tahiti is as follows: You put your arm round her neck, and she hers round your waist, and hangs on your breast in a limply affectionate manner. It is as much *selon les règles* as walking arm-in-arm, and is much prettier to look at. But the man should be tall, for to see a stumpy little French sailor clawed in this way by the big brown object of his affections is a thought ludicrous.

At last we came to a place where two streets crossed each other. Each corner-house was a grog-shop, where a lot of jolly Frenchmen were singing in chorus, a crowd of natives standing round and joining. Another knot was collected round the doctor, who was holding forth about European politics (the war between France and Prussia had just broken out) to a learned native, who translated all he said to the eager by-standers, while I was being addressed by a brown lady in her native language, which edified me exceedingly. Behind each bar the ideal French barman presided, with the sleeves of his dingy white shirt rolled up, brawny, bull-necked, black-haired, and shaven. Here and there an unmistakable Yankee skipper might be seen among the mob, with an occasional English Jack, or Scotch storekeeper. The shifting crowd grew larger, and the singing noisier, till on a sudden a native policeman appeared as if from the clouds, and begged, prayed, entreated, commanded the crowd to disperse. Some one twitched his stick out of his hand, which caused a roar of laughter and a fresh torrent of eloquence from the brown bobby, which lasted till the mob good-humoredly did as they were told. Handcuffs have not yet been introduced into Tahiti, pieces of string being used as substitutes by the native constabulary when duty calls upon them to arrest a criminal or a disorderly person. If the offender is a person of active muscles and independent spirit, the capture becomes a very exciting and amusing spectacle for the by-standers.

The lighted shops and stores surrounded by the beautiful trees, the gayly-dressed girls, the rollicking sailors, the pleasant smell, the perfect cleanliness, the universal mirth, civility, and good-nature of every one, the utter absence of quarrelling, jostling, or rudeness, made a very novel, picturesque, and pleasing nightscene.

"Society-Islandism" is very catching. In an incredibly short time you feel a kind of early Christian brotherly love coming over you, a delicious indolence, a refined gentleness of manner, and a blunting of the edge of your moral ideas. Tolerably virtuous and proper as I was, I always had a secret consciousness that I should not be the least surprised to find myself lolling about the groves after the manner of the natives, making lazy love, and utterly regardless of past or future. Things that would strike you anywhere else as wrong and degrading, seem somehow only natural and beautiful in those lovely islands.

I feel that this aimless, pointless dreaminess, is pervading the chapter I am writing, making it utterly dreary to an incident-and-information-loving European reader. But if any such kind critic should come to me, and in the barbarous manner and language of the North inform me that my article was intolerably prosy and stupid, I should smile blandly, and say: "My dear fellow, don't be so horribly abrupt and angular! As many poets have arranged their rhythm to suit and suggest the actions they were writing about, so I have made the style of my composition a reflection of the life and the people I was describing. It is just the sort of thing, too, to read in that country. Nothing startling, to make you fix your attention exclusively on its pages; no deep thoughts or curious information to worry your brains with. Just the thing to dream over as you are sucking your cocoa-nut under the palm-trees; just the thing to go to sleep over at the end of every two sentences, while a native or half-caste young lady watches by your side with a fly-whisk or a fan to keep those abominable insects from settling on the tip of your nose.

By-the-way, those brutal flies are the only things that refuse to be Society-Islandized. Under the most softening influences they still retain the tiresome energy and vulgar conceited obtrusiveness natural to their race. They are the Scotchmen among insects.

If you are wearied with the busy—I mean lazy—hum of men, you go out in a canoe on to the great coral-reef that forms the harbor, and, dabbling your hands and feet in the cool water, gaze dreamily down at the gorgeous sights beneath you: the beautiful coral, with its mysterious caves and fissures, from which you almost expect to see real water-babies appear; coral, some of it like great crimson fans woven from the most delicate twigs—some of a beautiful mauve or purple—some like miniature models of old gnarled trees—some like great round mounds of snow-white ivory, chased and carved with a superhuman delicacy—some like leaves and budding flowers—while all about are scattered magnificent holothuria and great red and yellow starfish, that look as if they were made of leather, with horn buttons stuck all along their feelers for ornament;[1] and echini, with their dense profusion of long brown spikes, covering them so completely as to make an unlearned person like myself wonder how they can get at their food or mix in society. Still

[1] This is the "slate-pencil fish," a species overlooked by Mr. Chas. Reade.

more beautiful when they are dead and their spikes are gone, and nothing remains but their round white skeletons, splendidly embossed in long lines with purple-and-pink knobs. Fish of every shape and color swimming lazily in and out of the black-looking caves and fissures, or coasting round under the overhanging edges of the coral precipices. Some of the finest cobalt blue, some golden, some pink, some more like beautiful orange and purple butterflies than natives of the sea, with long white rat's-tails, swimming or floating frontways, sternways, sideways, with apparently equal ease and partiality. Some variegated like harlequins; many, not with their hues more or less blending into each other where they meet, like Christian fishes, but mathematically divided by regular distinct lines, as if they had paid for their colors, and had them laid on by the square inch.

Oh, a coral-reef is the thing to dream over! So gloriously beautiful, so wondrously fantastic, so treacherously dangerous, and so damnable to walk upon. In the first ten minutes your shoes are cut to pieces; then you step unexpectedly into a deep hole, and bark your shins against its edges. On getting clear of this, you most likely tread upon an echinus,[1] and with a howl of agony make a wild attempt to stand upon one leg and pick the spikes out of your injured foot, whereon you lose your balance and sit down violently upon some of his (the echinus's) relations. The only thing then to be done is to lie quietly where you are, like a

---

[1] The species of echinus alluded to here can *thrust* its spines into the skin, of its own proper motion. I have watched them most carefully, and have seen them do it.

stranded whale, swearing feebly, until some kind companion makes his appearance, and extricates the spines from the injured parts with his jack-knife.

And what glorious places for boating expeditions those Society Islands are! Threading your way between the patches, inside the outer reef, you can sail along the coast for miles in smooth water and beautiful scenery, with one picturesque bay after another to be explored. And though you be but a common sailor, with empty pockets, everywhere you are certain of a hearty welcome from everybody and every thing, including those confounded mosquitoes. One man comes out to steer you by signs toward the best landing-place; another, as soon as your boat sticks, trots out to her, and without more ado directs you to jump on his back, and carries you ashore, as if you were but a fly on his gigantic shoulders; and on the beach you are received by the various members of the family, who set to work to entertain you, and supply your necessities as best they can. When you have had a short palaver, and have declined with some difficulty the various hospitable offers that have been pressed upon you, you return to your boat, and find in her a quantity of cocoa-nuts, bananas, bread-fruit, and similar delicacies; indeed, in one instance, I remember finding the paterfamilias in the act of lugging the last of his fowls, a tough-looking old cock, down to the beach by a string that was fast to his leg; I laughingly declined the present, at which he seemed a little hurt.

And then, when all is ready for a start home, and even the youngest baby has been held up to lisp out a parting " Ya rana," and you have shaken hands with all the village, till you are tired, some stately matron cries out, "John! just launch a canoe, and pilot the gentleman out to the mouth of the bay, in case he should stick anywhere," or words to that effect, which John accordingly does, and you start away home; the last thing you see being a kindly smile, and the last thing you hear a cheerful "God bless you!"

It may be a confession of weakness, but I must own I like this kind of thing. I like being petted and made much of, as long as I am sure that there is no affectation, humbug, or mercenary feeling about it. "Bah!" cries the cynic, "their kiss-me-cum-cuddle-me blarney is only skin-deep, they have made a prince of Jack to-day, and will do the same with Bill to-morrow." "Well, my friend," say I, "your feelings may last a little longer than theirs, but are they immutable and everlasting? and at any rate my brown friends deserve admiration for their natural unsophisticated impulse toward kindness, affection, and unselfishness, short-lived though it may be, for it is a rare enough thing in this world, especially where many people of your sort are to be found."

When the nights are calm and dark, away go the natives to spear fish by torch-light. They use several kinds of weapons, according to the size of the prey they are hunting, but the ordinary spear is like a small metal broom, made of a lot of iron rods diverging outward from the staff on which they are lashed, between which the little fish become jammed without being much injured. Silently your canoe glides over the coral-reef through the clear, shallow water, and you stand up with the torch in one hand and the spear in the other, all ready for action. A blaze of light shines close to you, and suddenly the figure of the bowman in some other craft becomes revealed like some splendid bronze statue, the torch lifted on high, the form bent slightly forward, the eyes intently fixed on the surface of the water, and the right arm raised to strike, while behind you dimly distinguish the black, crouching figure of his comrade, noiselessly and almost without motion propelling and steering the long, narrow pirogue. Whish! Down drops the end of the torch— he's got one! So he has, sure enough, for I hear the tap, tap of his spear against the side of the boat, and the squatter of the fish as he drops into the bottom of it. I see one! and make a desperate lunge, whereby I lose my balance and topple over, luckily not overboard, dropping my spear into the water, on one side, and the rather heavy reed-torch on the other, which leaves us in utter darkness, in which I hear, not weeping and gnashing of teeth, but a most unmistakable gurgling and chuckling from my native companion, usually the most polite and dignified of mortals.

We arrived in Tahiti just in time to celebrate the feast of St. Napoleon. The shore was thickly lined with gigs and whale-boats that had brought in the natives from all parts of the country, to say nothing of the neighboring islands. The festivities were about to commence in full swing. Regattas, horse-races, reviews, court processions, and hymns! ye powers! to be sung for prizes by the different districts. Hymns at that time were associated in my mind with uncomfortable pews, swell bonnets, etc., and I wondered whether the judge would be low church or dissenting, and give the prize to the choirs who sung slowest and dolefulest, or whether he would be high church, and reward those who could rattle out "Adeste fideles" in the most triumphant style. Little did I know what a South-Sea hymn, or "himene," was like. Little did I know that all styles of music, from the most comic to the most sacred, came under the same title, and that even dances, more graceful than moral, were sanctified by the sacred name of hymns.

August 16th.—Bang! bang! Twenty-four guns at sunrise in honor of the day, rousing me just as I had dropped into a blissful slumber in the cool of the morning. I repent it deeply, but I fear that the expression that rose to my lips was more forcible than choice. However, I dozed off till about seven A. M., when I was awoke again by some one coming on board. Such was my pertinacity that I managed to get to sleep again till eight o'clock, when another dose of twenty-four guns, not to mention those of the frigate, shook the vessel through and through, and compelled me to get up. At mid-day more guns, as before.

After luncheon came the regatta, gig, whale-boat, and canoe races, the best of all being a great double-canoe-race, some fifty men or so in each craft. A glorious sight it was; all the way there was not five feet advantage to either, and they kept so close side by side that a man could have jumped from one to the other. Every paddle caught the water at once with the regularity of clock-work, making the canoe lift and spring forward at each stroke like the rush of some great sea-serpent, while in the extreme nose stood, or rather danced, the chief or captain, yelling, swearing, stamping, and giving the time to the performers; at one moment whirling his long paddle over his head, and looking very much inclined to sweep the opposition leader in the rival canoe into the briny deep by a dexterous stroke, at the next making furious scoops at the water to add an inch or two to the speed of his vessel. Neck and neck they ran all the course, and when at last they passed the Astrée that was acting as flagship, not a foot could have divided them. When it was all over, and the cheering had subsided, they lay under the stern gallery of the frigate, where old Queen Pomare and her maids of honor were watching the fun, and beat time with their paddles against the sides of the canoes to the music of the band, producing a wonderful effect.

In the evening we went off to hear the rehearsal of the "himenes," or native singing, which was to take place in the gardens of the governor's palace, where, at the same time, a swell ball à l'Européen was going on. Edging our way through the laughing, romping crowd outside, the doctor and I succeeded in getting in; but, going out again to fetch Mitchell and the skipper, we found ourselves in a fix, as the temper of the bullet-headed little French sentinel had completely given way under the continued fire of banter he had been compelled to receive, without a chance of retaliation, from the native young ladies, and he doggedly refused to let us reënter the gates. So here we were stuck, feeling very much like the foolish virgins in the parable, or four male peris gazing into paradise; to all the doctor's logic and honeyed words, the little brute only snapped, "Montrez votre passe," to which we could only reply that we had an invitation from the governor himself which we had left on board, at which he only sniffed with the profoundest contempt for such a shallow imposition. We were beginning to have vague ideas of upsetting our Liliputian friend in the thick of the crowd and rushing the gate, when a swell naval officer appeared, and being struck, I suppose, with our respectable and ingenuous appearance, passed us in without more ado, and civilly fetched an A. D. C. to admit Mitchell and the skipper.

The scene that burst upon us was quite indescribable in its strange, wild, motley beauty; the gardens were lit up by countless lanterns hanging from the branches of the trees, the walks thronged by natives, French officers in full glory, white, brown, and beautiful half-caste ladies in ball dresses, and a sprinkling of motley civilians like ourselves, while all the rest of the space was filled by the different native choirs, each, I should think, several hundred strong. Each choir was divided into two halves, one of which sat shoulder to shoulder in long rows three or four deep, while the other half, similarly disposed, faced them, leaving a long aisle down the middle, where the chiefs of the district, arrayed in old native dresses, consisting of short capes with numerous many-colored flounces, walked to and fro, gravely directing the singers.

The effect of the music was quite indescribable. Many of the tunes were, I believe, of European origin, but so completely nativized that their authors would scarcely have recognized them. They had a character of their own, utterly unlike, and far finer than Arabic, Turkish, or any savage melody I ever heard. There were many parts harmoniously arranged; one set of singers devoting themselves entirely to making a bass "*boom,*" something like the drone of a bagpipe, others confining their energies to various long-drawn, high, falsetto notes, brought in at different times, and varied to suit the music.

The most striking features were the extraordinarily perfect time, hundreds of men and women clapping their hands together at started intervals with a noise as sharp as the crack of a stock-whip, and the strange metallic ring of every voice, which, though scarcely beautiful in itself to an unaccustomed ear, had a wild and curious effect, that was in perfect keeping with the savage grandeur of the whole scene.

After doing the necessary poojah with the swells, and being shown round by our good-natured consul and a French officer, the doctor and I were left to our own devices, and enjoyed ourselves to our hearts' content, roaming from choir to choir as each struck up in turn, and sitting down among the singers, who, with native politeness, immediately offered us a corner of their mats to sprawl on. And very pleasant it was. Wandering about among the merry crowd, speaking whatever came into our heads to anybody we pleased without fear of offending, or being sat upon, squatting down among the performers, and carrying on a broken but laughing conversation with the ladies of the chorus in the intervals of the music, listening to its execution till the last sigh (Tahitian music always ends with a kind of deep sigh) had died away, and the clear, inspiriting chant of some distant choir rose suddenly and ringingly in triumphant rivalry; watching the countless pretty little pictures of love and tenderness on all sides, young men and maidens comparing souls, and anxious mothers attending, when they had the chance, to their remarkably patient and long-suffering offspring that were rolled up in many-colored handkerchiefs, and strewed about the ground like bolsters in every direction. How strange, and new, and beautiful it all seemed, and yet, and yet—when I write it all down it seems as flat as ditch-water—it is like exhibiting the skeleton of some beautiful woman with the purpose of giving the spectators an idea of her loveliness! I think I shall head this chapter with a notice that no one but poets are allowed to read it, for none but a poetical imagination would be able to conceive the gorgeous coloring that gave birth to these dry pen-and-ink sketches. What seemed more odd to me than any thing was, that scarcely any except ourselves were impressed with the beauty of what they heard or saw. Was it but an illusion produced by our too vivid imaginations?

The French officers haw-hawed and pooh-poohed, and almost professed themselves bored with the whole concern, evidently considering that "better is the meanest *café-chantant* in the city of Paris than the most glorious festivity in the whole of the Pacific." Beauty of scene and even beauty of character lose much of their striking charm by their constant presence, and so it is less remarkable that the natives could not appreciate the loveliness of the picture of which they formed a great part; but I shall not forget one woman, who, when I expressed to her that I thought the abominable brass band that the swells were dancing to, a horrid nuisance, and not to be compared to the

Tahitian "himenes," gazed on me with an expression of shocked wonder, such as a Calvinistic preacher would direct upon a bold freethinker, or the august Pio Nono on some more harmless freemason; and then, having debated solemnly whether I was making fun of her or was only a harmless lunatic, she turned away without an answer, and gravely continued her singing.

Toward the end of the rehearsals Queen Pomaro and the commandant appeared on the scene, and a dance was got up for their especial benefit. One division of singers stood up and made a circle, or rather oblong, and kept up a strange wild chant, while a boy and a girl performed their gambados much in the style of the Egyptian Ghawazee, twisting, wriggling, and undulating all over in a by no means ungraceful manner. After a little the girl pretended to be tired or out-danced and slipped aside. Instantly the music changed into a kind of satirical burst, and she reappeared. Then more performers joined in, and the singing and dancing grew faster and more furious to the end, when every one cheered loudly. It was curious to see how the old queen's face, usually apathetic, brightened up. Her lips parted, her eyes glistened, till she looked as if she would have liked to kick over the old governor on whose arm she was leaning, and perform a *pas seul* on his prostrate carcass.

But the sight of the evening was the "scratching-dance." After a lively prelude, all the singers threw themselves on to their left elbows and unanimously and violently scratched their right legs, and then *vice versa*. What it all meant I don't know, but I fancy the words were a shade broad from the way the spectators laughed.

At last it all came to an end, the mats and bundles and babies were gathered up, and amid much squeezing, and laughing, and singing, the divisions filed one by one out of the gates, to the sound of drums and other barbarous instruments, to seek their night-quarters, while we went on board, regularly bewildered with the charms of all we had seen and heard.

August 17*th*.—In the afternoon we mounted some strange little American carriages, and drove out to see the races. The road was very gay and pretty; natives dressed in their gala-clothes, French officers mounted on caracoling steeds, which they were teasing and showing off with that absurd affectation of coolness and nonchalance so common to them; jolly-looking naval swells, some on foot, others crammed into little buggies with their laughing, bubbling-voiced half-caste friends; every large animal with four legs, and every thing that could run upon wheels, being put into requisition.

Society in Tahiti is divided into two sects, between which is a great gulf fixed: the first consists of the white merchants and shopkeepers who have pale-faced wives, and the second of the half-castes and their friends. In a cynical temper I christened them the mean whites and the dirty browns. The former have all the virtue, and the latter all the charms, by which they attract all the naval officers and distinguished strangers into their circle, which causes the others to regard them in a most unchristian spirit. They are certainly very pleasant, nearly always handsome, and with charming manners, simple without rudeness, easy without vulgarity; free from the angular good qualities of their white cousins, and eke from their petty meannesses; bubbling over with fun and good-humor; loving virtue, and I fear also vice, for its own sake more than for any thing that may be got by it. If the old proverb that "God made white men, and God made black men, but the devil made half-castes" be true, all I can say is, that when his Satanic majesty was at Tahiti, he showed a very pretty taste in creation.

On arriving at the course we were placed in the grand stand, a splendid erection, capable of containing at least thirty moderate-sized people, and soon after appeared Queen Pomare, to whom I was introduced by Mrs. Miller, our consul's wife, together with her relations and suite. I never saw any one look so thoroughly bored as she did; and I fancied she seemed half inclined to resent being made a puppet of by the French officers, who kept telling her what she had to do and say. Poor old lady! would that the imperious "Oui-oui" had never placed foot upon your sacred shores! The French officials complain that she is very obstinate sometimes, and small blame to her, say I.

The racing was of course execrable, but very amusing. Races with saddles and without; a trotting-race, in which the sole competitors were two horses too far gone to be able to gallop; and a human running-race, in which all but two shut up at once, leaving them to make an exciting finish at the pace of seven miles an hour.

After the races we were invited by a hospitable

civilian to his house among the palm-trees, to partake of beer and lemonade. There we found a lot of visitors, naval and military, male and female; and after a pleasant chat we drove home along the shady broom-road.[1]

At seven in the evening we joined the Millers, and went with them to the garden of the queen's palace, where the "grand himene" was to take place. This erection I have christened the Tower of Babel, as it is always building, is never finished, and, they say, is never intended to be. The French use it somewhat like the man in the pictures, who is always represented galloping on a donkey with a bunch of vegetables at the end of a long pole, which he keeps dangling just in front of the donkey's nose.

There the whole population of Tahiti and the neighboring islands, with the exception of the sick and aged, were assembled. The bare stone verandas of the palace were filled on every story to suffocation, and the open space below densely crowded. All shades of beauty were represented, from the swarthy Tahitian to the washed-out white. All dressed much alike, in the long, loose, cool-looking chemise of white muslin or linen, their luxuriant tresses set off by brilliant flowers and masses of snowy reva-reva, a gauzy white stuff,

---

[1] Not properly a specific name for any particular drive. Nearly every village in the Society Islands consists of a long row of houses stretching round the bay about sixty or a hundred yards from the beach, behind which is a dense belt of foliage backed by precipitous mountains—the wide, smooth path between the houses and the beach is invariably called the broom-road. This word is simply the native word "purumu," and describes the purpose to which the slopes are put after dark. For the meaning whereof, overhaul the Church Catechism or Williams's Maori Dictionary.

looking like strips of silver paper, made out of the shoots of young cocoa-nut trees—(ah! well I remember who first taught me to make it, but never mind that now!)—and their flashing, melting eyes, directing their fire here and there, for a Tahitian lady well understands optical effects. Alas, that they should so often prove optical illusions!

Most of the choirs this night were arranged in distinctive dresses; one in particular I remarked, where the performers were decorated with green boughs, like the pillars of a church at Christmas, the chiefs and directors wearing the ancient costume of the country, as before described, the general effect being rather marred by a pair of black-cloth trousers from some Yankee store, which were added for the sake of decency.

Oh, that I could give an idea of the exquisite time and harmony of their wild part-songs! Each choir sang in turn, the auricular committee, with the commandant and admiral, attending the singers; and at the end of each performance the directing chief of the district yelled out: "Vive l'empereur! Hurrah! Vive l'impératrice! Hurrah! Vive le prince impérial! Hurrah! Vive la Reine Pomare, Monsieur le Commandant, le commissionnaire, l'admiral!" "Vive tout le monde," in fact. One of these directing chiefs, the leader of one of the most crack companies—for there were degrees of excellence among them—took my fancy amazingly. He was evidently a South-Sea Michael Costa. As soon as his "*divas*" had struck up, he appeared to take no more notice of the performance, but strolled gently up and down, gazing calmly at the twinkling stars, with an expression of countenance as if he were calculating the distance between the sun and the moon, or analyzing the theory of light, until the cantata was finished. Then he looked quietly round on the spectators, as if to say, "See what perfection I have trained them to," and gracefully condescended to set an example of loyalty by leading the cheering.

We strolled about the gardens all the evening, carefully stepping over or picking our way between the numerous babies that were scattered about the ground in such profusion as to make it very difficult to walk without committing infanticide, receiving information from the civil naval men among whom we had already an extensive acquaintance, and interchanging ready laughs and symbolical compliments with the young ladies we were jammed against in the crowd. They were so clean, graceful, good-humored, and merry, that I would have defied the most sour-hearted Methodist preacher to have kept up a cool dignity among them long. At one time we were standing close to two of them, when one turned round to the doctor with a smile, and asked him for his cigar. He presented it with great civility, and the young lady, after a few modest sucks, handed it back with the utmost grace. I grinned in spite of myself, but the doctor made an elegant bow, and puffed away coolly, saying that there was nothing like falling in with the customs of the country. We soon got accustomed to this little courtesy afterward.

After the merits of the different performers had been settled, the captain of the Entrecasteaux took us to see a dance, and introduced us to a little French gentleman well versed in the language and customs of the country. After a spirited burst of singing, half a dozen girls rushed out of the ranks, and did the wriggling-business, a dance common all over the world, from the Irish jig to the nautch of India. We were standing just inside the oblong space, and presently one of the girls came and danced to the little Frenchman, who, much to my amusement, accepted the challenge, straddled his legs, twisted his body, and went through the regular rigmarole till the close of the performance. Then Mr. B——, the interpreter, made a speech on behalf of the governor from the veranda of the palace, while I took a last stroll under its bare walls, and soon after the natives began to file out of the gates, the lights died out one by one, the crowd dispersed, and the whole scene faded away like a beautiful dream.

On arriving at Tahiti, we heard the news that war had broken out between France and Prussia, but we little thought that we were about to witness the last *fête Napoléon* that would take place in the South Seas. *Eheu, fugaces*, etc.

August 18th.—To-day I went with our kind consul, Mr. Miller, to pay a visit to Queen Pomare, who had graciously consented to accord me an interview. Not being a Yankee, and hearing besides that her majesty was as apt to be bored with these formal introductions as I was myself, I did not look forward to it with any great amount of pleasure. But it turned out better than I anticipated. On our way to the palace we picked up Mr. B——, who kindly consented to act as interpreter, the queen, though she can speak a little

English, disliking to use any but her mother-tongue. We were shown into a long, low room, detached from the rest of the building, with seats round the sides, and some tolerable pictures on the walls, including one of Pomare herself. At last she appeared, a very quiet, but dignified and good-natured old lady. There is something that carries respect with it to my mind in the name of queen; an early prejudice radicals will say, but so it is. And she was a fallen queen, more or less; and this it was, I suppose, that brought the most quixotic part of my nature to the surface, for it is a fact no less strange than true that I, usually the most rough-mannered and brusque of mortals, bent down respectfully and kissed her hand, whereby I retained a not unpleasant smell of cocoa-nut oil in my nose for the rest of the day, and caused no small astonishment and amusement, I suspect, among the lookers-on. Anyhow, she was pleased, which was the main thing. We talked about my cousin, Lord G——, whom she remembered very well at Tahiti; and I went my way, after a short time, much gratified at having seen the famous savage queen I had read and dreamt about in my childish days.

In the evening we went to hear the band of the Astrée play opposite Government House. It was very pleasant and pretty, as the natives are invariably fond of music, and thronged round in crowds, laughing, talking, romping, and spooning. I fell in with some naval acquaintance, who, in the sublime innocence of perfect immorality, showed me a good deal of the manners and customs of the Society-Islanders. Then I met with my dancing-friend of the night before, who distributed his favors among the crowd with a most amusing fervor and impartiality, and a superb conceit of which only a Frenchman is capable. He introduced me to many of the swell chiefesses of the districts, who were very cordial, and promised me a reception if I would look in upon them at their country-places; the warmth and earnestness of which Jawleyford himself could barely have surpassed.

But at last I began to say to myself, "This society is not improving, young man; if you don't steer clear of what's-his-name, you'll go to thingummy." So I sought out the doctor and the Millers, who invited us to tea, together with the admiral and his officers.

The threshold of a kindly host is "*tapu*," and it is bad taste, or something worse, to describe or criticise what passes within its walls; yet I cannot refrain from mentioning the many pleasant evenings we spent with our good-natured consul, Mr. Miller, and his charming wife. Every night there was an unconventional reunion for every one who cared about agreeable conversation: the kind-hearted, shrewd old Admiral Cloué and the officers of the French fleet, a few French residents, official and non-official, with an occasional stray missionary, or a half-caste young lady, formed the usual party. All subjects were discussed with good-natured freedom, our host and hostess—with a natural tact uncommon enough in the highest society—putting no restraint upon their visitors, beyond showing a trust in their manners and taste. And as for the languages spoken—the Tower of Babel is all I can compare it to! each person used the tongue in which he fancied he was most likely to be understood.

K—— and I first addressing the more gifted of our audience in English, and then laboriously translating our metaphysical ideas into the most canine French, and receiving our answers perhaps in that language, perhaps in Spanish. It was confusing a little, but it had all the exciting pleasure of putting together a child's puzzle. What good-tempered chaff and wit there used to be! what strange South-Sea stories used to be told! One man describing how the savages used to feel the insides of his thighs in a perfectly easy and familiar manner to see how they would "eat." Another relating how whole ship's crews had been devoured in the Pomotou group; and how, when a man-of-war was sent to avenge the outrage, the natives all dived into the caves in the coral, and, though they could be heard, could not be got at, until the widow of the murdered skipper fitted out a small schooner that took them by surprise, and obtained her the satisfaction of beholding the chief that had eaten her husband and two children. Another informing us that in the Fiji a slave had been fattened on purpose to be killed and eaten on the visit of Prince Alfred; but whether they allowed him to try Banting when his Royal Highness did not make his appearance, or served him up to a select party to reap the reward of their care and trouble, deponent sayeth not.

One learns little odds and ends by strolling about the streets of Papiete. It is curious to think that the unique garb of the women, that has such a tropical appearance, is nothing more or less than the "*sacque*," the old dress of English and French women some generation and a half ago, immortalized by numerous caricatures of the time, but now only to be seen in the slow-changing Pacific Ocean, where it was introduced by the earliest missionaries.

It is not wise to hold conversation with an English-speaking native for more than ten minutes; during that time he will talk Shakespeare and the musical glasses, so to speak, or discourse on any subject you please, but in the end he invariably comes round to proposals that are apt to be offensive to one who is not yet completely Society-Islandized. The natural, innocent, kind-hearted creature means nothing but kindness and hospitality by his offers, but quite unintentionally he is apt to bring a blush to the cheek of the young person who is not yet sufficiently naturalized as to have shed his breeks and adopted the blue and white *sulu* or kilt of the country. When this metamorphosis has taken place, the backsliding individual is looked upon, not without reason, by the more religious and decent of the community, as little better than one of the what's-his-names. I remember seeing a fat, pallid, greasy Frenchman, clothed in nothing but the aforesaid garment, a large grass hat, and a pair of gold spectacles, looking like a study of Silenus in the nineteenth century.

The chief occupation of the natives is gambling. When a man has lost his whole fortune, probably some five or six dollars, he simply goes up into the mountain and brings down a load or two of fruit, with which he begins life afresh.

August 19*th*.—Louey and I took a sail down the coast inside the reef; the lagoon was crowded with boats and canoes of all sorts and sizes, full of laughing, singing natives returning to their homes, every kind of sail being hoisted, from new white canvas to the undergarments of the lady passengers. We noticed many acquaintances of the preceding evenings, and many and loud were the "Ya ranas," and the offers of drinks out of bottles, which we wisely declined, though we were fearfully hot and thirsty from pulling in the blazing sun.

Racing, laughing, and chaffing, we travelled along the coast for some ten miles; canoes and boats as far as we could see ahead and astern, when a tempting, shady bay opened out, and we picked our way into it through the coral, intending to lunch and recruit ourselves in peace and solitude. Soon, however, appeared a strange, dried-up old native whom I had met at the himenes, and, through my greenness and ignorance of native manners, had put down as an unmitigated old scoundrel. In a queer mixture of English and Portuguese he asked us to come up to his house, introduced us to his family, who set to work to get us shells and cocoanuts, wanted to cook us some dinner, and behaved like a courtly old gentleman, in fact. When at last the time came to go on our homeward way, we received an affectionate shower of farewell blessings from him and his wife, and his daughters, and his sons, and his brothers-in-law, and his aunts, and his uncles, his first cousins, and his second cousins, etc., as if we had been intimate friends for five years at the least.

It would seem or be thought strange in Europe if a young lady whom you had seen scarcely ten minutes and had not spoken ten words to, were coolly to propose deserting her kindred and friends, and accompanying you, bag and baggage, to the other end of the world, but in the South Seas it is but an ordinary occurrence, scarcely deserving of mention.

I remember at Samoa two ladies of high degree, fat, brown, and forty, paying their court with such irresistible ardor that, after telling most shameless lies about a ferociously jealous wife in England, by way of making a polite excuse for not taking them, I was fain to bolt ignominiously for fear they should win their end by sheer persistency, like the widow and the unjust judge in the parable.

August 23d.—This day we went for a picnic at Point Venus, so called because it is the place where Cook observed the transit of the planet, but many in Tahiti seriously believe he discovered it there, as it were some strange beast, while others declare the name is derived from a worship of the heathen goddess that the ancient mariners used to celebrate on that spot.

We met together at the consul's, who with his wife and children, the admiral, and his secretary Mr. M——, Mrs. B——, the doctor, and I, made up the party.

We then bundled ourselves with some difficulty into some extraordinary uncomfortable little Yankee carriages, my companions being Mr. M——, a very agreeable, amusing young man, and Mrs. B——, a half-Spanish, half-American widow, whose husband was eaten some time ago. A merry little soul she was, with eyes that always twinkled, and a tongue that never stopped talking except to laugh, always in a blaze of fun or feeling, and discussing every thing as if her life depended on it.

What a jolly drive it was! Arguing in a circle on every subject under heaven, talking the wildest nonsense. (How rare and pleasant it is to meet any one who can talk good nonsense and understand it, instead of getting up and knocking the wind out of you with a boring fact!) Hearing the histories of various people as we passed their houses—and Tahitian life-histories are usually strange and checkered—and enjoying the beautiful scenery all the more for the high pitch of our animal spirits.

The road ran for a long way parallel with the shore, under the shade of the trees, crossing innumerable little streams, mostly filled with native girls washing themselves or their garments, for the Society-Islanders are the most cleanly race I ever met, very different from their Maori cousins.

When you are riding about the island, it is very pleasant to dismount occasionally and refresh yourself with a bathe in one of these rivulets. Not unfrequently while you are performing your ablutions you are struck by a fruit thrown from the trees on the bank. On following the direction of the shot you most likely find yourself in the presence of some dusky charmer; but not unfrequently your admirer turns out to be a horrid old chiefess, and if you blight her young affections a row ensues.

Then the road wound up the sides of the steep mountains. Precipices above and below it; in fact, a South-Sea Cornice, but far grander, and more beautiful, for here the most perpendicular hill-sides are covered with a luxuriant vegetation. Perhaps we should have enjoyed it more if we had not been in some danger of going over the said precipices, owing to the imperfection of our harness, as we descended on the other side. This consisted of a pole, with a cross-piece of wood at the end, to which the horses were attached, and which, being only fastened to the pole with string, kept sliding first one way and then the other, as soon as the strain came on it, jamming one horse inward and shoving the other right away. There being only one trace, and no splinter-bars, the vehicle twisted about in an exciting and uncertain manner.

At length we finished the descent, and, having arrived at our destination, strolled about the native settlement. In the chief's house we found a party of French officers surveying. Most of the native houses are built of hibiscus-poles, planted in the ground about two inches apart, giving them the appearance of enormous bird-cages. The roof is ingeniously constructed of plaited palm-leaves. When you retire for the night you fasten up a shawl or blanket against the side to keep the wind off you; but the natives suffer much from cold or rheumatics, at which I don't wonder.

In the more considerable villages there is a large building of this kind which is public property, and where the mayor and corporation, the local board, or whatever answers to those things in Tahiti, hold their meetings, and where also the people collect together to perform himenes.

Then we were shown the chapel, by the priest thereof, close to which was the old Protestant one in ruins. "Un clou chasse l'autre," remarked the doctor. After this we proceeded to the tamarind-tree planted by the immortal Cook, where we rested while some of the party went off to go up the light-house that has been built here. What hidden feeling is it that makes humanity desire to get to the top of every thing—spires, light-houses, pyramids, and what not? And it is curious that the two things that tend to make men most unbearably conceited, are getting to the top of something or seeing a sunrise. I would give any man who wilfully committed either of these acts, solitary confinement for forty-eight hours.

Then we had luncheon in the chief's house, followed by a pleasant stroll about the village. We noticed that all the fowls had feathers on their legs right down to their toes, and the doctor started a theory that they were bred so by the missionaries for the sake of decency.

We came upon a curious little hut with a kind of door at one end, which, when opened, disclosed nothing more or less than a coffin. It is a custom among the natives to keep them above-ground for a time, to be visited by the relatives of the deceased, a sensible and decent practice enough compared to the ghastly ones that may be found in some places in Europe. I remember in Sicily, when a young lady of good family died, she was dressed in ball-clothes and stuck up at the end of the drawing-room, to receive all her friends, who paid her a visit in evening-dresses to bid her a last farewell. I don't think this case was exceptional.

Then, after a very merry drive home, we dined on board the Astrée, where we were shown some very ingenious breech-loading cannon; and then, after a short stroll ashore, to bed.

August 24th.—Up before daylight in the morning to drive to Mr. Stewart's plantation at Atimaono. He

TAHITI. 39

had kindly sent over a carriage for us, and dragged by two little mules, driven by a sturdy Scotchman, we were soon rattling along the road, bound for the other side of the island. We met lots of natives bearing fish, mostly mullet, to the morning market, as long as we were within three miles of Papiete. There is no way of going *through* any Society island, as they are all a mass of great mountains, gorges, and precipices, so our road lay all the way along the shore, amid groves of bananas, plantains, etc., among which the huts of the natives were sprinkled. Some appeared lazily in the door-ways as we galloped by, some we saw gnawing pensively at pieces of bread-fruit which served them as an early breakfast, others performing their toilets in the little rivers that we were continually splashing through, nearly all looking up to give us a cheerful "Ya rana." I won't answer for the spelling of any native words that I use, but what does it matter? The missionaries made it a written language, and I have just as much right to spell the words after my own fancy as they had.

The scenery was splendid. Wherever there was a break in the glorious tropical forest, we could see on one side the barrier reef-line of great white breakers curling over without ceasing, though the deep-blue sea beyond seemed as smooth as glass, while between us and it was a line of bright, pale-green water, in which an occasional man or woman might be noticed wading or poling, fish-spear in hand, in search of a dainty breakfast, and then some ten miles off the picturesque island of Eiméo, rising fantastically from the bosom of the horizon, its ruggedness and grandeur set off by a gigantic and distinct hole bored right through the centre of its loftiest peak, while on the other side of us a mass of splendid cliffs and mountains would be revealed, hanging almost over our heads, with deep, narrow gorges running up between them into the very clouds.

About every hour we stopped to change horses, when we took the opportunity to stretch our legs, chat with any people who might chance to be about, and ornament our hats and heads with crimson hibiscus-flowers; for you will find, if you go to the Society Islands, that, unless you are a wooden idiot, you will do things quite naturally that you would look upon as stark staring lunacy anywhere else.

Soon we began to feel the fresh trade-wind in our faces, a great relief, after the stifling atmosphere of Papiete, and the third stage brought us to the boundary of the plantation, after which we drove through a long avenue of bananas with cotton-fields behind them, till we came to Mr. Stewart's house, a fine building on the shore, built with large rooms, and well suited for a hot climate, where we were very kindly received by its owner.

Mr. Stewart and the plantation of Atimaono have a strange history, too long and complicated for me to attempt to give a full or judicial account of, especially as every one tells a different tale on the subject. I have heard him bitterly abused, but with so little sensible reason, that I strongly suspect that the jealousy of the smaller white merchants and settlers is the chief motive of their virulent attacks.

He came out here as agent to a company with a

grant of land, and his troubles seem to have begun at once; the grant was delayed, so he set to work to buy land from the natives out of his own pocket. A report was then circulated that the natives were forced to sell to him, which, whether true or not, was peremptorily denied by the governor. As soon as the plantation was fairly under way, specimens of inferior cotton were sent to Europe as the produce of Atimaono. Infamous libels were circulated in the American papers, describing the horrible cruelties of Stewart and his myrmidons on their unfortunate workmen; the sick were left to die, the dead left unburied, the men cheated out of their pay, etc.

Mr. Elea, the overseer, in particular, was represented as a most blood-thirsty monster. He had hung women with child up and flogged them, he had roasted Chinamen alive, etc.' Mr. Stewart was a perfect wicked baron of the middle ages, brutally assaulting every one who came too near to his castle; to all these accusations Mr. S. answered by demanding a public inquiry, which was granted. This cleared away the whole cloud of lies, every thing being found and reported in the most perfect order, every regard being paid to the health and comfort of the coolies. The only serious complaint made by the Chinese was a curious one—that they were not allowed to hang themselves as payment for gambling-debts.

But the troubles of Atimaono were not yet over. Certain men, among them the *juge impérial*, formerly a blacksmith, entered into a conspiracy to ruin the plantation, for which Mr. S. is now bringing an action against them. He has won his way in spite of all opposition, and little heeds the snarling of his enemies. *Vive le succès!* Of course I do not know enough to be able to judge exactly of the fairness of what I have just written, but I must say that a happier, healthier-looking set of men than the fifteen hundred workmen I saw at Atimaono could not be found in a long day's walk among the manufacturing classes of England.

K—— was lodged in a little room built right out in the sea, so that he could catch fish out of his window if it so pleased him. The other day when the plantation doctor was lodged in this place, it came on to blow heavily, and one night the bridge between it and the land was washed right away by the sea; the medico turned out of his bed, and was rather horrified to find himself alone in his glory on a desolate and rather shaky island.

We spent the day very pleasantly, reading and loafing about till dinner-time, when Mr. Stewart treated us to some native dishes, which I did not appreciate so much as his capital French cookery. Besides the admiral, who had also driven over from Papiete, our dinner-party was made up of several people employed in different ways on the estate, and very pleasant company they were. Some good types of what I call the cosmopolitan Micawber, men whom one comes across oftener in the Southern than in the Northern Hemisphere, who try their hands at every kind of wild speculation in strange places, generally clever, energetic, and brave, but often too restless, too dreamy, or too sanguine, to meet with permanent success; men whom you may meet one day living in affluence, and next month earning their bread by the work of their hands, waiting for another chance to turn up. I delight in these fellows; more often than not they are gentlemen by birth and education, whose chance of success in life has been ruined by the very qualities that make them so charming, their good-nature, love of freedom, independence, and wild adventure. Some that I have met are the most delightful companions in the world. They have tried every thing, know every thing, and have been everywhere. They are vagabond adventurers, respectable English society may cry. So were Sir Walter Raleigh and Francis Drake, say I; but it is this class of men that macadamizes the world; and I don't think they are worse as a rule than nine-tenths of the respectable men in white chokers and faultless boots that one meets at an English dinner-party. I have known specimens who could set an example that would make society blush, as far as kindness, unselfishness, and honor go. There is one appearing before my mind now, known but for a short time, yet not easily forgotten. Well do I remember his massive, well-shaped head; nearly all these men have fine heads; his *worn* yet handsome and merry face, so full of humor, kindness, and fun, that it used to warm the cockles of my heart, would brighten up the dullest physiognomy in a room when he entered it, and produce a good-humored laugh at the first word he spoke. A man with the mark of the "vagabond dry rot" plainly written upon him, yet one that few could help loving and even trusting. Often he used to tell me in his quaint, laughing, philosophical way the stories of his many wild speculations in different parts of the world, and how they had ended in his becoming "flat broke" as he used merily to call it. Full of wit, kindness, cleverness, energy, and courage, yet unable to make or at least keep his own fortune, and consequently worthless in the eyes of the great mass of the world, which judges mankind a great deal more by the rule of the "almighty dollar" than it is willing to own. One who could share his last sixpence with a friend, or risk his life without hesitation for a noble purpose; one still young, yet in spite of his never-ceasing fund of mirth and humor evidently broken and worn out. He used to give me an inner feeling of sadness and pity, even while I was laughing at his exuberant fun. And the next-door neighbor to a man like this, or perhaps even his chum, living in the same hut on terms of equality, may be an old whaler or run-away man-of-war's-man of the worst type, who is utterly devoid of all feelings but the basest, and has broken every one of the commandments, not to mention committing a few other crimes scarcely comprehended in that interesting catalogue.

Ye worldly old philosophers of the London clubs, who fancy you know life, should make a trip to the South Seas to study it in its vivid incongruities. Here at Atimaono, a comparatively speaking civilized spot, the book-keeper was an infantry-major, the store-keeper a captain in a light-cavalry regiment, and the barman the son of rich parents and grandson of the mayor of a great town in the British Isles. There are ups in this world, and there are downs, as Mr. Plornish wisely remarks. Such is life south of the equator!

August 25th.—In the afternoon we drove down to the cotton-mill, and I was much interested in watching the work. The cotton was brought in in baskets and thrown into a kind of trough which, by an ingenious process, winnowed it through the bottom, cleaning it of all the black berries, or whatever the proper name of them may be, and coarse stuff. Then it was poured into the top of an enormous strong box, stamped down, and shut in; then it was compressed by machinery as tight as possible, and, on the great iron clasps which fastened the sides of the box being unfastened, they swung open on hinges, disclosing a square, white, compact mass of cotton; a few split bamboos were lashed round this to keep it in shape, and then, being sewn up in strong canvas, it was all ready for exportation.

All the laborers were Chinese or Hervey-Islanders, the latter strong, healthy, savage-looking people, who build their huts on a platform of poles and enter them by a ladder. There would be a fine case of hereditary instinct for some naturalist or philosopher to work out. Doubtless, there was originally a purpose and a reason for this peculiar style of architecture, but, though that has now disappeared, the practice it gave birth to still remains.

In one place the laborers were employed repairing carts, making wheels, and doing carpentering generally. In another they were building a ship; while in one of the buildings we came upon an ingenious old Chinaman making a beautiful *épergne* of silver and mother-of-pearl shells. I could not help being struck with the universality of Stewart's genius, and his wonderful power of finding his men's *spécialité* and setting them to the right work; and he seemed to be one who had the rare gift of combining justice with strictness.

I saw at once the absurdity of the libels about cruelty that were published against him and his overseer, Mr. Elca. That two men might torture and tyrannize over the same number of negroes in the old slave States might be possible, because in the case of a rebellion they would be certain of support from their fellow-planters; but here, where the slightest scandal or disturbance on the estate would be hailed with joy by nearly every white merchant in Tahiti, and the mass of people to be managed are not negroes, but clever, desperate Chinese, proverbially careless of life, such a system would be impossible.

I saw a list of the regulations of the plantation, the heaviest punishment being imprisonment for five days. The ordinary penalty for small offences is, I think, twenty-four or forty-eight hours of drudging labor, during which time their pay is stopped.

I was much amused by observing two Chinamen in disgrace doing penance by carrying ballast into one of the ships, watched by a big Hervey-Island savage with a stick; the unutterable disgust visible in the countenances of the two prisoners, and the pompous grin of their temporary commander, as he followed them to and fro and kept them up to their work, were very ludicrous.

Down by the sea was an enormous yard, full of pigs, and such pigs! Of all sizes, from a Guinea-pig to a Shetland pony; of all colors, from a zebra to a negro. And as for shape! They were thin where they ought to be fat, long where they ought to be short, more like great wedges with the sharp end uppermost than any thing else I can think of. Such gaunt, horrible monsters were never beheld; the scene was like the nightmare of a dyspeptic farmer.

There has only been one serious disturbance among the laborers since the commencement of the plantation, when they quarrelled about some gambling-debt, and set to work stabbing each other, and so on. One of the ringleaders was guillotined as an example.

While we were here the overseer came in, bringing some forged notes, very cleverly made, that had been uttered by ingenious John Chinaman for the purpose of swindling the simple natives. These last get on, however, with the Chinese more amicably than might be expected, which is chiefly owing to the low moral feeling of the Tahitians, who get money from the Chinese by the aid of their female relations.

As the afternoon wore on, the Hervey-Islanders—men, women, and children—began to flock round the store, and on a bell ringing each came up to receive a spoonful or two of molasses, of which they seemed inordinately fond. It was served out by the storekeeper from a great tub, and the whole operation reminded me forcibly of Mrs. Squeers and her brimstone and treacle.

Then we drove through the cotton-fields and returned to dinner. The next morning we bade farewell to our kind host, and drove back to Papiete.

Swiftly, too swiftly, the days passed away. From the natives, the French, and, above all, from Mr. and Mrs. Miller, we received the greatest kindness. In the mornings reading and dreaming on board, or talking lazily with friends on shore; sailing or paddling about

the reefs when the heat of the day was passed; and
when the cool night had cast its veil over the island,
strolling about the quiet paths in the dim moonlight,
or enjoying the pleasant society that could always be
found at the house of our hospitable consul. What is
the use of trying to describe dream-land? Its beauty
is that of the dead, calm ocean, unbroken by a rugged
or prominent line, and much of that which its loveliness
consists in seems always to my mind too sacred to
be painted or written.

If I were a mendacious mendicant, I might have
enlivened this chapter with hair-breadth escapes, romantic
adventures, fights, love-stories, etc., *ad libitum*,
after the manner of most books of travels; but, in spite
of my several years of voyaging, and the time I have
spent in the South-Sea Islands, I have not yet become
utterly demoralized on the score of veracity. I don't
know how it is, but I never, or very seldom, do meet
with any romantic adventures. I did at last manage
to get shipwrecked; but even that disappointed my
expectations as far as romance was concerned. I suspect
they are like miracles, not common to those who
don't look out for them and meet them half-way.
However this may be, I consider I am hardly treated
about such matters. I don't, as I said before, get a
proper share of romantic adventures. I never see
ghosts; I never have mysterious, prophetic dreams that
come true; I can't get mesmerized, nor even turn
tables successfully, and as for miracles! if I was in one
parish they would be sure to take place in the next one.
I once went to the Church of St. Januarius in Naples,
thinking that at last I should succeed in witnessing a

miracle, or an imitation of one; but when it was performed, I could not make out that any thing happened at all, and so went home disgusted.

Soon, too soon, the time came for us to leave the South-Sea Capua. I was so happy there, that I verily believe I should have been content to dream away my life, without care or ambition. I was Society-Islandized, in fact. It could not be, and it was best for me as it was. Perhaps after a time a man's feelings and thoughts would become degraded and numbed by such a life; he would lose that power of enjoyment that made it at first so charming and pleasant to him. Peace, and quiet, and perfect freedom, are useful medicines, but not a wholesome diet: Their charm lies in contrast; there is no spark without the concussion of the flint and steel; there is no fine thought, even no perfect happiness, that is not born of toil, sorrow, and vexation of spirit.

"Be virtuous and you will be happy," is an old English proverb, which in Tahiti should be rendered, "Be happy and you will be virtuous." And the latter version is as true as the former. To be *perfectly* happy, you will find that sympathy is necessary; you must make others happy too, which is the essence of virtue. You cannot sin against God except by sinning against your neighbor *or yourself*, and so I hold that my brown friends are a good and happy people, in spite of what stern Judaical moralists may say to the contrary. It was with a heavy heart that I put up the wheel, to let our little schooner go bowling and tearing out through the narrow channel, and it gave me pain to look back and see the dear old island growing fainter and dimmer as each minute passed.

I wonder if I shall ever see it again? I promised and vowed that I would, and was sadly answered: "You say so now; but when you go home, you will find new duties, new pleasures, and new friends; you will never come back again."

Truly we are often compelled, bitterly against our will, to write "finis" under the pleasantest pages of our life.

> One day I was watching a boat
> Borne on by the wind and the tide,
> And into the rushes 'twould float
> That grew 'neath the bank on each side.
>
> For a moment perhaps it would stay,
> But their arms could not hold it for long;
> They broke, and the boat swept away,
> For the wind and the current were strong.
>
> As down the swift stream it was hurled,
> I fancied I heard these words spoken:
> "Few partings there are in this world
> In which friendly ties are not broken.
>
> "All are hard at the best to burst through,
> Some are bitter and painful to sever,
> While some, but alas! very few,
> Will stand time and distance forever."

CHAPTER II.

EIMEO, OR MOREA.

August.—EIMEO, as seen from Tahiti, is a wonderfully beautiful island, peaked and jagged in a way seldom seen. Some of the isolated peaks may be rivalled by those of the Dolomite Gebirge (as little visited when I first knew them as Eimeo is now), but there are some which are nearly unique in their forms. But we must make comparisons nowadays with bated breath, for fear the *Alta California* should be down on us with some fresh discovery of strange loveliness. If photography is to be trusted, the scenery of that part of Western America must equal if not exceed in beauty, any in the world.

We easily found our way into the western harbor, through the fringing reef, though there are one or two nasty lumps and patches to be looked for in the passage. The reef gives one generally the idea of a fringing reef which is being gradually changed into a barrier-reef by subsidence. Inside the harbor the water is tremendously deep, and you have to run a long way up to get an anchorage.

The harbor is a "gorge," and one of the noblest gorges I have ever seen. Green precipices rising upward of two thousand feet, sheer from the water, fringed round their feet by cocoa-nut and orange-trees—trees, not bushes; I think I never saw any so large elsewhere.

Far up on the green cliff-side may be seen the large leaves of the "faïes," or wild-plantain, a never-failing source of food, but one which often requires no little strength of limb and steadiness of head to gather, and still more to bring down to the sea-shore. A sort of vegetable chamois over which many a life is lost.

A charming little boy of a good half-caste breed (his mother being an Englishwoman and his father a Frenchman) told me a legend, in good biblical English, anent a great red scar on the green cliff-side. How that "a man went gathering faïes on the Sabbath, and God was angry with him, and he fell down and made the mark on the hill-side."

These "islands of the blest" are not without their drawbacks; even faïes, though it grows wild, sometimes grows very wild indeed. The plants we can see from the deck of the yacht would require a sturdy climb to reach; I should think they are at least fifteen hundred feet above the water's edge; pleasant for the father of a family, with a sore foot or a swelled leg—two very common complaints in these parts. Better a store of potatoes and a keg of salt-fish, after all, though it may require a more sustained labor to obtain them.

The trap-dikes are very grand here, running positively like walls and towers from above to the sea, through the mass of green. By moonlight it is almost impossible to believe that they are not ruins of some old fortification. Some are as regular as that old stepped wall which runs up the rock of Gibraltar.

One of the highest and most acute peaks is perforated right through, just below the summit, which aperture we can plainly see from the ship, and might walk through if we were so minded, which we are not; a climb of two thousand feet, with the thermometer at 120°, being no joke. This aperture can also be seen from Atimaono in Tahiti. Of course, it was caused by an ancient hero throwing his spear through the mountain-peak. These sort of things always are.

The upper end of the harbor softens into a pretty bit of delta, backed by high green hills, and with a sparkling stream running through it. This is cultivated with great success as a sugar-plantation, and the white-walled, red-tiled building connected with the establishment comes in very prettily. It seemed rather a dead season with them, but the resident representatives of the company, a cheery Italian doctor, and a more grave *ex-colonel de la ligne*, did not seem much depressed on the subject.

When a European meets you in one of these out-of-the-way places, he either sulks and says nothing, or else gives you at once a slight autobiographical sketch of his previous career, and is most careful to explain the circumstances which brought him there, as if his presence required some explanation. Mighty queer histories some of these worthy beach-combers have, I have no doubt.

On the shore were certain gigantic baskets, or rather wattled buildings, consisting of two sides, a bottom and one end, some twenty feet by twelve, which puzzled us very much. Our young friend tried to explain that they were to catch fish and sharks in, though he so utterly failed to explain how, that we concluded that they were ladies' bathing-machines, so contrived to shield their beauties from the impertinent gaze of the 'long-shore loafers. Having, however, by this time some little insight into the proprieties of these islands, we merely accepted the theory provisionally, and for want of a better.

The time came when we found, as usual, that our theory was wrong.

Sitting on deck one day, we observed a deal of fire-lighting, singing, and general hustling and bustling, under the orange-trees on the shore, and forthwith paddled across to see what the fun was. It needed no interpretation of the cries of welcome to tell us, for, looking over the side of the boat into two or three foot water, we saw that the bottom was literally paved with small fish, something between a dace and a char; they were positively in myriads. Unable to resist the temptation, we took a throw with the casting-net, whereby we got nothing but an ugly lump of old coral, the bottom being much too broken for that style of thing. Our ill success was greeted with derisive cheers from the opposition, who then invited us to see how they did the trick.

Three or four women walked into the water with no small merriment, bearing an aboriginal kind of seine, made of the leaves of the pandanus thickly interwoven in a line of coir. Making a long sweep, they drew it cautiously in a semicircle to the shore; and, when at the proper distance, they inserted a small edition of the big baskets, and swept in the beauties by hundreds, a most original and successful way of going to work. Had they tried to land the fish, they would certainly have succeeded in wriggling away under the leaves.

I think, among all the fish-glories I have seen, this was the most glorious one. These thousands and thousands of silver-green backs and crimson bellies all flickering in the sun! It was like looking at bushels of diamonds, emeralds, and rubies, all being shaken together, and one fairly winked with their brilliancy.

Not only are these "fishlets," known to the natives by the name of "*urio*," most beautiful to the eye, but they are most pleasant to the taste, being even as a mixture of whitebait from Greenwich, fresh char from the König Sea, and—the best other fish you can think of. Scale them not, clean them not, cast them into the frying-pan, and continue eating, not till you are satiated, for that will never be, but till there are no more to eat.

It is a curious fact, which I have not noticed myself, and so cannot warrant, that the only singing-bird on this island is a kingfisher. (Why fisher? They hardly any of them fish, and even the English one is a poor hand, wounding more than he catches.) Day and night he pipeth pleasant notes, not unlike the beginning of the thrush's song, "che-whi-schew."

Sitting on board in the afternoon, we saw Admiral Cloué and his tender, the d'Entrecasteau, slipping quietly to leeward on some private expedition. The admiral seemed, when we left him in Tahiti, to be by no means easy about the war. "Men in plenty we have, and our men are brave, but where are our generals?" He is a fine old fellow, and scorned the idea of taking German merchantmen out of Samoan ports. "No; we will make neutral ports of them, and perhaps help to civilize the native rulers by showing them that we respect their authority."

I always expected that the native of the Isle of Pines, or the New Caledonian, would eat me if he could, they looked so like it. But these folks grin and laugh whatever I do, right or wrong. And somehow it puts me in mind of the two Australian crows at the Kawau, who were found dancing and laughing joyously round Miss Annie's pet canary, which they were slowly pecking to death. 'Tis but a vain fancy, however.

Saturday, September 1st.—Along the channel inside the reef, to the eastward harbor, which is very lovely, but I think not equal to the one in which we are lying.

September 2d.—Called on Mrs. Simpson, the widow of the late missionary, a most agreeable and lady-like woman, whose mere presence and example must have been of infinite use. She speaks the purest biblical English; which may be accounted for by her having lived forty years of the seventy of her life in this island, with few books but her Bible. Her grandson, a boy of some eight or ten years old, being a private and particular friend of my own, took me a long walk by the Broom-road, bearing with him his fish-spear, composed of a light shaft of hibiscus, with a brush of iron wires, little larger than netting-needles, lashed round the larger end. Indeed, our walk was principally undertaken for the purpose of procuring similar instruments from a cunning man who dwelt at the far end of the big village. We beguiled the way by trying to spear the land-crabs, as they popped sideways into their holes in the road; a difficult and delicate task, requiring much skill. We rested the shaft on the tips of the first two fingers of our left hands, and projected it with those of our right; but the crabs were very shy, and, though we made some beautiful shots at the entrance, the crab had always retired into his back-parlor before the missile reached him. Wearying of this we tried the sea-shore, and there the sea-urchins and holothuriæ, being more passive targets, suffered severely. I also think that, quite accidentally, we speared a fish, but he was so spiny that we had to knock him off the spear on to the rocks, and he fled again to the sea.

Then we came to the village, consisting of neat wattled whitewashed cottages, raised above the ground on stone supports; a practice which, though it favored ventilation, oddly enough at the same time encouraged dirty habits. The cottages themselves seemed cleanly and well kept, but their inhabitants seemed much of a muchness with those in the next harbor, who live in huts made of interwoven cocoa-nut branches. They were particularly indelicate in their habits; they were, however, most friendly and kindly, and it was very pleasant to see how fond they were of my boy-companion, and how confident he was of their affection.

The spear-maker was from home, but there was something to repay us for our walk in the shape of certain large canoes hauled up on the strand, each of which had a large forked spar, some twenty feet long, projecting from its bow. My young friend informed me that these were used as a sort of Anakim fishing-rod; lines being fastened to the end well baited, and the canoe kept well up to the bobble of the sea. "And they catch fish, so large—so large!" quoth he, indicating a size as large as, or larger than, himself.

Under his guidance I walked into the old missionary-house, once a commodious slab building, but now I fear on the high-road to ruin. It was curious to see how every small household article, glass, table, basin, ewer, had remained exactly in the place in which they were left, when the missionary's widow had closed the door behind her for the last time. The place was evidently strictly "tapu." I was puzzled to find, among a quantity of low-church divinity, some very incongruous French books, such as drill-books for such and such a "régiment de la ligne" and Jasmin's poems. It was not till I returned to headquarters that I learned that the missionary's daughter had married the gallant French ex-colonel, and that my young friend was the consequence. As we returned, a native woman gave the boy a gelatinous matter of a pearly gray-color, made from arrow-root, and wrapped up in a banana-leaf, which he thought very nice, and I, luckily for him, very nasty.

P—— and Loucy, the suspected Russian Finn, went exploring inside the reef to Cook's Harbor. They represent the passage as by no means clear or pleasant, and, as the wind was dead ahead, they had to down sail and pull. Where the reported "ship-channel" is, is by no means clear.

It seems to be difficult to decide whether Cook's Harbor or the one in which the yacht is lying is the most beautiful. Possibly the difference between a handsome woman and a pretty one. "I landed," says P——, "close to the head of the bay, near a small creek. All round the harbor was a beautiful shady avenue, close to the water's edge, brightened by the crimson flowers of the arrow-root, the fresh green of the banana, and the richer, redder green of the taro-plant.

"Here we ate our luncheon and the mosquitoes ate us, and it is a question whether the latter had not the best of the bargain. (These infernal mosquitoes and the flies, says P——, are the real cause of the demoralization of the white settlers in these parts; it would be impossible to live without keeping some one to brush away the plagues, and as male labor is difficult to obtain—you have to run into danger.) Then approached a jolly old dame, who talked and laughed at the top of her voice for ten good minutes. I could not understand much that she said, except that her strong point was, that she hated the French (an almost universal sentiment in these parts); and that, in order to avoid them, she should intensely like to accompany me back to England—a proposition which I firmly, but I hope politely, declined. Then we landed at another point of the harbor, where there was a benevolent old gentleman, and a woman and child, who (with the exception of the last, who howled) greeted us with the usual 'Ya rana.' The old man, in the usual broken English of the island, asked me about the war, and when the English were coming back to the country. All which I answered as well as I could. At the mention of the French he made a very wry face. After a little conversation he said, 'Come, I give you cocoa-nut;' and, calling a boy, he shouldered a long bamboo and a stick sharpened at both ends, and marched off toward the feathery cocoas. In spite of my remonstrances he insisted on knocking down dozens before he could find any he considered good enough for me. On deciding he placed his sharp stick in the ground, and proceeded to peel off the outer shell by striking it against the other sharp point in a very workmanlike manner, though one fancied every moment that he must impale his own old paws. In very young cocoa-nuts you have merely to cut through husk and shell with a knife, when out springs the cool water as briskly as champagne when the string is cut.

"When he had placed the nuts on board, he seized a tough-looking old cock, who was looking very melancholy at the end of a piece of string, and proceeded to add him to the cargo. I laughed, and told him that I had no money. 'I no want money,' quoth he, a little offended, still dragging along the unfortunate cock. However, at last I got him to understand that I did not want it, having plenty on board, and we embraced and parted excellent friends.

"We ran back under easy sail, picking our way between the coral-rocks, without accident, but I don't envy the man who tries it, in a dark night, blowing fresh!"

September 3d.—Tempted by P——'s description of Cook's Harbor, the Dingey and the Fish Fag were commissioned to pull round the point, and a hard pull it was, as it blew half a gale of wind dead against us all the way, the rough coral-bottom creating a nasty short sea, which nearly stopped the little Dingey altogether. At last we turned the corner and discovered the location of P——'s old friend of yesterday, who kept up his reputation by giving us unlimited cocoa-nut water. There was a Kanaka who spoke very good and forcible English, having served on board a whaler for several years. He informed us, among other important facts, that all their pigs had been killed by "those dam rascals of Frenchmen." "Ouis-ouis," said P——, whereupon the old lady, recognizing the slang, kept on repeating "oui, oui," over and over again, like the dormouse in "Alice," and they all laughed till they were hoarse at the new and exquisite joke. "What are these sticks in the holes for?" asked P——. "Kill those dam crabs, make their dam holes everywhere," quoth our enlightened friend; and certainly, if saying it would do it, he would have d——, I mean stopped a river in full flood.

Hillo! Walker's original! or the Aboriginal Walker, the twopenny postman! and up shambled a uniformed Kanaka on a stumbling pony, with an enormous letter-bag with one letter in it, which he ingenuously showed us, and would, I believe, have given us, if we had asked for it. The baby of the establishment was given him to nurse on the pommel of his saddle, I suppose because he was imagined to have a share in it, which the babe appeared to deny with the most strenuous howls.

On our return, we landed on the reef, and "floundered" about in the water, sometimes up to our ankles, sometimes up to our waists. We saw an infinity of fish, many large ones in the very surf itself, and I think if I had had my young friend's spear I should have made a good bag; having only the common "grains" with me, I got nothing; not even an enormous squid which I speared through and through two or three times, but which always forced itself off again, and escaped eventually into a hole. Those horrible, lidless eyes, and nothing else, of the squid, always struck me as uncanny, especially when you suddenly come upon one staring at you out of a dark hole.

The real principle for catching reef-fish is compression, not penetration, pinching the fish between the wires, not boring a hole in him. Of course with the larger fish, penetration must be resorted to, the weapon growing larger and larger, till it becomes a veritable harpoon, which will hold most things, except perhaps a porpoise, which we have never yet managed to get on board though we have been well into many a one. When a porpoise is wounded he dashes away, with the whole herd after him—whether to eat him, or to see what he had left them in his will, I have never been able to determine. The ordinary "grains" is a very valuable and firm-holding weapon, but cannot be thrown far. You want to be over your game to handle it properly. In this way I once, after a tremendous fight, killed a black scowling trygon, or "stingaree," which weighed one hundred and thirty-five pounds. I really think that these black trygons are the most repulsive and ruffianly-looking of created beings.

The grains will not do every thing. There is a legend of P—— and Loucy having tried to kill a wild-pig with them, and failing most signally.

At low tide day or night all hands go on to the reef and get fish for food and squid for bait. Scalken would have been the man to paint the night-fishing. The torch gives a ruddy glow to the skin of the holder, which is very rich and warm, more especially when standing out against a jet-black sea and sky, as is generally the case, a perfect calm and dark night being indispensable to good fishing.

A Society-Islander, with his feet firmly planted on the sides of his canoe, and bending over the water in act to strike, would make a grand study for a sculptor. The roundness and development of the upper part of the back and arms, from constant use of the spear, is most beautiful; and when not disfigured by elephantiasis, which is too often the case, the lower leg and ankle are perfect; as superior to the coarse limbs of a Maori, as the fetlock of a thorough-bred is to that of a cart-horse.

CHAPTER III.

HUAHINE.

September 5th.—SAILED for Huahine. Saw a very long-flighted flying-fish, with large red pectorals like a gurnet, which possibly it was. Flying-fish *do* fly, moving their pectoral fins with extreme rapidity, like a pair of twin-screws. Moreover, they raise and lower themselves over the tops of waves, and do *not* dip into them to wet either their whistles or their wings. I do not think that their flight is necessarily the proof of submarine persecution; of course, they fly if the bonito is after them, but I suspect that, often as not, they fly for the mere fun of the thing. Why else do they make such wild dabs at the bits of light in a ship's side at night? I remember, between Panama and Rapa, I used to see the cabin "bull's-eyes" surrounded by a circle of scales every morning, left there by flying-fish, attracted by the light within, and possibly asking for a passage.

I should consider two hundred yards a very good flight for a flying-fish, and very few there be who do it, twenty or thirty being the general range. It seems limited, in some degree, by the difficulty of keeping the body horizontal. The tail droops more and more and

HUAHINE.

more, and at last, splash! he goes into the sea. It struck me that as the flying-fish grew scarcer they grew larger, as if only the very big and strong individuals could reach the outside of the circle. Whenever I have seen them in the New-Zealand seas, they have been large and solitary. The largest I ever saw (twenty-two inches, if I recollect right) flew on board the Tauranga, a small steamer, in which I was taking a passage to the Bay of Islands, in New Zealand. It went slap into the engine-room, and smote the engineer a smart rap on the cheek. He, supposing that his stoker had assaulted him, used language which I need not repeat, and threatened reprisals. On explanation being given, however, the fish was discovered, and handed over to Dr. Hector for preservation in the Colonial Museum, where it may now, I have no doubt, be seen by the curious.

From Panama to Wellington, from New Zealand to New Caledonia, from Auckland to Tahiti, and back again, a fair number of miles, I have watched the flying-fish carefully, and I never saw one seized by a bird in its flight. Nor have I ever seen such an occurrence in the Atlantic or West-Indian seas. I cannot doubt that it happens somewhere, because I have seen pictures of it, but in the seas *I* know it must be rare. Possibly other lands, other manners, and likely enough other flying-fish and sea-fowl.

I should as soon think it possible for a kiw to catch a rifle-ball in full flight, as for any real sea-bird to seize a flying-fish on the wing. The albatross I dismiss at once, his chances of trying are too few to bring him into question, as far as the South Pacific is concerned. The frigate-bird, or man-of-war hawk, decidedly the swiftest flier among sea-birds I have ever seen, seems to have given up fishing on his own account altgether, and makes use of the tern as his fishmonger. The tern, if the sea be smooth, has a neat little way of picking up small morsels from its surface, and, if necessary, makes a very respectable gannet-like splash; never, however, as far as I have seen, immersing himself, and always keeping his wings in motion, to get him up again.

The gannet, a splendid yellow-headed species of which is common in the South Pacific, is, I think, the finest of all fishing-birds from John o'Groat's House to the Chatham Islands. But even he could never catch a flying-fish, his strong point being "perpendicular," not the horizontal pace. Soaring high, he marks his prey beneath him, and shutting up his wings (like a wood-pigeon darting into cover) he plunges downward with a splash that makes one's head ache to look at, and after a semicircular dive of five or six yards he emerges, sneezing and flapping, with his prey safely lodged in his throat.

I have seen a good deal of gannet-life, both domestic and public. On Nepean and Philip Islands, in the Norfolk-Island group, I used to find the fond gannet mother sitting affectionately by the side of the snow-white fluff she called her child (*paterfamilias* having made himself scarce long before we reached the party) till I was within two or three yards of her, when she solemnly disgorged the two fish she had cooking in her throat for her darlings' supper, and followed her mate's example. These two fish on Nepean Island were nearly always a species of anchovy, with the brown line of flesh, or fish, strongly marked; they were closely pressed together, and had evidently undergone a process of maceration if not of digestion. The New-Zealand "sala," like his Maori fellow-countryman, is of a more warlike nature, and fights fiercely for the sanctity of his nursery.

I once saw the most stout-hearted of British skippers fairly driven off a rookery of them with his breeks in rags and his legs in holes, positively obliged to retreat and arm himself with a big stick before he could make his ground good. Even after the old birds were driven off, we had to walk warily among the sharp-billed powder-puffs, as they never missed a chance of giving us a sharp prod if we came within their reach.

I have watched the osprey fishing carefully, and never saw him swoop at a flying-fish; if he did, I would back the fish.

One rarely sees him on the flying-fish ground, generally contenting himself with beating the shallow water inside the reef; generally, as far as I have seen, grabbing his prey in a very slow, hovering fashion, without any of the murderous lightning dash of the falcon.

I have seen the sea in the Indian Ocean alive with big fish, and sea-birds darting down to secure their prey. But I suspect that it was a case of the flying-fish chasing the bril and the seer-fish, and the bonito chasing the flying-fish, and the birds picking up the wounded bril, not the flying-fish, in full flight. I must repeat that I never saw a bird, a real sea-bird, capable of bagging a "rocketing" flying-fish; if I knew the bird that could, and could tame him as John Chinaman tames the cormorant, what glorious fish-hawking I would have!

September 6th.—As soon as it was light we ran down for the land, rounding the northern corner of the island. The skipper, aloft on the foreyard, soon made out the opening in the reef, and we stood in for it, opening out a beautiful bay, with trees and white houses sprinkled along its shores. The wind was dead out, and the channel very narrow, and the first board we stood on a little too far, and the little ship shooting ahead in stays, we looked for a moment very like landing on the top of the reef, which would have been mighty unpleasant with the surf there was on.

But even this momentary uneasiness could not prevent our remarking the beautiful effect produced by the fresh breeze catching the top of the breaking roller, and sending it up in a long, wavy wall of sparkling diamonds.

As soon as we were well through the pass the brown pilot came on board, and, disdaining to explain why he had not appeared before, merely remarked to the skipper, "You too much saucy the reef," as if he suspected him of trying to do him out of his dues.

Our friend, to prevent our pleading ignorance, in case of our committing any little peccadillo on the island, presented us with the penal code, elegantly written in an ancient copy-book. It struck us as having been compiled more for the sake of the rulers than the ruled. After studying it carefully, we came to the conclusion that it was all a matter of dollars, and that having dollars you could do what you like, just as at

HUAHINE. 69

home. Some one proposed that we should "square" the authorities with a five-pound note, and go in for an unlimited "swop" as long as it lasted, begging them to tell us when we had sinned to the full amount. It is not dear; a man could be frightfully wicked for a ten-pound note if he confined himself strictly to crime. If he threw his money away by paying the queen ten dollars for a deserter, or two for making a man go ashore against his will, or another two for stopping on shore after nine o'clock at night, and luxuries of that sort, why, then the thing would come more expensive. Of course, you do not pay unless you are found out, but in order to prevent that you must be very careful, as there is a set of disreputable beings here who prowl about at night and peer through the bars of the houses, with an eye to dollars.

The island is governed by a queen (now in Tahiti); she is governed by a prime-minister and a house of peers, who bully them both and have all the real power in their hands.

Went on shore and called on Mr. and Mrs. Saville, the missionaries. I consider that the missionary's wife is a missionary herself; and, in a large number of cases, the most efficient one of the two.

The well-filled book-shelves showed their owner to be a man of education and culture. He is also a doctor, not a mere *dilettante*, but an ex-student of the London University. I think it is an excellent thing for a missionary to pass at least one session in the wards of a hospital before he starts; that is if he have a fancy for it, if not he is likely to do more harm than good.

He accompanied us back to the yacht, and gave us

the island news. How they had "revolushed" the other day (pardon the slang, there is a species of *lingua Franca* in the South Seas wonderfully catching), and he fears will shortly do so again, which will be a bad thing for his people. There is the rub; Christianity is the religion of peace, but, as men will and indeed must go to war, we must have a religion to suit both states of existence. A *coup d'état* is also expected at Raiatea, our next island. Some fiend in human form tried to console him by saying that even that was better than a "riot-here," but he was punished by his joke falling utterly flat. Here a revolution is a purely political affair; there it generally causes a heavy fight, so we may come in for some fun.

All the morning the schooner was crowded with natives, many of them ill, coming to be doctored. "Elephantiasis is very prevalent here, even among the European residents. The early symptoms are—" Here the doctor was stopped, this not being a medical work. Queen Elizabeth, having a spite against a youthful rival, would have banished her to this island, had she known of its existence; a horrible revenge, for her ankles would have been clean spoilt in a twelvemonth perhaps.

After luncheon we cruised inside; the life-boat, I suspect, making an experiment or two to test which was the hardest, her mahogany planking or the coral. The results were in favor of the coral, which cuts like a knife.

In a lovely cove we found a number of women and children immersed to their middles, like a graduated row of Pandœan pipes, fishing with the rod and line in a highly-artistic manner. The bait was a little pounded crab, a very small bit of which was used. They cast their line very deftly, and when they hooked a fish paralyzed it by a most crafty swing round their heads, and pouched it. I never saw better fishing; no, not even among the bank-fishers of Thames or Trent; their striking was perfection. The amusement seemed to be entirely confined to women, and the immature of the opposite sex; as we gazed at them a feeling of shyness and an inclination to giggle seemed to come over them now and then, but the latter most of them could not indulge in with safety, as they carried their bait where the Eton boy carried his "wums;" altogether they looked singularly like a row of brown herons.

On our return, called and gossiped for an hour with Mr. Saville and his family. It is hard to say how thoroughly refreshing the sight of his two darling little children was, even to the bachelor half of us; even a brown gentleman who came in evidently submitted to the same influence. I do not know why, but there is always something curious to me in the relationship between the colored man and the white child. The child invariably assumes an attitude of the most intense superiority over her brown friend, patronizing while loving him; while he as invariably bows down and worships with a tenderness and courteousness which is very beautiful.

More island gossip. The missionaries having taken the power of performing legal marriages into their own hands, the natives have ingeniously contrived to hold their own by assuming that of civil divorce, and some curious cases arose in consequence. There is a white man living here, called Mr. What's-his-name, whose wife being, I suppose, tired of nursing, got divorced from him one fine day when he was ill and unable to appear in court. Having now got well, he has appealed again and again for a fresh trial, but in vain; and is likely to remain a divorced man to the end of his days. Now this is not a question of White *vs.* Brown, for the ex-Mrs. What's-her-name is a full-blooded Lima Spaniard, real *sangre azul*. Is it not quaint to find a brown society divorce-court deciding a case of White *vs.* White?

The natives here insist on choosing their own "sacred" music. A most pious effusion of the lower school of divinity was "offered up" to the tune of "So early in the morning."

Sauntered back along the shore, among the native warrés. They are built as usual of upright bamboos or hibiscus-sticks, supporting a roof which forms one large room.

"Come in; you need not be afraid. They are all my own people," quoth our friend, to our slight amusement. If he had an idea of the queer places into which we had poked our noses during the last few years, he would not have fancied that we needed encouragement.

And so, shaking hands with everybody, we went on board.

September 17*th.*—At ten o'clock in the morning we made ourselves tidy to go to a "school-inspection," and with the recollections of similar inflictions at home we pulled ashore in a very low state of mind.

School-inspection! it was a *fête* or bacchanaliad! On the very beach we were received by a perfect torrent of muslin, smiles, and laughter, which swept us into the school-room—a large, open, cool, well-planned building, with all manner of kindly greetings.

As they all settled down, we found that there were three classes of scholars—girls, boys, and grown women—all got up in their best clothes to do us honor, and not only that, but crowned one and all with the most beautiful and tasteful wreaths it has ever been our lot to see; there was not one single wreath round the forehead or neck of a girl or boy which was not admirable, in the judgment with which the flowers were selected and arranged, and the scent!—orange-flowers being used in profusion; "'twas as a bridal!" They had been employed since early dawn in gathering and arranging them. It is not always that this flower-wreath-wearing is permitted in school. They may wear them to the door, but must leave them outside. The naughty little dears have invented a flower language for themselves, and make love under "teacher's" very nose without a word or a glance passing.

After infinite wrigglings, gigglings, and whisperings, it was proposed that a song should be sung in P——'s honor. Songs of this sort are sung to impromptu words like the "Schnada hufflem" of the Tyrolese, and it required no little encouragement to induce the shy little prima donna to begin. At last she commenced in a wild, high-pitched key, and was gallantly seconded by an elderly lady in spectacles, who had a private and particular "skirl" of her own, which was supposed to be very perfect; it put me much in mind of the strange, falsetto notes so common in Arab songs: altogether it was most pretty and pleasing, and their idea of time seemed absolutely perfect, and, though different possibly from our own, they evidently seem to have a decidedly musical talent: in fact, they can sing any thing, even the alphabet, out of which apparently dry subject they have made a really pretty song, a sort of "A with an A with a B-A-Ba" ballad, which, when closed with clapping of hands and joyous laughter, is by no means to be despised. Every now and again one of the more advanced pupils would give us her slate filled with monstrous sums, and retire to her place, blushing and giggling, which struck us as being the most original form of flirting we had ever seen. Unfortunately, we were bad arithmeticians, or I firmly believe that we should have discovered that there was a way of making love in a rule-of-three sum. There is nothing the darlings could not do; I am firmly convinced that they could dance the multiplication-table if they tried.

Another pretty song they had was descriptive of all manner of employments—digging, weaving, etc.—accompanied with appropriate motions; arms, hands, and legs, being freely used. The one they delighted most in was the rowing-song, in which they pulled with ever-increasing vigor, till at last they tumbled one atop of t'other, with shrieks of joyous laughter and infinite innocent romping.

There was one wee brown boy in a chair who was as good as a play in his way. To watch how thoroughly he threw himself into the spirit of the thing, gracefully waving his arms and legs in time to the singing, was delightful; I do not think that he could have been more than two years old, but he evidently had the old spirit in his very blood.

Some of the young princes and princesses were presented to us, all of a decidedly high-caste type, and very well-mannered. They all had almost flaxen hair, and their complexions were not darker than those of Marseilles children of the same age, if as dark. Among them was the ex-King of Raiatea, a nice, bright-looking lad, dressed in white shirt and trousers, who seemed to trouble himself mighty little about his lost grandeur.

The school-inspection being over, the whole of the scholars, little and big, passed before us, every one, as they passed, giving a pretty shake of the hand, and depositing his or her wreath at our feet, till we were knee-deep in flowers. It was the prettiest, newest, freshest thing that either of us had ever seen. The dresses, flowers, and cheerful laughter, gave a sunshine to the whole affair which it is impossible to describe. We loaded ourselves with their beautiful wreaths, wherewith to decorate our cabin, and strolled down to the beach, like heathen deities out for a walk, attended by their worshippers.

Just as we pushed off from the shore, our eyes were simultaneously attracted to a most lovely vision: a tall and graceful girl, dressed in a long white muslin sacque, leaning on the shoulder of a brown girl. Her whole form undulating with grace as she walked, her eyes were full and swimming with light, her beautiful lips full, red, and rosy; her hair, poor Heine says—

> "Like a warm moonlight night,
> Streamed from her broad-crowned temples down,
> And curled all dreamily beautiful,
> Around her sweet, pale face."

Oh, such a beautiful creature! such a real, ideal Cleopatra!

We thought that we had discovered a new race of Kanakas, and wondered what island had the privilege of producing such beauty. We asked, and found, alas, that she was only the divorced Mrs. What's-her-name from Lima!

In the afternoon P—— and Louey started in the lifeboat, on a voyage of exploration inside the reef, their point being a strait which divides the island into two halves. After a long sail with baffling winds, we reached what appeared to be an enormous bay, with a small island across the entrance. Beating through the channel between it and the land, we found ourselves in a mighty basin, surrounded by towering green mountains. At the opposite end one could see a narrow channel winding in and out between them. It was a perfect fairy-land! Working up through the channel, we found ourselves in another deep bay on the weather-side of the main island, and, after beating out to seaward for some time, reached a little village. A kindly native waded out into the shallow water and piloted us in. As soon as the boat was made fast, he carried me ashore as easily as if I had been a baby. The people were kindly and hospitable, as usual, offering to load the boat with fruit to any extent.

To my great delight, they showed me the often-described, seldom-seen, manner of making fire by friction. One of the boys took a long, dry hibiscus-stick, about an inch and a half in diameter, cut a piece of bark off it to get a flat surface, squatted down upon it to keep it steady, and worked away with a little pointed stick till a groove gradually appeared, at the far end of which the dust produced by the friction collected. This soon began to smoke, and in about a minute caught fire, showing that the savage had practically understood the "correlation of forces," long before Mrs. Somerville or Dr. Tyndall.

Meanwhile, Mr. Saville, a most intelligent native, and I, with a native rejoicing in the name of Riti, or Rice, had been on an excursion in another direction. Our friend Riti had obtained his name from having attended one of Queen Pomare's children during its illness. It seemed that the child asked constantly for rice; and so, after the fashion of these parts, the name of the thing brought descended onto the bearer thereof. There is a gentleman here whose name, being translated, means merely "a drop of tea." And the great name Pomare itself, which has passed through so many generations, means simply "he who coughs in the night." The great object of our expedition was to examine some very extensive and sacred "marais," a few miles down the bay in which we were anchored.

A very pleasant walk through the scrub on the raised coral-beach at the foot of the older hills, brought us to the edge of a lagoon, which was separated from the sea by a wide-sweeping reef, covered thickly with cocoas, bread-fruit, and iron trees. We took canoe, and paddled a mile or so, to a large and curious village, a real "Phal-banten" affair, built principally over the water on piles and large stones. Some of the houses were of considerable size, the walls (?) formed of hibiscus or bamboo poles, with sufficiently large intersticces between to admit of a very free current of air, which the inhabitants seemed to enjoy exceedingly. The floor was covered with sweet-scented dry grass and bright mats, the general effect being very clean and tidy. The mats seemed to be used as some sort of separation between the different branches of the family. Each set being evidently distinct from the other, and having its own little objects of use or luxury grouped upon it. The general impression was really a very pleasant one.

The opening of this lagoon into the sea is the Thermopylæ of Huahine, the scene of the defeat of the French by the islanders, in 1847. Headed by a tough old Scotchman, they fought very bravely, killing a great number of their adversaries, and even capturing a gun, at least for a time. Our friend Te Riki, who was in the fight, pointed out all the principal points of interest, and even the identical stones behind which his men sheltered themselves. The gun seems to have been excellently placed, so as to command the narrow path from the village; but the natives made a flank movement over the ridge and killed every artilleryman. "Here stood the officer behind, and when all his men were killed, he advanced and fired the gun himself for the last time, being instantly shot down." Almost the only ammunition the Kanakas had was composed of the heads of nails, extracted from barrel-hoops, a mighty nasty sort of thing at close quarters.

They gallantly buried the dead Frenchmen with greatest care on the reef outside.

To and from Thermopylæ, the village girls and boys followed our steps in a small crowd, and evidently carefully treasured up Te Riki's descriptions of the great fight. Passing a bush of tea-tree, whose leaves had the proper brown-red color, they made a rush at it, and in a moment had woven themselves all manner of head-dresses, collars, and ceintures, after the ancient manner. These wild-leaf dresses have a great attraction for me, and great taste is always shown in their arrangement. Seeing that we took an interest in the affair, they began to weave, and twist, and twine all manner of adornments for us, and clicked and screamed with delight when we put them on. The people of this village are the most natural and unsophisticated of any I have met with in all my wanderings; I fancy that it is a rare thing for them ever to see a white man, except the missionary.

The great "marai" on the hill-side above the village is now overgrown with scrub, but one can still make out its principal features. It consists of a series of terraces of stone, placed without any particular regard to regularity, against the hill-side—lanes being left between them. They were partly places for religious rites, and partly places of meeting for the discussion of public affairs. Along the edge of one of the principal terraces is a row of upright stones, said to have been placed there at the first subdivision of the land between the emigrant tribes, and still called "the stones of dividing." Te Riki assured me that the history of each of these was perfectly well known to the chiefs at the present time, and he pointed me out the particular stone which referred to the land possessed by his tribe. I wonder whether the Maori-Meri-Ponanin, which is often connected with land-titles in New Zealand, is a relic of this custom?

I asked about human sacrifices. Te Riki denied that they had ever taken place on this large public marai, and pointed out a peculiar deep lane, walled in on each side, up which the pigs used to be driven long, long ago: he said that human sacrifices were offered up occasionally in times of great national distress, on the smaller private marais, which are very numerous along the shores of the lagoon. He repudiated the idea of their ever having been eaten, with disgust and scorn.

One large and very sacred stone resting on three others, apparently as it had fallen from the neighboring hill, was pointed out to me as having been the high altar, and possibly was the cause of the marai being built around it. It was exactly like the so-called Druidical altars of Brittany and Cornwall.

Wherever a savage race finds a big stone supported by others, they believe at once that it has been so placed by supernatural means, and worship through it the tremendous forces which did so. Then they try and propitiate these forces by giving presents to their representative. In time comes a man more crafty than the rest of his tribe, or possibly slightly mad, and declares that the forces have come to him in his sleep, and told him to take care of their representative and its presents. At first the priest and chief squabble on the subject, and the chief is apt to get the worst; sometimes, however, the priest gets clubbed, and, as civilization advances, both see that it is to their mutual advantage to pull together to a certain extent. Population increasing and food becoming scarce, part of the tribe have to migrate, taking with them a priest who, finding no sacred stone in the new country (probably a rich alluvial plain), builds one, and so wags the world! From the storm-dropped stone at Huahine you get the gilded dome of St. Paul's.

We crossed the lagoon in a canoe to the reef, which was densely wooded, and inspected some more marais. One very large one was built of enormous slabs of coral-rock set on their edges, and the interior filled up with smaller stones. It was built on the flat ground and regularly terraced. I should think it some thirty feet by fourteen feet high.

Here a big bunch of the fibre of the cocoa-nut at the mouth of a hole, told of the presence of the cocoa-nut robber-crab, or rather shelnm-lobster. We worked hard to get him, and I am sorry to say brought down a good deal of the marai in the excitement of our hunt; however, he was either not at home or had a bolting-hole, and we got him not. He climbs here and cuts off the cocoa-nuts: some say that he comes down on the top of the cocoa-nut; others that he comes down the way he went up. Who is right I know not, for I never saw him. Oh, it was hot! and what whirlwinds of poisonous flies whizzed around us! In sheer desperation we burst through the jungle, and emerged, mosquito-bitten, sweat-bedabbled, into the hard white sand, and into the roaring, tearing, fresh trade-wind, that sent the blue sea foaming to our feet.

Besides the marais, we visited a very remarkable cyclopean causeway, said to have been built by a numerons tribe in a single night, in order to procure a famous beauty as the wife of their chief; it being supposed proper to do something heroical and out of the common on these occasions, to show the lady the value placed on her charms. The Duke of Bridgewater is said to have devoted himself to canal-cutting because the woman he wished to marry refused him. Had he cut his canal first and proposed afterward, the case might have been different.

Returning home in the dusk, my friend Mr. Saville, who was sitting in front of me in the canoe, nearly had a severe if not fatal accident from a curious cause.

There is in all these waters a gar or guard-fish (hemiramphus ?) some two feet long, with a hard and sharp prolonged lower jaw. This fish has an unpleasant custom, when suddenly startled, of leaping out of the water with such extreme velocity as to transfix any soft substance which happens to be in its way. Cases of severe wounds, even death, from this cause are by no means unknown. In this case Mr. Saville was saved by the fish striking him obliquely (as I plainly saw, not being a foot from him); had it hit him fairly end on, between the ribs, the consequences would certainly have been serious. As it was, he was quit for a thump and some fish-scales on his coat. I have often observed the same power of making a strong rush among the small gar-fish of New Zealand, a rush strong enough to bring them into a boat. These latter fish have a wide distribution; I have caught them in the harbors of Suez, Auckland, New Zealand, and Tahiti.

Our walk home, pleasant enough in itself, was rendered still more so by the evidences of kindly feeling between my companion and his flock. If any good is to be done here by religious teaching, these new missionaries are the men to do it. They have most certainly gained both the affection and respect of the people, and are looked upon as friends, not as servants.

Beguiling the walk with gossip, my friend Riti, a most grave and proper man, confessed to have just married his eighth wife, some of the others being dead and some divorced, but he does not seem quite clear which is which. The real history of this marriage-and-divorce question cannot be entered upon here, it being fitter for the pages of the *Lancet* than for the drawing-room. Though, for that matter, it seems by no means impossible that that excellent medical journal may find its way into every lady's boudoir, if things go on as they are going. There are many social "questions" of this sort, which are often discussed but never answered, because a feeling of natural decency forbids those who really understand the subject from airing their knowledge in general society.

Arrived on board, Mr. Saville's "boy" (here as in the Indies all male servants are boys, irrespective of age) demonstrated the art of fire-rubbing to us again, and we carefully preserved the sticks as curiosities.

In early times there arose difficulties in the infant church at Huahine very like those hinted at by the fathers of the early church of Corinth.

The "communicants" would drink far too much sacramental wine, and wink in a highly-improper manner after having done so. This sort of thing could never answer, either one way or the other, being in fact both improper and expensive. So the wine was stopped, and a mixture of cocoa-nut water and molasses (why molasses?) was substituted, to, I should imagine, the infinitely increased confusion of a question quite intricate enough before.

Possibly, however, they had read their "Faust," and knew that

> "Wine is grape, and grapes are wood,
> The cocoa-nut yields wine as good."

September 8th.—Mr. Saville came on board at breakfast-time to tell us that the regent, the queen's speaker, and some of the principal chiefs, requested P——'s presence on shore, in order to present him with a gift, as a token of their kindliness and good-will. On shore we found a large portion of the population waiting to receive us, and accompanied by them we walked up to the queen's house, and were solemnly introduced into her reception-room. We were there received by the chiefs, and our flaxen-haired friends the princes and princesses, and better-behaved and better-mannered princes and princesses it would be hard to find. We shook hands all round, and pelted each other with the flowers of compliment through the kindly medium of Mr. Saville.

The present consisted of about two boat-loads of yams, bananas, cocoa-nuts, etc., besides three small pigs and half a dozen fowls. P—— thanked them, and invited them on board in half an hour, during which short time Mr. Saville bundled off to his school to tell his young people to be ready to join whatever might be going on a little later.

The regent and chiefs, with the royal children,

came on board at the appointed time, and evidently admired our pleasant little craft immensely, having never before, I fancy, seen any thing but small coasting-schooners, in which the captain's cabin is any thing but "all same one house." What delighted them most was the galley below, and they could not make out how we could keep a fire in it without burning the ship; and, though one would have supposed it hot enough in all conscience on deck, they positively enjoyed the extra heat: I believe that the way to deter these people from being naughty would be to preach a future eternity of ice. It is a great mistake to suppose that the idea of the "fire-punishment" must necessarily have arisen in a hot climate; I have seen the natives of hot climates suffer from cold, but never, if I remember, from heat.

The Queen of Huahine's speaker is as unlike Mr. Denison, as far as personal appearance is concerned, as it is well possible to imagine. He is most fearfully diseased and distorted. In other respects, some resemblance might be discovered, as he is a most courteous, and, we are given to understand, talented man.

Our visitors were mightily tickled at the care we had taken of "the boy's" fire-sticks, marvelling how men who could command countless matches, could be interested in such relics of barbarism. P—— presented the ex-King of Raiatea with a striped blue rowing-cap, and his brothers and sisters with infinite pots of jam, which were highly appreciated. A sack of flour was placed in the boat for the chiefs, a great treat for them, and with much hand-shaking they went on shore.

Then there was peace on board till two o'clock, when a fresh rumpus began. The school-children, and very fine grown children some of them were, collected on the beach, and the boats were sent to fetch them, the life-boat and the "fish-fag" being loaded to the water's edge; the life-boat on one occasion bringing off no fewer than thirty-seven very strapping young ladies. Luckily the water was smooth, or even *she* might have capsized; not that it would have made much difference, they would have swum on board singing. They were evidently in a high state of delight, laughing, cheering, and clapping their hands in ecstasy, at the prospect of an outing.

P—— and the skipper received them at the gangway, and stevedore Mitchell "took tally" as they came on board; a hundred and twenty-two regulars, besides some thirty strange sheep, who came off in private canoes.

First they explored the cabin, pouring down one hatchway and surging up the other; and when they had exhausted the marvels of the lower world, they seated themselves on the deck in close ranks and began to sing. What a wonderful picture it would have made! and what a pity it was that there was no one to do it justice, either with pen or pencil! The dense mass of merry faces and flashing teeth and eyes; the gay wreaths and flower-crowns; their bright, pure, graceful dresses; the lithe swaying of their bodies and movement of their limbs as they sang; and the occasional unanimous clap of their hands from one end of the ship to the other. Captain Cook himself never saw any thing better!

To get from one end of the schooner, one had to climb "outside," so closely packed were they; and the mighty bunches of green and golden bananas which festooned the rigging added no little to the picturesqueness of general effect.

After giving us half a dozen songs, each prettier than the other, they began to leave the ship, pouring over the side like a snow-wreath, laughing, singing, and decorating us and the sailors with their beautiful flower-wreaths. P——'s right arm fairly broke down with the repeated, or rather uninterrupted, hand-shaking.

Surely such a school-feast was never seen before; and I know not where you could find such a set of well-behaved, affectionate children to make another.

The pigs presented to us turn out to be hideous little animals of some aboriginal breed, at least one-third head, and very ugly head too. They gave one the general impression of having been squeezed from their youth up between two tight boards. And their manner corresponded with their appearance; wickeder pork, for its age, I never saw alive! When stevedore Mitchell civilly offered one a banana, it flew at him and barked like a dog, to his no small discomfiture. Then it dropped on its fore-knees, and seemed for some time to be rapt in religious contemplation. After fortifying its soul with prayer, it quite suddenly, and quite *à propos des bottes*, attacked one of our little Maori porkers, who was poking about the deck thinking no evil, and a tremendous fight ensued. Maori was so fat and round that for some time the new "chum" could not raise a bite out of him, more particularly as he steadily presented the fattest and roundest part of his person to his adversary. At last a new idea seemed to strike the latter, and he took poor Maori by the tail and made him squeak again. Maori, paralyzed for a time, retired into a quiet corner, thought the thing over, and, his native fighting-blood gradually rising to boiling-point, he came out with a rush, and, with many a prod, and poke, and bite, finished off his slab-sided assailant in one last and decisive round.

He turned out a clever and original pig, but never became really civilized.

Idled away half an hour watching a young man and some boys (among whom was my young friend the ex-king, now dressed in nothing but the "paréu") practising spear-throwing at the stump of a cocoa-branch stuck into the sand. The spear here is thrown-rather underhand, the shaft resting on the two forefingers of the left hand, and propelled by the tips of the first two fingers of the right. They threw up to ten or fifteen yards with fair accuracy, the young man nailing his palm-branch at nearly every throw; but it seemed more adapted for fishing than fighting. They are not to be compared with the New-Caledonians or the Pine-Islanders, who drive light spears of hard wood with tremendous force, by means of a "hitch" made of the wool of the flying-fox. By-the-way, their best spears almost always have a head with a nose and chin like Punch's carved on them, as also have often their canoes. I wonder where they got that ideal face, so utterly unlike their own, from?

The West-Australian blacks, however, with the throwing-stick, would give them both points and beat them hollow. I have seen them make very fair sticks at swallows on the wing, without of course killing them, but going mighty near them.

Seeing a mighty bustle of folk on the reef, paddled up, and found them preparing a labyrinth of fish-traps for an expected high tide, making leads and *cul-de-sacs* of coral as artful as any set nets for salmon. Curious to see how crafty the natives were not to lift a lump of rock out of water, but to carry it along beneath it.

An evening, as here at Huahine, is a mighty pleasant affair. From the moment we land, a cloud of light infantry attend our steps; running, jumping, spear-throwing, and larking generally. Now and again, as we lounge along in the bright moonlight, a dusky beauty, with a charming shyness, gives a sweet-scented flower, and then subsides among the feet of her young companions, overcome with the sense of her own audacity—very much! They may be a little naughty, but that is no reason why you should be naughty, and there is no doubt that the man, who wishes to pass through these islands pleasantly and with the love and respect of their inhabitants, cannot do better than show that he is above the mere profligacy of the whaler or the beach-man. Apart from other considerations, by doing this, you find that you are trusted by women who would never have approached you, had they fancied that you were a mere idle voluptuary. And, really, I have met few women who appreciate the mutual-trust system more, or who are more worthy of it.

It really seems to open up a new life to them when they are talked to as reasonable beings, and nothing more.

To compare the "Broom-road" of Huahine with the streets of an English town after nightfall, would be a most infamous libel on the former. What immorality there may be, is infinitely less immoral in Huahine than in England, as one might easily prove did one care to go into the foul subject.

Sauntering along, attended by our train of dusky beauties, we met our Cleopatra of yesterday, Mrs. What's-her-name? What's-her-name? Why, what should it be but Maria Dolores! and a very pretty name, too. And gentle and kindly, and speaking a soft and pleasant form of English, was Maria Dolores! And, moreover, quite ready to have any amount of baskets full of the flowers of compliment, showered over her in that stiff tongue. We rambled and scrambled together over the hibiscus fences, and in and out among the houses, without the slightest regard to the laws of trespass; and peeped and peered about without much regard to those of domestic privacy. Cleopatra enlivening the walk with many a choice bit of island scandal, which would have done good service in a St. James's Street club; but generally rather too highly flavored to be admitted into the pages of this proper and decent chronicle.

A pretty little girl and boy coming up to kiss P——'s hand, he asked her who was supposed to look after the royal children. "Oh, nobody," she answered, with a graceful carelessness; "they look after themselves." And I must say they seemed to do it very well.

The whole beach was alive with fish-scraping and fish-cooking, the products of the artful arrangements we had watched in the afternoon. And we might have

HUAHINE.

loaded a boat with the cheerfully-proffered presents. The cookery was carried on in the real old "Maori" way, by means of hot stones, and any one who can find a better (barring the mystery of the wet newspaper) let him tell it me, and I'll do what I can for him.

Hearing a rub-dub-dubbing approaching, we feared that our 'long-shore cruise was coming to an end, and meeting the princes beating the "rappel," we expressed our sorrow at having to go on board so soon. "Oh!" quoth Cleopatra, with her loftiest air, "laws were not made for *you*." And we continued our saunter with ever-increasing satisfaction, every patch of bright moonlight or dim shade producing some fresh group of prettiness; but we are not going to tell you *all* we saw that evening!

Farewell, Huahine! surely you take your name from "Wahine"—γυνή—woman!

CHAPTER IV.

RAIATEA AND TAHA.

September 9th.—ALAS, alas! That abominable invention of civilization called time, has decreed that we shall tarry no longer at Huahine, the woman's island. It is, indeed, a perfect little garden of Eden; plenty of Eves, but no snakes. They have not tasted the tree of knowledge of good and evil as yet. Nature is almost their only law, hard as the missionaries have tried to elevate them to a sense of sin.

Kind little Mr. S—— came on board at nine to say good-by; and, in spite of many assurances that we should find Raiatea not nearly so pleasant, we weighed anchor at ten, and, exchanging farewell salutations with the royal flag, stood out of the cozy little harbor. It seems to me that I can't leave any one of these islands without feeling low and sentimental. I know each time that another leaf of the pleasantest part of my life-book is past and finished.

At about one o'clock, steering by the directions we had received from Huahine, we found ourselves off the northeast end of Raiatea, where a pilot came off to us to show us the passage through the reef. And a strange reef it was; like a great necklace, enclosing both

Raiatea and Taha, the neighboring island, while to complete the simile, a quantity of gigantic emeralds, consisting of most lovely little islets, were threaded at regular intervals upon the white surf-line. Looking through the passage between Raiatea and Taha, we could see in the far distance the splendid peak of Borra-Borra, rising like some giant's castle out of the sea.

I noticed that the little reef-islands lay generally in couples, with bold water between them, giving them the appearance of poetical gate-posts, placed there on purpose to mark the entrances to the lagoon.

We shot through one of these narrow gaps, and run down toward Uturoa, the chief settlement, where we came to an anchor. Immediately, as at Huahine, the penal code was handed to us by the pilot, this time in a washing-book; given to us as it were some criminal bill of fare, the exact price of the most delightful offences being stated to half a dollar. The laws read horribly strict, but they are seldom carried out to the letter, unless the king happens to be short of spirituous liquors, and wants to raise his revenue, when he has only to put into force the one relating to every one being in their houses by nine o'clock P. M., to screw a couple of dollars apiece out of half the population. When I asked Queen Moé whether I should have to respect this rule, she gave me to understand that I might be as naughty as ever I liked with impunity, which was very nice.

I had been intrusted with some letters by Queen Pomare, the directions on which would fill Bedlam with post-office officials in six months, besides a letter of introduction to Queen Moé from her cousin in Tahiti, and soon after our arrival we proceeded on shore to deliver them. First we reported ourselves to the missionary, Mr. V——, a most agreeable and kind-hearted gentleman, whose wife has suffered terribly in health from the heat of the climate. Having no children of their own, they have adopted a charming little native girl, after the custom of the country. The Society-Islanders are death on adoption, as a Yankee would say. Nearly every one has four parents, the real ones and their feeding ones; the second couple being responsible for their bringing up and education, which consists chiefly of teaching them to spear fish, the crabs which infest the shore and dig it into holes, representing their A, B, C, and are considered in the eye of the law as being nearer relations than the real papa and mamma. It must be rather hard on the young native to have to keep the fifth commandment double. The children are often bespoken before birth, and handed over as soon as they are weaned. I don't know what this custom originated in, but I have a fanciful theory that it was introduced by the fond fathers to check that engrossing, offensive, and boring pride which possessed their helpmates whenever they had produced, and were engaged in rearing, a child of their own. A woman with a new baby, or a man with a new book, is a monomaniac and a bore.

Relationships in these small islands are intricate and confusing enough, but when this adoptive element is introduced they become utterly maddening and hopeless.

Then we went down to Queen Moó's, with her letters and a parcel from her cousin Moetia. We were shown into her reception-house, a large bird-cage room on a platform about two feet from the ground, while some one went up to her private house to announce our arrival. These buildings have one great advantage worth introducing into civilized society, which is, that you can always look through the bars to see who is at home before paying your visit.

At last she appeared, a tall, graceful, wonderfully pretty girl. She had rather a large but well-shaped head with an unusual amount of forehead, under which were a pair of the biggest, roundest, shyest, gentlest, quietly-laughingest (bother the adjectives!) eyes I ever saw, a small *retroussé* nose, and a most lovely little mouth that puckered up her cheeks into cozy little dimples whenever she smiled; the lady-like gentleness of her manner, and the quaintness and *naïveté* of her words and ideas, were most charming.

Tamatoa, her husband, is a most awful sweep, committing the most fearful extravagances when he is drunk, which is his normal condition. The other day, when slightly elevated, he took a Snider rifle, purporting to polish off a minister or two by way of a lark. Having loaded it the right way, he thought to increase the effect by shoving a lot more ammunition down the barrel, by which exploit he nearly succeeded in blowing his arm off. This the queen told us with the greatest coolness and gravity.

But, like most men, he has his good points, the chief one being that when he is drunk he goes away on the loose; and when he is sober, shuts himself up altogether. He is the son of Queen Pomare, but, instead of taking after his sainted mother, imitates the noble example of his father, a very naughty old man.

Outside the house I was introduced to several native lions; among them Queen Pomare's mother, a wonderful old lady with an eye as keen and piercing as a hawk, old as she was. We have just arrived at a political crisis in Raiatea; Taha (the next island), the Ireland of this kingdom, has demanded a separate government, because King Tamatoa wastes so much of the revenues on orange-rum and other spirituous liquors. No one knows how it will be settled, and a war is looked upon as more than probable.

This orange-rum drinking is a regular and elaborate ceremony—no light, casual intoxication. Large parties of men and women go up into the mountains for the sole purpose of drinking themselves drunk and enjoying the sensation. It is a weak, vinegary stuff, I believe, about two pailfuls or so being required to make a man jovial. They keep on brewing and drinking for a month or six weeks, till at last some one gets killed, or drinks himself to death, when they return to their villages and are penitent until their digestions are restored.

A good deal of intoxication, said Mr. V——, arises out of connubial differences. There is a quarrel, and the weaker vessel gets drunk and takes up with another man out of spite. On this the injured husband drowns his sorrows in the flowing bowl, and solaces his spirit by consorting with some friend's wife. On this the woman gets sober, and, with that faithful cleaving to her first love for which her sex is so remarkable, forgives his iniquities, and goes for advice to the missionary, who makes up the quarrel and sends them off reunited with a blessing.

They remember my cousin, Lord G——, very well here, and call him "the silver arm." Nearly every one, even the missionaries, are nicknamed in these islands; my title being, I believe, "the cocoanut tree." I noticed a small schooner aground near the royal mansion, with her hull, masts, and rigging, all falling to pieces; this, I was told, was the chief line-of-battle ship, or crack frigate, of the Taha navy, that had been taken in the last war.

September 10*th*.—L—— and I sailed away in the life-boat in search of adventures in the direction of Taha. We picked our way along inside the barrier-reef with some difficulty, owing to the numerous shoal-ridges. In the court-house, or "raiatea," the principal chiefs were still vehemently discussing; boats and canoes kept crossing and recrossing between the two islands, and, as no one knew at what moment the signal for war might be given, and the peaceful passengers turned into desperate pirates and privateers, it was all rather good fun.

In about an hour we had crossed the channel between the two islands, and soon after passed the principal village on the southeast end of Taha; and stretching still farther on opened out a fine bay, some three miles deep, nearly cutting the island in two.

Then, seeing a large boat ashore on a beautiful little island on the coral-reef, we stood out toward it. We found there were two islands with a deep channel through the reef between them, and beaching our boat close to the stranger soon came upon two natives roasting bread-fruit. They explained that there was a great fishing business going on on the other side, which we proceeded to see.

Sure enough appeared about twenty natives on the reefs, up to their necks in water, attended by a few small canoes, all shouting and bobbing round a kind of circular net which they were gradually dragging toward the shore—rather, I should say, lifting, for you cannot drag a net over a coral-reef. At last they brought it close to us, into about three feet of water, when the two men who were standing with us, respectable, clerical-looking old fellows, began to get violently excited. One seized a huge fagot of stakes, with which he ran violently down toward the sea, while his friend did likewise with a bundle of spears, three-pronged, two-pronged, but more often long, single harpoons, with a barb on one side. The stakes were planted in a circle to support the net that was hung upon them, and then each native seized his weapon, began spitting the fish inside with the most extraordinary skill and precision, and dropping them into the canoes alongside. There was wild excitement, and how they avoided prodding each other's toes I know not. Some of the men, evidently the masters of their art, stood a long way back from the mass as if they were fielding at cricket; and when a fish escaped from the net chased him in the shallow water, shying their spears at him with nearly invariable success, a feat that Loucy and I applauded tremendously.

Then the haul being over, and half a canoeful being secured, they came back to where their simple dinner was cooking, laughing, shouting, and racing through the clear water like a lot of mad mermen. Bread-fuit is a delightfully simple thing to cook. You make a lot of hot ashes and pitch it among them, and then go for a walk. If there are any little pigs about, they go and scratch their little sterns against it, which turns it round and round, and, when you reappear, your dinner is ready. All the little pigs at the Isle of Pines had bald sterns and tails in consequence of this practice!

The natives presented us with some fish, and we sailed across to the other island to lunch, in defiance of mosquitoes.

I was very much struck with the big, sailing, outrigger canoes, and the pace they run. They carry one enormous sprit-sail on a mast stepped far forward, and raking tremendously. A great cross-piece of wood is lashed across the canoe where the mast is stepped, to which three or four shrouds and stays are fixed. One man, or two, according to the strength of the breeze, stands out on the weather-side of this cross-piece, which keeps the canoe upright. A pole like the tail of a passionate cow runs outward and upward from the stern, which gives one the idea that the builder was drunk, and had put the bowsprit on the wrong end of the vessel. A rope runs from the end of this to the point of the sprit, to keep the great sail from swagging over too much.

They are of enormous length, with no more draught or beam than a racing-wherry, all their stability under sail being effected by the leverage of the great outrigger and the additional effect of the men on the cross-piece. These peculiarities give them a speed in running quite incredible to any one who has not seen them, and they work to windward better than one would expect, to look at them. Of course, in the case of a sudden calm they inevitably capsize; but the natives are amphibious, and don't care about that. The steerer holds his paddle perpendicularly against the lee-side of the canoe.

Then we ran back among the fishing-canoes for the chief settlement of rebellious Taha. I managed to get pretty close inshore by the help of the signals of the people on the beach, and, as soon as the boat stuck fast, a brawny native waded out and transported me to the beach on his shoulders, to the amusement of the population, who gave me a very kind reception. After a little broken conversation and the usual present of fruit, they asked me if I should like to see a white man who lived there; and I was guided to a nice little cottage, where a pretty half-caste woman asked me to come in and make myself at home. Soon after, the owner of the house arrived, a man of the true Pahcha-Maori stamp, brown, restless-eyed, plausible, civil, and good for nothing; and we sat down for a talk, surrounded by a group of admiring natives. "You're rather in difficulties with your king, I believe," said I, by way of starting the conversation. "He's an awful scoundrel, isn't he?" Whereon my friend replied in a mysterious whisper: "He is all you say, sir, but I mus'n't say nothing; these natives understand more than they pretend to very often, and I might get into trouble." So politics were barred. How unlike the glorious freedom of my own country, where any foul-mouthed rascal, with the gift of the gab, may get up and abuse her Majesty in public with impunity! "Speak not of the king in thy chamber, lest a bird of the air carry the matter;" a proverb that should be slightly altered to suit modern times, when it is not the bird of the air that carries the matter, but the beast of the area.

My friend declared that there was no way of getting any money on these islands, as the natives would neither sell nor let their land; and, even if they would, no labor could be got. "They've got their grub hanging over their heads, and their water at their feet; and when they want fish they can go out and get it as soon as they like. If I could only get two nights' frost, to make them work for their breakfast, I might do what I liked." Then I said good-by, and he asked us how we intended to pick our way home among the reefs. I got the bearings and directions by heart, as well as I could, and went down to the beach. Then I was carried aboard again, solemnly attended by the chief people of the town—all out of good-nature, for I was not known, and to all their questions about myself and the schooner returned vague and mysterious answers—and one of them said he should like to come with me and show me the way, if I would let him. "Jump on board," said I. And a very pleasant passenger he proved, showing us all the short cuts through the reef, giving us lessons in the native language, and learning English in return; expressing his hopeless inability to speak words with many consonants by laughing, shaking his head, and touching his tongue, to explain that he could not spit it out.

As soon as I got on board I heard that the queen had been inquiring for me, and hurried ashore, where

I was introduced to King Tamatoa, a powerful, bullet-headed, but not very ill-looking man, very decently dressed in European clothes. Like Mr. Bob Sawyer, except when he's elevated, he's the quietest creature breathing.

After a short conversation, with her majesty as interpreter, I departed, promising to come again to-morrow to be taught to make reva-reva.

September 11th.—After luncheon, the doctor and I went ashore to the queen's. Close to her reception-room was another bird-cage building, the House of Parliament, only yesterday the scene of a stormy and critical debate, but now occupied by the peaceful votaries of music, five or six of whom were squatted in a circle performing native ballads, while a young man accompanied them, melodiously playing a flute through his nose. Men, women, and children, lolling around on their mats, lazily enjoying the performance. A Pan and Dryad effect. Then the queen showed us how to make reva-reva, from the shoot of a young cocoa-nut tree, an operation simple enough when seen, but very difficult to describe intelligibly. She then tried to teach me to do it; but my fingers were too clumsy, and I generally managed to tear the delicate stuff. She would have made a wonderfully pretty picture, engaged in this work; and, when she asked me wonderingly what I wanted to see it done for, I felt inclined to give that as the reason.

Then appeared Tamatoa, and in his right mind, who signified his desire, through the missionary, to make me the usual present of pigs, fruit, and fowls, while the queen gave me a beautifully-worked araroot-crown, decked with reva-reva, besides many fine plumes of the latter article.

I think I shall introduce Society-Island manners into England, with some slight omissions. When visitors call on me at W——, on their departure, I shall put into their carriage a couple of sacks of potatoes, ditto of flour, cloves, etc., a dozen bunches of grapes, half a dozen melons, peaches, etc., a few fowls, and some fine young pigs from the model farm; and perhaps a house-maid to make the thing quite complete.

In return for this my lady visitor will present me with her bonnet, shawl, jewels, or perhaps her boots, or my gentleman visitor with his best shiny hat, watch, walking-stick, shirt-studs, or metal buttons if he has any.

Then the king, queen, and the Bismarck of Raiatea, a handsome, intelligent, jovial man, came on board with us, and we had some amusing conversation on all kinds of subjects, her majesty interpreting. "Do you bathe much here?" said I. "No," replied she, "I fear the beeg fish. I see the Frenchman bathe in Papiete, and the sharks bite their legs," for which she didn't appear to be the least sorry. They were very anxious to know all about England, whether there were bread-fruit and cocoa-nut trees there; what kind of houses were built; and how the people lived; carriages drawn by horses, great, fast-running pigs they call them, they could understand, having seen specimens in Tahiti, but we broke down at the description of a railway-train; the only definition by which we could convey the idea was a man-of-war that ran along the shore upon wheels.

In the evening we went for a stroll along the shore, and fell in with a party of exceedingly intoxicated natives, who begged my cigar, and would have retained the doctor's pipe, a proceeding he objected to decidedly. But, drunk as they were, they were perfectly good-tempered and civil. These, and a few ladies of shady character, were the only people we met. Unlike Huahine, this is not a nocturnal place, for it is constantly exposed to the trade-wind, which the natives consider cold, and which, moreover, produces a most unpleasant smell of rotting coral-stuff.

September 12th.—The doctor and I went ashore to church. It was a very pretty sight to see them all in their best clothes, neat little hats, and fresh flowers.

They didn't seem to care much about the service except the hymns, occupying the rest of the time by reading the hymn-books, whispering little jokes to each other, and laughing and telegraphing with their eyes. A good part of the congregation kept outside the doors, looking in occasionally to see how things were getting on. The sermon was in the native language, and Queen Pomare's mamma, after taking a note or two on a piece of foolscap paper with great gravity, curled herself up on a bench and went fast asleep; as did also the missionary's big dog, which I considered wrong and rather too cool in an animal of his associations— so trod on his tail to wake him up.

I did once know a bishop's wife who always took a nap during her husband's sermons, and I always felt an intense respect for her moral courage.

In the afternoon the doctor and I went for a stroll, and, walking along under the pleasant shade of the bread-fruit trees, arrived at the farther end of the village, and sat ourselves down on the sad sea-shore, surrounded by a group of admiring natives of all ages and sexes. I can quite understand and sympathize with the feelings of the brindled gnu in the Zoological Gardens, who always charges furiously at the visitors who come to stare at him. It requires a long training to be able to think and talk comfortably and unconsciously under the steady gaze of twenty or thirty eyes.

Sometimes one of the girls would get up and pick an orange, present it slyly, and retire giggling about twenty yards, sit down again, and stare as before. I was particularly struck with a lively baby of an observant and humorous turn, who seemed delighted with our appearance, and crowed approvingly and continuously, until we attempted to draw nearer to make his acquaintance, when he changed his note, and howled till we ceased to advance.

As we walked back we met the whole congregation coming out of chapel with a broad grin on, and much hand-shaking ensued. "These are some of his riverence's servants," said the doctor, when I heard "Good-afternoon," behind me, and turning round saw "his riverence" laughing at us, and we proceeded to his house.

He told me that a war does some good here by killing off the bad characters who are usually foremost in getting it up. As there are no prisons here, and no punishment but a nominal fine, these fellows accumulate till they become quite a drug in the market.

Water-spouts are very common about these islands; not long ago a large one came into the lagoon, ran all along the water close to the shore—the natives shying sticks and stones at it—ran up the beach, smashed all the Venetian windows of the chapel, and took the roof right off, leaving an old woman saying her prayers in the middle of it, very much astonished, and half expecting she was going to be taken straight up to heaven!

While we were at dinner, the pilot came off to me with a note from the queen, rather a curiosity in its way. The address was charmingly simple, "For the lord!" the writing was good and the spelling tolerable, only there was not enough of it; the words being run into one another in a most confusing manner. The substance of the epistle was, that she had heard that I had been out last night walking, and had been insulted, or assaulted, by some drunken people; if it was true I was to tell her, and the king would put them in the law, as she expressed it. This is very delightful, to have a real live queen to watch over my safety and keep me out of mischief.

I fear it will be long before Queen Victoria will exercise a like maternal protection over her humble servant—God bless her!

I wrote back a warm, civil answer, saying I had met with nothing but kindness from her people; for which, perhaps, the king won't thank me, it being two or more dollars out of his pocket.

The royalties of the Society Islands are all, more or less, members of one family, connected by various mysterious and confusing relationships. I have been very much struck with the tone of perfect equality in social life observed between the royal families in these islands and their subjects. It seems to me essentially unbarbaric, and is one of their numerous marks of high-bred feeling and unsnobbishness, to coin a most awkward word. Yet, in spite of this social equality, there is a powerful instinct of loyalty among them, even in connection with such a man as King Tamatoa.

And what is still more strange, and shows still more what thorough gentlemen and ladies they all are, is that, though the king and queen talk and live with the meanest of their subjects naturally and apparently without any feeling of superiority, yet all have the greatest respect for high birth, or, rather, good ancestry. No matter how poor and insignificant a man may be, if his pedigree is good, he is the social equal or superior of the highest dignitary of the land.

As England is getting so radical now, and professing to be so much above that kind of thing, it would not be a bad idea for the Heralds' Office to remove to the Society Islands.

They treat idiots and madmen here with great respect and consideration, which perhaps is the reason that—Never mind! There is an "old foolish man" here, as Moó calls him, who has got into his head that I am his grandson, and comes to her perpetually to inquire what time I am coming on shore. He is very proud of me, she says. Lord help him, he must be mad indeed!

An American brigantine, the Timandia, came in to-day from Tahiti. She carries a three-cornered main-sail without a gaff, the gaff-topsail sheets going right down to the end of the main-boom.

The population of Raiatea is, I believe, about fifteen hundred souls; Taha is rather less.

When the men go to war, their lady-loves gird up

their loins and accompany them to battle to take care of them and carry their ammunition; sometimes, I believe, they take part in the fighting. These lazy, good-natured folks appear to be no cowards.

September 13*th.*—The morning was wet and cloudy, so the school-people, who were to have paid us a visit, had to wait till the afternoon, when it cleared a little. Soon we saw them coming along the shore in an apparently endless string, two and two, like the beasts going into the ark, chattering and laughing furiously, and singing their wild choruses; all dressed in their best, with new crowns and reva-reva on their heads, instead of the wreaths of fresh flowers they sported at Huahine.

All our boats were soon engaged as transports, and off they came, cheering and singing and making the boat roll, utterly regardless of a capsize, which I momentarily expected.

They came on board to the number of one hundred and seven—not so many as at Huahine, but much bigger. I took a lot of them down into the cabin. "You sit there," said the principal pupil-teacher, laughing and pointing to the divan, which I did, and held a regular *levée:* they poured down the after-companion, and each girl was presented in turn, shook hands, and gave me the crown from her head, beautifully worked and plaited into various devices, and decked with reva-reva or flowers, and then passed on through the galley and up the fore-companion. It was a wonderful skylark; the slightest mistake, such as a young lady shaking the wrong hand, or dropping her garland, was greeted with screams of laughter from her friends, while the abashed maiden would flee swiftly and hide her diminished head among the crowd.

"O Lord!" thought I, "if my friends and relatives could see me now, seated in state, in a flannel shirt and trousers, receiving homage from the nobility and gentry of Raiatea, what would they think?"

Then we proceeded on deck, and a lot of the small boys began clambering about the masts and rigging. "They won't do any mischief," said their pastor. "Not, unless they break their own necks," replied I, as I observed one infant of tender years slide right down a stay from the mast-head. "Oh, there's no danger of that, they can all climb like cats or monkeys;" and, directly after, two little brats, certainly not more than eight or nine years old, were on the trucks. Then we had some singing—every thing has to be altered to suit the temperament of these people—the multiplication-table, always connected in my mind with a fusty Colenso or a slate, was here a dance and a song combined; the alphabet was sung to the tune of "Auld Lang Syne;" one hymn to that of "Jolly Dogs" nativized, and another to that of "O Susannah! don't you weep for me!"—"Green Sleeves" moralized was nothing to it.

Then a gang of them began quietly to perform a little dance, Mr. V—— consenting to wink at it. Two little imps of girls came out of the mob, wriggled their bodies, and waved their little arms, after the approved fashion, while the rest of the girls formed round them and sang. It was very amusing to see the way they all "dried up" whenever Mr. V—— looked over his shoulder; though occasionally they became so inspired by the performance, as to require a gentle tap on the head with an umbrella to call them to order.

Then they all departed in high good-humor, laughing, cheering, and skylarking, from the prime-minister's wife to the house-maid's baby. And for years after they will keep up the tradition of their visit to the ship that was a house inside, and had a fire to cook with below-deck; and a place that when you touched it poured out water that came from the other end of the vessel, and so on, *ad libitum.*

The beauty of these people's faces improves with age, a rare thing among brown races. The ruggedness of their strongly-marked features looks natural and fine when they begin to grow old, and sets off the bright, healthy-minded good humor of their expression.

September 14*th.*—The doctor went ashore in a medical capacity, and had a look at all the incurables of the island. Elephantiasis is fearfully common, both among the whites and natives, and is an intermittent disease.

He also visited the school, and found that the text for the copy-books of the upper classes was "Lord P—— and Doctor K——." This is, I think, the first time I was ever made use of for educational purposes.

After luncheon I went ashore to see the queen, and found that the whole population were away picking oranges for the Timandia; but the king had ordered them back, fearing that the Taha natives might seize the opportunity for an invasion. The poor little woman said she was very frightened; and indeed she seems far too gentle and civilized to live in such a savage state of affairs.

I gave her two tortoise-shell head-ornaments from Ceylon, while she presented me with her pretty little arraroot hat, etc., etc. "Compliments pass when gentlefolks meet." These hats are made from the dried leaves of the arraroot-tree, washed and rubbed in some peculiar way, which gives them an appearance far brighter and more delicate than straw. The devices and patterns into which they are worked are very beautiful and ingenious.

Tamatoa, as I have said before, is not a model young man. One of his latest exploits was to borrow, without leave, the missionary's whale-boat, to go off on an orange-rum drinking excursion. It was delightfully wicked to go for such a purpose at all; but how much more so to do it in a missionary's boat! And then he and his friends, returning from the orgy in a jovial frame of mind, took it into their heads that it would be a most delightful spree to ride the boat right over the coral-reef through the surf. The natural consequence of this was, that the boat was considerably damaged, and the oars lost. When they reached home I believe Mr. Vivian was not pleased.

Not long ago, this naughty king had an attack of conscience, or perhaps indigestion, and he resolved to amend his ways. Great was the rejoicing even in this world over this precious sinner who had repented, and an account of his conversion was sent home by the pleased missionary to their magazine at home. Alas, alas!—

"When the devil was sick, the devil a saint would be;
When the devil got well, the devil a saint was he!"

Soon, too soon, he relapsed into his evil courses, and the account of his repentance in the missionary magazine came out to Raiatea just after the performance of some of his most abominable bestialities.

September 15*th*.—The doctor, Louey, and I, escorted by the native pilot, set off in the life-boat to see the " marais," or sacred stones, the last vestiges of the old religion of the country. The sail along the coast inside the reef was very beautiful. On one side of us the many-colored coral-water in long streaks of green and yellow and purple, bounded by a long snow line of breakers, broken at intervals by fairy-like little islands covered densely with bread-fuit trees, screw-palms, and cocoa-nuts; beyond, the deep-blue sea—bluer than the Mediterranean—looked at through sun-spectacles, and on the far horizon the peaks of Huahine mingled with the summer clouds.

On the other side, the beautiful bays, and grand mountains of Raiatea, changing every minute as we crept along. The wind was very light, and the heat was awful. I could feel the skin crackling and peeling off my nose: and I must confess that, in spite of the beautiful scenery all around, the subject of my meditations was beer—beer—nothing but beer.

At the end of some seven or eight miles we arrived at our destination, and ran ashore close to an extraordinary little hut, built right out in the sea, and communicating with the land by a plank—perhaps the hermitage of some old priest?

A short walk through the forest brought us to the " marais "—strange places they were; built of enormous slabs of rock or coral, arranged in an oblong shape, and the space inside them filled with shingle and coral, so as to form a platform about eight feet high.

I think the largest was about fifty yards long; we scrambled up on to it by help of a tree, and stood on the spot stained with so much blood shed in the *name* of religion. What horrible stories these stones could tell, if they could speak!

How strangely universal this devil-worship, this low and blasphemous doctrine of God getting angry with the beings of His creation, and requiring sacrifices to appease Him, is!

It was, I suspect, a creation of the priestly mind, that mind that has extended, through all ages, from the earliest times down to Doctor M——; and is so singularly alike at this day all over the world, from the Maori Tohunga to the Presbyterian minister. They invented it, first, because they used to get the benefit of the offerings that were presented for sacrifice; secondly, because by representing God as a terrible vengeful monster, that they knew how to manage better than the rest of the world, they got and held their power over the people. This second reason is the main one for keeping up the sacrificial, vengeful part of Christianity nowadays, though in the Roman Church the first cause is by no means extinct.

Lord! to think what thousands and thousands are paid every year to the priests for " persuading God " to take people's souls out of a horrible place of torture called purgatory, latitude and longitude unknown.

If a man were to get the true statistics of the amount of money expended in English law-courts to obtain justice, and the enormous quantity of men who lived and thrived upon the same, people would cry, "What a monstrous shame!"

What should be said to the thousands of men who live well and make money by professing to make peace between the Omnipotent and All-wise God, and the beings that He, knowing what He was about, I suppose, created? It makes me mad to think of it. All honor to the simple clergyman who devotes himself merely to the care, education, and welfare of his people; he earns his salt as well as any man in the world. It is the priest who sets up for supernatural powers, who claims for himself or his profession some superior share in the favor of the Almighty; and thus works upon the superstitions of the foolish, the ignorant, and the cowardly, that excites my loathing and contempt. When will men have the courage and energy to destroy this many-headed hydra? Not for a long, long time, for there is a considerable leaven of fools in this world, and men who have never known freedom cannot feel the vile chains which bind them, and are even afraid of being loosed.

"There at least," thought I, "a great step has been made in the right direction, and no longer will Samuel hew Agag in pieces *before the Lord!*"

What made the human sacrifices of the Society Islands so strangely ghastly and horrible, was the fact that the wretched victim was always chosen from one of certain families, set apart for that special purpose for generation after generation forever. How this caste originated I do not know. Many of these families used to put to sea secretly in canoes, preferring an almost certain death by drowning or starvation to the terribly uncertain fate that was always hanging over their heads.

When a man came to the priests to beg some heavenly, or rather infernal, favor, they would tell him, either from whim, malice, or some reason best known to themselves, that the god required a human sacrifice, and, naming the victim, present the supplicant with the death-warrant in the shape of a sacred stone. He hides this carefully somewhere about him, and, collecting a few friends, seeks out the doomed man. At last they find him sitting lazily under a tree or mending his canoe, and, squatting down round him, begin talking about the weather, fishing, or what not. Suddenly a hand is opened—the death-stone discovered to his horrified view! He starts up terror-stricken, and tries to escape—one short, furious struggle, and he is knocked down, secured, and carried off to the merciless priests. Ugh! it is an ugly picture.

Sometimes these men have succeeded in shaking off their captors, and fleeing to the mountains—have lived and died there unseen and undiscovered.

It was too hot to shiver, but the very shady, green, quiet beauty of the place made its history the more horrible.

There we saw traces of the great cocoa-nut-eating crabs; they run up the trees, nip off the cocoa-nuts, and, inserting one of their powerful claws into the eye, tear off the husk, and eat the nut. The natives put things like small crinolines on the trees a few feet up to stop their ascent.

Then, after refreshing ourselves with luncheon and cocoa-nuts, we set off home. Mr. Vivian dined with us, and told us a great many interesting things.

September 10*th*.—After luncheon, the doctor and I

went ashore to bid farewell to Beauty and the Beast, as we call their majestics. But the Beast was away on political business at Taha; so, after giving Queen Moé notice to finish her mail for Bora-Bora, we adjourned to Mr. Vivian's house. The doctor and Mrs. V. went into the next room to see a half-caste girl, who had something the matter with her foot. Meanwhile Mr. V. gave me a discourse on the subject of half-castes, describing them as the most whimsical, provoking, inconstant, mendacious, and immoral of women. Presently Mrs. V. came back, and her husband went out with the doctor to talk medicine. Mrs. V. sat down with her back to the door that led into the interior of the house, I being at right angles to her on the sofa, and we began talking. In the passage behind the doorway some natives were sitting and staring. Presently appeared the head of the doctor's half-caste patient, who began smiling and making little signals of like kind, rather to my confusion under the circumstances. It was almost beyond the powers of humanity to talk to a female missionary, and respond to the smiles of a beautiful young lady at one and the same time. But I couldn't help looking that way and laughing occasionally, especially as Mrs. V. was descanting to me at the moment on that young lady's unusual steadiness and sobriety.

Very soon Mrs. V. perceived that something was going on behind her, and kept turning sharply round, thinking to catch the native servants in some impropriety. Whenever she did so, Miss Toe dodged out of sight, which made me grin all the worse. And so the farce went on till the doctor and Mr. V. returned, when we took a cordial farewell of the good, kind-hearted people, and left them. As we went down the steps, the missionary made us an earnest but rather parsonical little speech, ending with " You will meet many dangers before you reach home, but you must remember that there's a power above you," etc. I felt dreadfully tempted to say that we should either be providentially saved or providentially drowned, but refrained from criticising a speech that was so kindly meant.

Just as we were going to dinner I got a note from the queen, saying that the king wanted me to show him how to fix the gun I had given him, and I went ashore. We should have made a strange picture, Beauty, the Beast, and I, sprawling on the floor of the birdcage house, putting the gun together, and explaining the use of its appurtenances by the dim light of a solitary lantern! The king wanted to buy my life-boat, but I " did not see it," especially as it would have cost the greater part of his yearly revenues, and perhaps caused a rebellion. The queen asked me to spend the evening with them, but I foolishly refused on account of dinner. If we had done so, we should have seen some fun, as Queen Moé's attendants are of a lively and saltatory disposition.

The captain to-day took the life-boat and sailed round to examine the channel through the reef, on the lee-side of the island through which we purpose sailing to-morrow.

September 17th.—Mr. Vivian came on board to say good-by, bringing with him a mat as a farewell present from Queen Moé, their majesties' mail for Bora-Bora, a native Bible for me from himself, and some hymn-books for the doctor. I gave him a copy of George Herbert's poems as a souvenir. He said that the queen had asked him to ask me whether I would give her one of our "little round pigs," as she expressed it, which of course I did, with many expressions of good-will. I have often been asked for a photograph on leaving, or perhaps a lock of my hair, but never before for "a little round pig." These Society Islands are certainly original places.

Then we got under way, and, running down without accident between Raiatea and Bora-Bora, we slipped out of the reef on the lee-side of the former island, and stood away for the great peak of Bora-Bora.

P. S.—I have since heard that Queen Moé's husband has been shot, and has left her an interesting widow, with only one infantine encumbrance. I deliberated whether or not to go back and propose for her, but reflected that most likely she would have dried her tears on somebody else's shirt-front before I could make my appearance, and that on the whole, perhaps, my over-fastidious relations might object to the connection. So I didn't.

CHAPTER V.

BORA-BORA.

Bora-Bora at a distance seems split into two, a tower and a steeple; but as we approached, the two blended into one, and one has a ruined cathedral, with a stately gray tower about it. Sheltered naves and transepts, and here and there a flying buttress still standing. But such a cathedral was never raised by human hands, for size or beauty. The tower, viewed as it is, seems a good three thousand feet high. The reefs about it are very extensive and dangerous, and we had to keep off a long way to avoid one of them; but, being almost entirely wooded, they make a gorgeous fringe at the foot of the grand gray rocks. We had a long work up through the opening, disturbing flying-fish innumerable; but, though there were abundance of sea-birds of all sorts about, I did not see one sweep down upon them. Among the flocks were divers very gurnetty specimens, the motion of whose pectorals was not nearly as pronounced as in the real flying-fish. We were boarded by a quaint old pilot, the most curious specimen of his profession ever seen. He coolly walked about the ship, peering through the sky-lights and down the companions, making little grunts of approbation when any thing took his fancy, and evidently perceiving that the yacht was something out of the common line. "Are we going all right?" roared the skipper from the fore-yard as we began to get into the narrows (and very narrow they were). "Oh, yes! O'right," answered the old gentlemen with such perfect coolness and indifference that even the iron-faced Jim burst into convulsive laughter, enough to break his face. Presently he condescended to go forward and give his directions, which he accompanied with wonderful spasmodic yells that almost incapacitated the sailors with laughter. He had another slight failing (considered from a nautical point of view). He could not say "Keep her off!" The nearest he could get to it was "Keep your duff," which he used instead, thinking, I suppose, that such a slight difference in sound did not signify much. This little mistake naturally caused some slight confusion at first, but, fortune favoring us, we gained our anchorage safely. The harbor is most magnificently beautiful, overhung by a heap of rock, three thousand feet high, and looking in the moonlight as if it were hanging almost over our heads. And noble basaltic cliffs, standing out from a perfect cascade of verdure. Nowhere but in these islands have I ever seen, positively, richly green cliffs.

If one of the smallest, Bora-Bora is certainly one of the most beautiful, if not *the* most beautiful island we have visited in the South Seas.

September 18*th*.—A walk on shore, to deliver our mails at the missionaries' house. The village was delightfully green and fresh, the bread-fruit, with its magnificent leaves, being very luxuriant. Mr. Pierce has not been long on the island, and has not yet mastered the language, but a few weeks' work may do wonders. As the missionaries invented a good deal of it—certainly all the writing and reading part—it is but fair that they should be able to learn it easily. We had a highly-pleasant stroll along the beach under the cool shade of the trees. The women seemed fairer in complexion than in the other islands, and are fine great animals, apparently averaging ten or eleven stone, and the men are proportionally large. There was a good deal of cocoa-nut oil being manufactured in old dugout canoes, a manufacture most decidedly more profitable to the pocket than pleasant to the nose. In our walk we were accompanied with the usual admiring tail of light infantry, and it came into our heads suddenly to turn and go back, whereon they all scattered as if a shell had burst in the midst of them, and one little girl was seized with most horrible panic, rushing away screaming as hard as she could to the arms of her papa, and refused to be comforted. I am sure I don't know why we should frighten the children; we are any thing but pale-faces, and brick-dust red is as pretty as brown any day.

Mr. and Mrs. Pierce called on board, and also a flaxen-headed boy, brother to the fair little princes and princesses at Huahine, and related in some mysterious way to Pomare, Moé, Tamatoa, the King of Bora-Bora, and all the rest of the South-Sea Island royalties.

Every island, though it possesses a distinct government, is always under a member of one great royal family, and the relationships are more confusing and intricate than those of the Bourbons. The king here is brother to darling Queen Moé of Raiatea; his wife is the sister of Tamatoa, Queen Moé's husband, Tamatoa is the son of Queen Pomare, who is related to Queen Moé, who is cousin to Moitea and Mrs. Brandon, who are also related to Queen Pomare. The flaxen-haired children are the children of the Queen of Bora-Bora, who is daughter or some such thing to Queen Pomare, and are also cousins to Tamatoa, Moé, and the King and Queen of Bora-Bora? Can any thing be clearer? The best of the matter is, that the chances are that everybody is somebody else's son or daughter. But that don't matter here!

September 19*th*.— *Our* Monday-Sunday in these parts, and so to church. The said church being a most excellently-planned building, capable of receiving five hundred people in comfort and coolness, and, thank Heaven, as utterly unlike the popular idea of what a church ought to be as one could well imagine.

The wall all window, the roof lofty, the shape oval, and the ends of the white hibiscus-rafters prettily ornamented with colored tappa, wrapped round them to conceal their juncture with the wall. The floor was covered with comfortable benches, but the greater number of the female population preferred lounging about on the mat-covered floor, exactly like a herd of great, soft-eyed, brown seals. They were dressed in a long, soft, muslin sacque, but the most popular ornament was a soft, rough-fringed bathing-towel, with a red border, one end twisted round the neck and the other thrown over the shoulder in a particularly graceful way.

I do not think that I ever enjoyed a church more in my life; it was really delicious to sit near the door

and listen to the wind whistling through those glorious
bread-fruit trees, and watch the strange green-stemmed,
silk-cotton trees, and the quaint hues and the quaint
things going on in and about them, to the land-side,
and to the other the glorious blue sea, with the white
foam of the barrier-reef for the edging. I am the less
to be blamed for these distractions, as the service was
conducted in "Maori" by a native gentleman in spectacles (spectacles are always great "medicine" in these
parts, though even without glasses) and even the missionary was obliged to content himself with giving out
the hymns; the singing was very good indeed, and I
am given to understand that they consider themselves
nulli secundus as far as that is concerned. Their great
prima-donna was not, however, in church to-day, being
engaged canticling on the other side of the island.

Some of the women were very handsome, and there
was a great deal of quiet fun going on here and there.
We saw the white hat of the skipper glancing about
outside, and once or twice he evidently attempted a
slight flirtation through the window, but the native
beadle soon "settled his hash," going out boldly to him,
and bringing him as "meek as a maid" into the sacred
edifice, where he sat for the rest of the service looking
as if butter would not melt in his mouth, to our great
edification.

The babies were charming, jolly, merry little brown
things who crawled about the mat-covered floor, playing
and crowing, without a squall in a ton of them; the
elderly women all *began* to take strict notes of the
sermon with a pencil and paper, just as we used to do
at school, and I should not much wonder if the greater

part of their notes ended as ours used to do. However,
there is, I believe, a sort of examination held on the
subject once a week, and there is a certain amount of
emulation in remembering as much as possible of the
sermon.

The people were civil and kindly beyond all praise,
and "yer hamering" and hand-shaking was incessant.

After sermon we went up to Mr. Pierce's, to have
tea and to meet the king and queen. The title of *her*
majesty is Taupoa-Wapine. The king is a splendid
young fellow, six feet three inches and a half in height,
and wonderfully well grown and proportioned, with a
well-poised, antique-looking head, not unlike a male
edition of his sister Moé.

Conversation was difficult, as none of the European
party could speak Kanaka (or rather Maori), and neither
the king nor the queen spoke English. Ultimately we
found a means of communication through the former,
who had spent three years in France, and spoke a remarkably good and idiomatic French. He is a most
gentleman-like and intelligent young fellow, with a
strong spice of fun in him.

We are given to understand that he is not king in
his own right, but merely a species of king-consort, as
it were. The queen, on the death (?) of her first husband, picked up with this young gentleman on his return from France and married him; I think I *did* hear
that she had not waited for the death of her first husband, but had simply sent him about his business.

Her majesty is stout certainly, very stout, and,
though only twenty-six, looks quite old enough to be
the king's mother, but it has been whispered to me that

she has lived very *hard*, and that in these parts means something very hard indeed. At tea, she did not shine much in conversation, but philosophically concentrated her faculties on sardines and cake. But Lord ! to see how civil we were, and how upright we all sat on our chairs, though hard and hot !

We are informed on the "highest" authority that the Bora-Boraborians will eat goats, but not the "long woolly-haired pig," the sheep, which seems strange.

September 20*th*.—A guard of honor from the king to show us round the island, consisting of the king's Portuguese servant (Joe, of course), a very small fellow, and a fellow-pilot, in the shape of a remarkably handsome, intelligent, fine-faced native, who was no less a personage than a full colonel of the king's troops. We had the colonel to show us the way, and Portuguese Joe as an interpreter. He was a most civil and polite man, but, from having picked up his English on the beach, always addressed us as "You fellows," which, when done in the most intensely respectful manner, had a certain smack of quaintness in it. However, we made a very pleasant cruise of it, sailing between the island and the barrier-reef; the latter, almost uninterruptedly clothed with hibiscus, cocoa-trees, and sunwood. But oh! how hot, how hot ! with just enough breeze to steal us through the calm water, but not enough to cool us.

To our right, however, the gray tower or buttresses, and sheer green, every turn showing us some new beauty. I think that altogether it is the most magnificently beautiful piece of rock-scenery I have ever seen. The tower seemed utterly inaccessible, but we were told that it has been ascended, God knows how! But these natives have a wonderful power of climbing, developed by their researches after the wild-plantain.

We landed on the barrier-reef to lunch, and the old colonel fitting his feet into a kind of noose of green withes, skipped up a tall cocoa-tree like a remarkably well-preserved old brown grasshopper, without touching the bare stem with any thing but his feet and hands. Loucy slipped the noose on to his feet and tried it, but, active little monkey as he is, he could make nothing of it, and after getting about half-way up with extreme difficulty, and barking his shins in the most unpleasant manner, he was compelled to give it up and come down again, ignominiously.

There were a good many small birds among the bushes, one of which was a small whistling parrot, with a purple back and white throat, which I am told is the king's favorite *gibier*.

After leaving Bora-Bora, I was told that there was a sea-bird peculiar to that island and found nowhere else. It builds on the highest cliffs, and carries its young down to the water on its wings. It is a great delicacy, and reserved entirely for the royal table. It is a great pity that we did not know of this before we left the island.

After a lively sail right round the island, being within the reef the whole time, we reached the yacht late. The colonel and the portingale were given a glass of grog apiece, and P—— gave each half a sovereign, blushing ingenuously, for it is rather difficult to know how to tip a real live colonel.

Wednesday, 21st.—The king and his primo-minister

came on board, bringing with them two beautiful crowns and an ancient native dress, from the queen, together with the usual boat-load of fruit. P—— presented the king with a revolver, with which, let us trust, he has shot neither himself nor any one else.

He remained chatting on board all the morning, and is a very sensible and well-behaved young fellow. He has the character of being a "good boy" among his people, and really seems to deserve it. Among other bits of gossip, he told us that when Gilley was here he practised at an island, and mowed down many cocoa-trees, to the no small disgust of the natives.

The people are not as well off as they look, which may be the means of inducing them to introduce some local industry, as cotton, etc.

When the fruit-season is over, they stow the bananas in great pits, and continue to feed on them till they are all rotten, a custom which produces much sickness.

Climbing the cliffs for the faïes, generally ends in a broken neck or two in the course of the year, and no wonder.

There are very few oranges on the island, so it is comparatively free from the abominations of orange-rum drinking.

The doctor went fishing in the reef-opening, with Portuguese Joe. The fishing, as usual among the coral, was very poor, and requires much skill and patience. One of their ways of fishing is worthy of a Thames basket-fisher. They saw off the convex side of a large, spotted cowry, fasten a hook to one end and a line to the other. They then fill the shell with a large lump of roasted bread-fruit, and bait with a smaller lump; in fact, much in the way balls of clay and worms are used at home. While sitting in the canoe, something passed us, swimming about a foot under the water, which I took for a turtle, but which Joe declared to be a sunfish. I have often seen sun-fish basking upright in the water, but this one was swimming, not quite on its side, but at a certain angle in the water, and the wavy motion of its fins gave it a very remarkable appearance, quite unlike any fish I have ever seen. Unluckily, we had no heavy spear in the boat, or we might easily have secured it. Joe tells me that about a month ago a very large one was killed in the harbor, and that it had three live young ones in it—so much alive that they began to swim as soon as they were put into the water. I cross-questioned him on the subject, but he declared that there was no mistake. There were three live little sunfishes in the old one. I do not remember to have heard before that the sun-fish was viviparous. The flying-fish were darting about us in swarms, and I had an excellent opportunity of watching their manner of flying.

Getting wearied of our bad sport, we landed on a small wooded island, on which is the Windsor Castle or rather Balmoral of the island, represented by a large open shed, one end being closed by interwoven palm-leaves. The royal bed was on the mat-covered floor. Two or three mattresses, one on the top of the other, and plenty of blankets neatly tucked over, more for show than use I should fancy in this climate. At the bed-head were his personal knick-knacks, gun, accordion, etc.; round the post were hanging numerous cocoa-nuts of fresh water, the holes being neatly stopped with green leaves. The principal furniture consisted of fishing-tackle of various sorts, fish-spears, and long bamboo rods. And here comes the king when wearied by affairs of state, fishing, and shooting parrots, with his private friends, while the queen remains in regal splendor on the main island.

P—— took a farewell stroll along the village road under the shade of the beautiful bread-fruit trees, certainly one of the handsomest-leaved trees in the world. They make a very little settlement go a very long way here, as there is no back to it, the strip of land between the sea and the mountain being very narrow. It is nothing but a long, single row of scattered huts, with a clean smooth road between it and the beach, made rather unsafe for riding, by the way it is undermined and filled by the great land-crabs. These "broom-roads" are quite a characteristic of the Society Islands, and have been formed by the utilization of the "naughtiness" system—all minor improprieties being punished by the penalty of making so many yards of road. I am informed that in old times road-making was carried out in exceeding good company.

Guided by a confused noise of loud singing and screams of laughter to the neighborhood of the church, we found the greater part of our crew, and the whole of the younger part of the population, playing a kind of foot-ball with round things made of the husks of cocoa-nuts rolled up tight. Their way of kicking was entirely different to ours; they threw the ball into the air and kicked it with the sole of the foot in the oddest manner—an oddity which was heightened in the case of the young ladies, whose long, white dresses were rather in their way, and had to be "rather high kilted"

for the kick. Then he went and collogued with some
workmen who were making a low platform on which
to build a house; then sauntered rather sadly through
the settlement, thinking how long it would be before
he came across such pleasant places and such kindly
people again. Most of the folks knew that we were
going, and came up to shake hands—men, women, and
children—even the mothers held up their brown bam-
binos to say good-by, at which most of them howled
dismally, almost the only sign of bad taste we have
found in the Society Islands. Why the deuce is it that
we frighten the babies so? We may not be handsome
enough to frighten a horse, but I don't think we are
ugly enough to scare a baby.

"Heigh-ho! this is the last day in paradise. After
to-morrow we shall see nothing but ugly copper-colored
savages, or dirty-black Fijians; and then we shall return to sordid, practical, white people, black coals,
shirt-collars, actions for breach, and all that," growls
the disconsolate P——.

He went to say good-by to Mr. Pierce, who was in
great tribulation about a divorce-case. (In the other
islands the native rulers have taken the power of
divorce into their own hands; here the missionary
most unfairly has to untie his own knots.) And the
case was this: Two young people had fallen in love
with each other, but, as usual, the parents would not
allow them to marry. So they took a canoe, instead
of a post-chaise and four, and paddled across to Raiatea,
instead of to Gretna Green. King Tamatoa being
found in a state which permitted him to understand
what was said to him, married them as well as he could

for the small sum of two dollars. And home paddled the young pair; but the parents still objected, possibly to the civil nature of the marriage, as thousands do in Europe, and went to the missionary for a divorce, which he very properly refused. Married is married, however you are married, and I am of Audrey's opinion, "Faith, the priest was good enough, for all the old gentleman's saying."

The missionary said that he has sent away a quantity of people who came for divorces, and described the subject with an amount of liberality and common-sense which was highly creditable to him. P—— tried to comfort him by showing that the frequency of demand for divorce was in itself a sign of improvement in the morality of the people, and that it proved some idea of fixed affection, when one was demanded after a slip. He said, and what he said in Bora-Bora is of equal importance in England, that the first step in improving the morality of these people must consist in an alteration of the houses, dividing them into separate apartments, instead of all sleeping together in one common room as at present. But he added that he did not think they were worse than any others under the circumstances, owing to the impossibility of secrecy, and the fact of their being nearly all related in some way or another.

September 22d.—Sailed with a light breeze and a heavy heart, and after an interchange of dips with the Goza standard, stood out of the harbor.

Too much association with white folks has made the pilot suspicious of evil beyond measure. First of all, he refused to take any coins which had not the

queen's head on them; and, when this particular was
conceded, he demanded to be paid entirely in half-
crowns. On being presented with a pound of tobacco,
he insisted on opening the paper and counting the
sticks. He was, however, passing honest, and returned
the harbor-fees, which by the king's orders had been
remitted in honor to the white ensign.

At the south end of Sawaii is an immense bed or
rather tract of lava, which has been poured out at a very
low angle. The sea has worked long tunnels into it,
which form "meres" like those in Pembrokeshire (the
existence of the finest of which, Bocheston Mere, I saw
flatly denied in a pseudo-scientific book not five years
ago!) The heavy ocean-rollers entering the tunnels,
are driven out through the small opening at the far end
in most glorious clouds and columns of spray; some
merely like the blowing of a whale, others like the
bursting of a shell, while others spout up in snowy
white columns a hundred and fifty feet high. The
spouting is ceaseless, and sometimes several will be
seen at once. The beauty of the thing is infinitely en-
hanced by the dead blackness out of which the snowy
puffs spring, and the vivid green of the background.

CHAPTER VI.

TUBAI TROPICAL BIRDS AND THE LABOR QUESTION.

"WHAT you want do next?" asked charming Queen Moé, of Raiatea. "One thing we want to do, madame, is to shoot boatswain-birds, the pretty white birds with long scarlet feathers, to show at home what lovely things there are out here." "Yes, yes, I know, but why shoot them? Why not catch them with your hands?" To this there was nothing to do but to murmur gently, and try and look as if we wished we could. "Yes," continued Queen Moé, seeing that there was a hitch somewhere; "don't shoot, go to Tubai, and catch them with your hands on the sand; I have often." This sounded strange, but Queen Moé was a person to be believed, and we asked about this island of Tubai, and heard that it was no very great distance from our next island—Bora-Bora.

So, on parting from Bora-Bora, we thought it but a chivalric duty to our beloved Queen Moé to go in search of the fairy-island where one could pick up tropical birds with scarlet tails, as one gathers shells. I hardly know why, but Queen Moé had made us believe so utterly in her, that had we never found the island, or had all the birds flown away as soon as they saw our top-mast-head above the horizon, we should have believed in the picking-up business all the same.

From Bora-Bora we started with the lightest of airs, and we had not sailed

"A league, a league, a league, but barely three,"

when we saw cocoa-nut trees growing out of the blue sea, just where Tubai ought to be. But "looking is one thing and kissing another," and it was four o'clock in the afternoon before we reached the island; we were very much puzzled as we slided gently onward by the look of the sea ahead. Long lines of apparent surf showing here and there, which one could almost swear were produced by coral-reefs. Even from the fore-yard it was very difficult to believe that they were nothing but the glint of the sun between the clouds—but it was so. I suspect that many a "reported reef" in the South-Sea charts owes its existence to the same cause.

The quantity of sea-fowl, as we neared the island, was immense. Hardly anywhere, either at Nepean Island, near Norfolk Island, or at Handa in Sutherlandshire, have I seen a greater gathering than there were here, fishing, fighting, or winging their way homeward with the family dinner. I wonder whether in bad fishing-weather the parent-bird arrests its own appetite in order to save a morsel for the "wee yans" at home? I should not wonder. I believe sea-fowl to have very strong family affections, though they care but little for nests. Their separate squattings, though they be but on the bare rock, are jealously guarded, and marked out as the new lands of a colony by the government surveyor. On two stacks of rock, near

Stackpoole in Pembrokeshire, thousands of sea-fowl appear for two or three days in November, chattering and screaming and evidently discussing some important question connected with the next year's nesting-time. This decided, they all depart, and not a bird is to be seen near the place till the next spring; surely they are laying out the sections in time, so as to prevent a row when the lady-birds were housed and impatient to lay their eggs. Rooks have also somewhat of the same habit. The island of Tubai was certainly inviting, though the invitation was rather of a squeeze-like nature, being, as far as we could see, a belt of cocoa-trees, guarded by a most ferocious surf; we made an attempt to land, however, in that most hard-working of boats, the Fish Fag or the Bet of Billingsgate, so called from her excellent fishing qualities, and pulled round and round just outside the break of the rollers, vainly endeavoring to find a passage through. Once or twice there were half propositions made to "ride a roller" and trust to Providence, but wiser counsels prevailed, and we gave up the attempt for the night, and consoled ourselves by getting specimens of the sea-fowl; now a most painful subject, for every one of the rare, curious, and beautiful skins we obtained that night is at the bottom of the sea. Some of the birds were so tame that we could knock them down with the boat's stretchers as they hovered over us; others, like the grand fork-tailed frigate-bird, gave themselves the airs of falcons and pursued the smaller terns; not to eat them, but to eat what they had eaten. The plaintive shrieks of the tern when he is being chased, indicative of his agony at the prospect of having to give up his own hard-earned dinner, or the supper he is bearing to his starving nestlings, are heart-rending. He generally has to do it, however. One day I myself saw a curious thing: a frigate-bird was hard pressing a small tern, and would soon have had possession of the result of his day's fishing, when another larger bird—entirely of a different species—interfered and drove off the pirate, flying away afterward on his own affairs with all the consciousness of having done a good action.

I really believe that birds have some sense of right and wrong. I remember once on Exmoor seeing two small cock-chickens commencing a fight, which was speedily stopped by an old matronly duck coming between them and bringing them to order by tweaking billsful of feathers out of each. I avenged one tern by slaying his persecutor, and was surprised to find that he was a much smaller bird than he looked; the great breadth of the wing and the long swallow tail aiding the deception.

The brilliancy of the green of the trees on the white coral-bank, and the purple and crimson of the evening sky, are not to be described, at least by me. After a long and fruitless pull we returned to the schooner, and hove-to for the night with six Society Islands in sight.

Friday, September 23d.—Still bobbing about this tantalizing ring of cocoa-nuts, but apparently as far off from picking up tropic birds, like shells, as ever. At last we descried a big white flag, and, with the aid of the telescope, saw a group of men about it, who, by various motions and wavings, evidently desired to attract our attention. Pulling for the place, we found two groups of brown men placed on each side of a narrow crack in the reef, not much wider than the boat, and a big rock in the centre, up and over which the surf was boiling in a most unpleasant way. It looked a very nasty place; but, as the men signalled to us to come, we backed a little till a big roller came in. "Give way, men, all!" and on his back we went, with a vengeance! steered deftly into the very eye of the crack. The boat was seized instantly on both sides by our brown friends, who lugged her into the shallow water before the next roller could break, and dragged her across the reef some two hundred yards, picking out the deeper spots among the coral, till her poor old nose rested safely on the real beach of pure white sand. A jovial set our friends were. Brown, savage islanders, who were civilized and nice, as all savage islanders are. I don't mean the savage island of the story-books, but the savage island of the Admiralty chart; the island where they ran at Captain Cook "like wild-boars." There was one Penguin-Island woman among them, who owned to have eaten human flesh in the days of her youth and innocence. I believe this is rather a rare case, as "long pig" is generally "tapu" for the chiefs and warriors.

These savage islanders are a pleasant-looking and cheery people, not unlike Maltese, but not nearly so well grown or handsome as the Society-Islanders. These islands being over-populated, they are willing to emigrate as workmen, and they are to be found wherever plantation labor is required in the Pacific. Here they are paid twenty-four dollars a year and found in every thing. There is no doubt but that an immense amount of this labor can be procured, if the confidence of the people is once gained, a far more paying way in the end than by using fraud and brutality.

At their head we found Mr. Blackett, a Nova-Scotian, who rents the island from the King of Bora-Bora, for the purpose of making cocoa-nut oil. He received us with the greatest kindness, and led the way across the cocoa-studded belt of coral-rock to his establishment, situated close to the edge of the inner lagoon, for Tubai is a real "atoll," a circular reef, enclosing a lovely lake within it. I should think that a walk of a quarter of a mile brought us to his place, the principal building of which was a large and comfortable house, principally built of interwoven palm-leaves. Within it was roomy and airy, and contained all sorts of luxuries, clean beds, good furniture, and a fair stock of books; and, moreover, with many nice brown women and girls hanging about, well mannered, clean, and well dressed—indeed, remarkably so—really *nice* people. Without there was a wealth of animal life—gigantic pigs of the purest English or Chinese breeds, too fat and warm to do more than wink, dogs, cats, and fowls, all tame and kindly. You could not make the most trivial remark to a passing cat without her putting her tail erect into the air, rubbing herself against your legs, and answering with a kindly mew. I will not insult Mr. Blackett by calling his establishment "patriarchal," that is, if the present Arab be a type of the patriarchs, which is more than likely. I will only say that it is what a patriarchal establishment *ought* to have been.

The working-stock consisted principally of a wee steam-engine, which drove one or more iron heads, studded with projections, to which were held the cleft cocoa-nuts, grinding down the "meat" into pulp most rapidly. This pulp, placed in long, canoe-like troughs, went through private processes of its own, and then was squeezed into palm-oil. At least, that is the best description I can give. I do not feel justified in revealing trade-secrets.

After inspecting the pigs, talking to the dogs, and colloguing with the cats, we went down to the lagoon, a nearly circular sheet of water, most beautifully blue or green, according to the depth, which is reported to have altered sensibly during the last few years. We embarked in the whale-boat, pulled by the larky, laughing, savage islanders, who were as full of fun as they could hold, and even more, and, after a row of some two miles, landed on a white spit of elevated coral-sand, with a few cocoa-trees and scrubby bushes scattered about it. Through a depressed bit we could see the surf flashing and foaming over the very spot we had thought of landing on the night before, and very glad indeed we were that we changed our intention.

The savage islanders and the rest landed, and immediate skylarking began, in a manner which showed that the relationships between employer and employed were on a good and kindly footing. For our part, not believing in our Queen Moé as implicitly as we ought to have done, we began shooting the tropic birds as they flew over us; but we soon gave it up, for two reasons: First, that we found that if we got a rocketter, the chances were ten to one that we cut *the* scarlet feathers out of his tail; and secondly, because we discovered that, by diligent peering under the bushes, we might pick up as many live uninjured specimens as we liked. I never saw birds tamer or stupider, which tameness or stupidity may be accounted for by the extreme smallness of their brain, which is really not larger than that of a sparrow. They sat and croaked, and pecked, and bit, but never attempted to fly away. All you had to do was to take them up, pull the long red feather out of their sterns, and set them adrift again. Queen Moé was right. On Tubai you may pick up tropic birds as easily as a child picks up storm-worn shells on the sea-shore.

It was really no small comfort to be able to get specimens of this beautiful bird without betraying their confidence by shooting them from the schooner. Small-brained as they are, they are gifted with an extraordinary amount of inquisitiveness, particularly in the early morning. As we bowl along before the flashing trade-wind we hear a few harsh screams, and up come a pair of "bosens" with their bright scarlet tail-feathers glowing in the morning sun. They make two or three swoops around us, evidently comparing notes, and then away into the deep blue, on their own private affairs. They fish generally like the tern, to whom I suspect they are cousins-german; but they have a way, sometimes, of hovering perpendicularly, with the bill pressed against the breast, that I have never observed but in one other bird, the black-and-white kingfisher of the Nile. When the "bosen" has sighted his prey in this position he turns over in the deftest manner, and goes down straight as a gannet, up to his neck, no farther, and remounts for a fresh hover. I have never had the good fortune to see the white-tailed phaeton fishing, often as I have looked for him. Indeed, I have rarely met him out at sea at all. The finest I have seen were hanging about the high cliffs of the Society Islands, and I do not exaggerate when I state that I have seen more than one with a glorious waving white tail-feather, two good feet long, though the bird itself was not much larger than a black-headed gull. What they do with their tails when they feed, passed my comprehension.

Not only did we find full-grown tropic birds but we found their eggs and young. The former about the size of a hen's-egg, prettily splashed with reddish brown, laid on the bare sand, under a bush. The latter really handsome creatures, about the size of a herring gull, beautifully marked with black and white (like a falcon). The bill at this stage of their existence is black, not red. When you find your young friend under a bush, he is ensconced in a small basin of coral-dust, without any nest at all, and his surroundings show him to be a cleanly thing. When you come upon him suddenly he squalls and croaks, and wobbles about, and is as disconcerted as a warm city man when you try to drive a new idea into him, unconnected with money. But he sticks stoutly to his dusty cradle, and never attempts to escape, saying plainly enough, "My mother told me to stop here till she brought me my supper, and here I am going to stay."[1]

We gleaned a few specimens for stuffing and two to be tamed by pretty Miss Esther, who I fancy could

[1] Though fairly enough deserving the name of tropical bird, the phaeton sometimes is found outside the tropics. We saw our first solitary flying to the westward in latitude 28.27, longitude 150.15. Our last Cape pigeon was in latitude 32.34, longitude 151.02, and our last albatross, in latitude 33.48, longitude 159.09.

tamo most things; and, collecting our savage island crew, paddled back to the settlement, mightily contented at having solved a question which had troubled us for some time.

As we went back, an opening in the reef was shown us through which a small vessel *might* enter; yes, she *might*, but how could she get out again?

There is a small, noisy parrot on the island, like those at Bora-Bora and Huahine, but we did not get a specimen. Mr. Blackett tells me of a small woodpecker who lives in holes in the trees, and kills his fowls, knocking them off their perches at night with his sharp bill. A theory was started that it was attracted by the glitter of the fowl's eye in her darkness. A pretty enough theory, but do not fowls shut their eyes when they go to sleep? And have I not heard something about their putting their heads under their wings?

I suspect this woodpecker to be a kingfisher.

There are two glorious *real* Labrador dogs here, very different from the clumsy, cross-bred brute we call a Newfoundland. "Bosen" and Tray, or, as pretty Miss Esther prettily pronounced it, Te-rai, are up to any amount of lark, and have even invented one for themselves; this is, fish-hunting in the shallow water on the reef; one of them starting the game, and the other pouncing on it as it shoots past them, turn and turn about.

After an excellent and merry dinner, which I remember included more hard-boiled eggs than had ever been seen at once before, we wended "homeward" to the sea-shore; on our way being shown a stone as big as a cricket-ball, firmly embedded in the stem of a palm-tree, a good three hundred yards from where the surf is breaking at present, showing what fearful rollers occasionally burst on the reef. After swapping libraries to a certain extent, for Mr. Blackett is "death on books," we parted with a hearty farewell, he to his house, and we, away over the blue sea, laden with pretty cocoa-nut cups, scraped as thin as the finest china—*chou!*

I object most strongly against making personal remarks, particularly anonymously, not being a weekly reviewer; but for the life of me I cannot help saying that we left on the island a gentleman who, from the way he shut one eye and smiled, put me wonderfully in mind of a very distinguished ex-colonial governor. I mention this fact, so well known in North America, because I want to air a theory I have formed on the subject, and which has cost me much thought and reflection.

One of the best ways of discovering the use of an organ, or custom, apparently useless among the higher animals, is to trace them back among the lower till you come to the point where they are indispensable. And something in this way I attempted to solve the mystery of the shutting one eye, when you were particularly on your guard. After running through a world of curious theory, I came at last to the Skye-terrier, who, when he has a difficult matter on foot (connected with rats and such like), always tucks up one leg and goes on the other, thus reserving one fresh and sound for any unexpected contingency. And so it is with this eye-closing business. The crafty Yankee closes one eye, because he knows that the human eye becomes fatigued after a time, when it has been peered into to see what is going on in the brain.

Think of what a comfort and strength it must be to shut the wearied one, and open the other, brilliant and flashing, just as your adversary has tired both his or hers!

Some folks, lawyers and ladies especially, take to spectacles for much the same purpose, and get an unfair advantage over you, looking into your eyes without letting you look into theirs. I know a very distinguished man who is so perfectly aware of this that he keeps his eyes fixed on the ceiling, in a rapt and devotional manner, the whole time he is conversing with you.

Wednesday, September 28th.—In the morning awoke by the singing of native songs, and going on deck found that we were close to a "labor" schooner, with one hundred and twenty-one men, women, and children on board, from the Hervey and Cook groups, bound for Tahiti.

Certainly, judging from appearances, nothing could be more happy and agreeable than their position; and if most general singing be a proof of ease and well-doing, they possessed both in a high degree.

I hear, however, that these people *always* sing, happen what may, after they have left their islands for a day or two, however rough the parting.

The worst of it is, that they engage themselves to work; that is, such work as they have been accustomed to at home—an easy hour or two in the cool morning, and the rest of the day spent in the *dolce far niente*. I am afraid that, when they find they have to labor through the long, hot day, they often wish themselves quit of their bargain.

Still I think that this shifting the inhabitants of these islands from one to another is a good thing if properly done, and is in fact the *only* way of civilizing some of the more savage tribes. Moreover, they *must* emigrate from some of the islands, or starve.

Let me warn future travellers that this island must not be confounded with one of nearly the same name in the Austral-group, the island on which Fletcher Christian, of the Bounty, intended to settle when he left Tahiti. We passed this Tubai, but landed not, as the "South Sea Directory" states that "the harbor inside is unsafe, and the anchorage outside insecure and rocky, with bad holding-ground." A pleasant place!

By-the-by, the said Fletcher did good service in his way by landing here again with four hundred pigs and fifty goats, and a native of Bora-Bora. However, his party could not agree with the Tabuiese, and left in 1789.

It has a high, broken, and peaky aspect, and doubtless contains many a lovely gorge and glen for the enjoyment of the man who is contented to be left there. As it is marked as a French island, it might be worth the while to stop there to study the French missionaries, who have the credit of performing infinitely more fantastic tricks than even our own, which is saying a good deal.

It is, however, a great pity that there is not some strict supervision exercised over the "labor-vessels" flying the British flag. There can be no doubt that there are great outrages committed by reckless ruffians, and revenged on the next arrival, innocent or guilty.

7

It was in consequence of his having landed at Eromango after an outrage of this sort, that stout-hearted Williams was killed, and by far the greater number of massacres of whites in the South Seas are produced from this cause. And no wonder! I have had a vessel pointed out to me in Auckland Harbor whose captain, I was assured, was in the habit of running down the canoes at sea, in order to pick up the natives and sell them. And this was considered rather an exceptional bit of humanity than otherwise.

A tenth part of the money spent in trying to prevent the Imaum of Muscat supplying himself with labor from Africa, which is no earthly business of ours, would keep up a smart little gunboat or two in these seas, which would be quite enough to prevent all the mischiefs of the labor-trade as at present carried on. This really is our business, as the ships fly our flag and our fellow-citizens employ the labor.

It is of no earthly use a big frigate popping in now and again into one or two of the largest harbors. We want a small, smart boat, able to go anywhere. There are really very few ruffians employed in the trade, and were these rooted out and a set of regulations laid down like those relating to emigrants, for instance; and, moreover, consuls appointed who understood the native languages, the trade might be made a very great blessing to all parties.

I should insist on the consuls being well up in native languages, for ignorance on that head makes him absolutely worse than useless when he has to certify freshly-imported labor. There is no want of men in these seas perfectly capable of filling the office, though few so thoroughly up in the matter as our consul at Samoa, who has, however, but little of this sort of thing to do.

I was told of a case in which the consul, with wild gestures, lugs the newly-imported "labor" by the arm about the office as a means of rendering *à la muette de portici*, "Were you taken away by violence?" and asks the question, "Were you engaged for one year?" by holding up his forefinger interrogatively. As no native would ever dream of saying anything but "yes" to a white consul, he gets answers which perfectly satisfy him, if not the unfortunate devil who has gone to the risk and expense of importing the men.

And these planters really require some protection. Think of a case in which a vessel is seized by a British man-of-war for being overladen. The natives not sent home again, but handed over to the acting British consul, who distributes them among his friends, to work on their estates for nothing, during the trial of the case at Sydney. The case is given against the captain of the man-of-war, who is promoted and returns home.

The men whom he took are now working on the estates of the consul's friends, and will be made to do so till their time is out. And the unfortunate importer, who gained his case and sold his schooner to defend it, is beggared without the possibility of redress; the brother of the late consul still brutally refusing to let him have even the last remains of the labor he has paid so dearly for.

I believe that I have understated the iniquity and injustice of this affair. And remember that the victim here was no long-shore loafer, no square-gin-drinking "beach-comber," but a man of birth and education; and who would, in all possibility, have made his fortune had he not have had the luck to win a lawsuit against a philo-negro captain of the navy.

There would not be the slightest difficulty in obtaining labor were confidence reëstablished between the white man and the brown. They are often willing enough to come; I can say that, in the course of our cruising in the South Seas, we might have picked up any number of men. In the Isle of Pines, I remember, that we had to force them out of the boat, so anxious were they to take a cruise with us.

I wish the thing could be done, but I fear there is some adverse influence at headquarters which does not think that it is in its interest that affairs should be put on a good footing, or that the islands should be colonized. I think I know what it is, and why it acts, and recognize its wisdom—that is, as far as its own interests are concerned. But I have no wish to poke my head into a hornet's nest—and *such* hornets! the real bilious black-and-yellow brood.

CHAPTER VII.

RARITONGA.

Friday, September 30, 1870.—Sighted Raritonga, and knocked about all night.

Saturday, October 1st.—Beat up to Raritonga. A long ridge of beautiful mountain, wooded right up its precipitous side. The cliffs and pinnacles of black trap-rock, sharply defined against the clear-blue sky. The reef is fringing, not detached, at least on this side.

To our astonishment we made out a large ship, standing off and on under the lee of the land. As we drew nearer we hoisted our white ensign, which she did not seem to like, for she first made sail, and then shortened again, as if uncertain what to do. Then she hoisted a color at the peak, which we could not well make out, but which looked American, and then, as if she had made up her mind what part to act, hauled it down again, and ran the Peruvian flag to the masthead. As we neared her we saw that her decks were swarming with infinite yellow faces of the most decidedly Chinese type, which increased our bewonderment. But it was no business of ours, though she evidently thought it was. We hove-to and went on shore, where we were greeted with the greatest kindness and hospitality by the missionary and his wife; also with equal warmth by every man, woman, and child we met: evidently the Raritongians are a fine and genial race.

Sunday, October 2d.—After many deliberations and doubts, we were persuaded by the jolly old pilot to trust the yacht to the keeping of the harbor of Raritonga. "Safest harbor in the world." It may be so; but still I wonder how those suspicious-looking ships' bones came to be scattered so thickly on the coral just at the entrance? It is a curious place, and I fancy few would take it for a harbor at all, were they not assured of the fact by the proper authorities. Unlike most of the island harbors, you do not enter by a deep and narrow break in the reef, into a snug and secure lagoon, but into a mere saucer-like depression in the reef itself, which really looks infinitely more dangerous than the open sea. We calculated that it was about twenty to one that you were wrecked going in, fifty to one that you were wrecked going out, and even chances that you were utterly cast away inside. However, inside we got—(where could not the captain take the Albatross? wet grass is enough for her!)—and divers performed the most marvellous submarine feats, their brown bodies wriggling and kicking far down below in the clear water as they tied knots and passed hawsers through the rings of the mooring anchors. Of these we had plenty; in fact, when we were made fast, the poor old dear looked like an astonished spider placed in the centre of some one else's web. We had the pleasure of knowing that every wavelet that seethed in over the reef chafed one or other of our warps against the sharp coral edges; a process by no means conducive to strength or security. One really felt like a nesting coot in a flood. However, there we were; and if we were wrecked we were not likely to be drowned, so we accepted the situation and began our prowls on shore.

As in the north world so in the south world—civilization and manners tend from east to west. As we drop down from island to island in the ever-fresh tradewind to the westward, we become sensible of an ever-increasing want of finish, a provincialism, in fact, among the islanders. They are still very charming, but their mouths and noses are altering. The face generally is growing coarser, and one begins to sniff the negro taint from far-distant Papua.

The Raritongian would, however, most indignantly deny the sniff; and, indeed, it is but a faint one. Nor would he for a moment admit the lessened civilization. For not only has Raritonga a newspaper printed in pure Raritongese, and therefore highly available to the general reader, but she has a real stone church—a church as the churches of Britain! Oh, that church! that church! that vile black-and-white stone abomination, paralyzing one of the most beautiful bits of scenery in the world! Truly, indeed, may it be said, with horrible sarcasm, to be like too many of the churches at home. For sheer, blank, unmitigated discomfort and ugliness, I will back it against the most civilized nonconformist ranting-box in England; Scotland, or even Wales. Upon my word, I feel inclined to say that this most intolerable and pretentious building is

the only really and truly hideous thing I saw in the
South Seas. Did I think that there was the slightest
chance of those who agreed to and subscribed for its
erection ever reading this, I would launch out into
still more truculent abuse. The thing is an abomination, and the man who designed it ought to be grated
slowly to pulp against its black and doleful walls. It
has even glass-windows! Glass-windows in this climate! Surely there was a glazier brother in the connection, and the thing was a job—a job more iniquitous
than the employment of Raphael for the decoration of
the Vatican! Galleries, too! Good Lord! as if they
had not half the island to build on, were they so minded. No! there were galleries in their own little narrow sphere at home, and so there must be galleries
here. What makes the matter worse is, that the native
churches in the South-Sea Islands are generally perfect
in their way—large and cool, low-eaved, with a wall
nearly all window, for the crisp sea-wind to whisper in
and help the congregation to sleep.

Not only is this church hideous, but the very church-
yard is utterly detestable in every respect. I do not
like to say too much on the subject, but surely those
horrible tombs were not built without some reason;
they must have cost the early converts something somewhere. Pah! it makes me hot to think on't.

If the same man who built the church built the
mission-house, and laid out the grounds around it,
hanging would be infinitely too good for him, for the
latter are as remarkable for beauty and arrangement
as the former is for their absence. One glimpse of
that most lovely mission-house would make the Duke

of Devonshire let Chiswick fall into instant ruin, from mere hopelessness of competing with it!

We visited the church, or rather attended afternoon service, in company with the king, a well-dressed and particularly gentleman-like man, who was kind enough to come on board with his prime-minister, to invite us to seats in the "pew royal." The congregation we thought more attentive than any one we had seen in these seas, but it was really painful to see both men and women dressed according to the lowest style of European "go-to-meeting." Instead of those long, delicate, graceful "sacques," of which we have become so fond, and head-dresses of fresh flower-wreaths or neat arsroot crowns, the women wore detestable waisted European garments, with vulgar and tawdry hats and feathers, which utterly destroyed all their native ease and grace. Where on earth did the earlier missionaries pick up that curious idea of the necessary identity of piety and ugliness?

In front of us sat a grave and reverent elder, with the most broad-church cut of black coat and white tie, and a mighty pair of spectacles, looking exactly like a very bilious Scotch precentor. He kept his eyes steadily fixed on his hymn-book during the singing, and bore his "burden" by keeping up that prolonged humming drone, so popular as an accompaniment in these seas: a harmless paganicity, for which I suspect he would have been "cut off from the connection" in some of the neighboring islands, or at least have been mulcted in hard dollars. This "hum" is by no means unlike the drone of a bagpipe, and I suppose answers the same purpose, whatever that may be. I have an indistinct recollection of attending a cottage-dance, somewhere in the Highlands, long, long ago; when, for want of better music, one man played the Jew's (or jaw's?) harp, and two or three others kept up a prolonged monotonous nasal drone, very like that of my friend in the front benches. It is here by no means an unpleasant noise, as they manage to give it a metallic resonancy which no "Pakeha" or "Papelangi" organs could ever imitate. It is something like the drum of the emeu, or the answering note of the wekka, indefinitely prolonged.

After service, having shaken hands with a good half of the congregation as they filed before us, we sauntered up to the mission-house; past a mighty sacred tree, overthrown by the hurricane, lying like a prostrate idol, and concerning which there is many a strange legend; past a cricket-ground in course of preparation, in which, if the natives take to the game, there will in time be formed an eleven hard to beat; and so—through lovely and well-kept grounds, on the edges of which the bushes were blossoming with pretty brown faces peeping at the strangers—up to the cool veranda.

One does not wish, Yankee-like, to gossip about the private affairs of those who kindly admit the stranger within their gates. Let us merely state that the warm-hearted, sensible Highland lady and gentleman who represent the mission at Raritonga are very different people from the typical missionaries of the South Pacific.

By no means believing that they can wash the blackamoor (or rather brownamoor) white by a sudden application of Calvinistic whitewash, they try to make him as good a brownamoor as they can, and their labor has certainly not been in vain. How easily this whitewash cracks and peels off may be seen or heard by any one who keeps his eyes or ears open. One fact which we heard from a "high personage" rather tickled us. A short time ago a native drum was brought to Raritonga from one of the neighboring islands, and the very moment the first finger-taps were heard, all the girls, down to the wee chits ten or eleven years old, began to wriggle and squirm like so many galvanized frogs; showing plainly that the old dancing-blood still ran in their veins, and that even its peculiar forms of expression had not been forgotten. In fact, the newer missionaries are quite wise enough to see that the natives do not care to "let them know every thing;" and the quiet, decently-behaved visitor may see a good many things which the others wisely blink.

The older missionaries reported (and possibly still report) that Christianity has utterly stamped out all these pleasant paganisms. The newer ones and *we* know perfectly well that it has done nothing of the sort, nor will it do so for a very long time to come. The Gawazee of Egypt and the Gitana of Spain have kept to their old dances, in spite of priest or mollah, for many an age, and so it will be here. If any real improvement is to take place, I should propose that each ball should be attended by the missionary and his wife. I will warrant that under these auspices any evil element will soon be eliminated, and the native dance be rendered as decorous as the quadrille. What right has an English or French missionary to say to a whole race, "You shall not dance, you shall not sing, you shall not smoke," under the possible penalty of eternal damnation in the next world, or the certain loss of dollars in this? He dares not preach the same doctrine in Europe, or, even if he does, he cannot help feeling that all he gains is the ridicule of the sensible and the applause of fools. As I said before, let the missionary and his wife encourage decent dancing by their presence, and the lower form of that healthy and natural amusement will soon be unknown.

Seated in the pleasant veranda, enjoying the cool green of the English grass lawn, the only one worth the name in the islands, and possibly smoking a cigar, we were joined by two native gentlemen, dressed in the most correct black coat and white choker (literally *choker* in this climate), a vile taste and a ridiculous, which I hope may soon give way to something better. I suppose that in the older times the converts, when thus dressed, supposed that they were approaching the image of their demi-god, the missionary. I think that I have observed in these regions that the farther from "the establishment" the more clerical the rig. The attire in which I believe one noble, true-hearted man— a real bishop—sometimes addresses his good words to the savage heathen of Melanesia would scandalize all Dissenterdom; though 'tis for the most part a time-honored garment, and, moreover, in his case, a comely and well-fitting one. Of course, the newer and more rational missionaries dress as suits the climate, and, I think, their profession. Why a minister of light and purity should dress in garments more suited in color to the worship of the devil himself I could never make out. One of our visitors was an honest soul, and, on our host producing some grated kava in a bottle, he immediately recognized it, and so we experimented on him at once by giving him a tablespoonful and a half in a tumbler of water. He said that it was just enough to make him comfortable, though as far as I saw it had no appreciable effect on him—not more, certainly, than a glass of beer or sherry would have on one of us. He might have fallen asleep, however, at afternoon service for any thing I know to the contrary. Our other friend, though outwardly white-bearded and venerable, was, I fear, a humbug. On being shown the kava, he gazed upon it with lack-lustre eye, as a thing unknown and void of all interest, and listlessly demanded its name. On being pressed, he confessed to have heard of such a thing among the unregenerate in his hot youth, but for *his* part—oh, dear, no!

As both we and his friend were rather piqued at this assumption of superior purity, we shifted the subject to the cheerful one of cannibalism, and demanded of him, categorically, whether, at a former period of his existence, he had, or had not, with his own hands, cooked a fellow-sinner. He confessed that he had, but denied that he had ever tasted his own cookery. A likely tale, quotha!

Had it not been for the introduction of pigs and other animals, it is possible that cannibalism might have existed here to this day. The pigeons are being rapidly thinned out by the rats, who are far better tree-climbers, even in England, than is generally supposed. The dogs, which I believe they had before the arrival of the Europeans, and which Dr. Grüfe tells me are specifically distinct from those of Europe, were mere dainties for the chiefs, and flesh must be had. By-the-by, it is whispered that even in civilized Raritonga bow-wow is to this day by no means an unpopular dish, but it is not polite to talk about it. As in Spain, you eat what is given you, and ask no questions, though the claws in your plate may put you in mind of Ponto or grimalkin, as the case may be.

Among other civilizations, the missionaries have introduced photography, to the no small marvel of the natives. My white-bearded friend laughed loud and long when he was told that his beard would return to its pristine blackness on being dipped into that shallow dish of clear, transparent fluid. He tried it, however, and the missionary was exalted into the seventh heaven of conjurordom. The case of a young lady, however, ended not so happily. She dipped her pretty finger-tips into the innocent-looking fluid in the "yellow room," thinking no evil. But on emerging into the blazing sunlight, her fingers began to develop into blackness still deeper and deeper, till she burst into a flood of tears, fully persuaded that she was going to the devil in some new fashion, for which she had not been prepared.

Gossiping thus in the veranda, we looked out into the blue offing, and saw the mysterious bark still hanging about, some fourteen hundred tons' burden, and reported to be laden with Cochin-Chinese. Rather an odd cargo, and looking as if the French had been bustling up in those regions.

The captain gives one account of her antecedents, and the mate another, which most clearly proves that the captain is a liar; but the captain has got the best

of the argument, by simply clapping his mate into
irons till he agrees with him, a straightforward course,
and one highly likely to produce unity. The Peruvian (heaven or the other place only knows why) wants
to shoot his semi-celestial rubbish on to the island, and
to sail away with a clear ship. As there are several
hundred Cochinese, and Raritonga is none too large
for its present population, the chiefs do not see it in
the same light, and, if the Peruvian persists, there
will be a fight. He is reported to have tried to wreck
his ship three times on the reef, in order to settle the
question easily. People do free and easy things in
these seas; and piracy, kidnapping, and murder, are
not utterly unknown. Hence grave doubts as to the
captaincy and ownership of the good bark Dolores
Urgasto.

Since the above was written, news has reached
England of the burning of the doubtful Peruvian bark
Dolores Urgasto, with five hundred coolies, during a
voyage between Macao and Peru. *Captain and crew*
(with one exception) *saved, of course.*

That we went on board the yacht this evening was
entirely our own fault, for the missionary put his
whole establishment at our disposal with the most
generous and unfeigned hospitality. But when one
has been seeing things all day, one likes to think them
over in the evening at home; and a home our kaurie-
lined, green-leather cushioned cabin has become to us,
both from lapse of time and old associations.

A young English gentleman staying on the island
sauntered with us down from the mission-house to the
schooner, piloting us through a net-work of narrow

paths cut through a dense thicket of bananas, guaras, cocoas, and coffee-bushes, which seems to have been laid out expressly for a flirting-ground. There was always a new path up which to turn if any one, or rather two, saw you coming, which, indeed, this evening seemed to indicate the existence of a perfect maze or labyrinth of paths. The pretty native huts were closely sheltered in the bushes, and numbers of women emerged from them and greeted us kindly. One gushing young thing, after squeezing ——'s fingers, kissed them tenderly, and then *fugit ad salices*, which a beach-man would translate, "cut into the coffee-bush." She fled alone!

The question of the queer Peruvian is settled. He is to have water and vegetables, and then to depart to his own place, wherever that may be. So there will be old floating of tubs of fresh water to him over the bar to-morrow.

In the evening, about eight o'clock, we heard a noise, as of one beating with a stick an unfortunate kettle, to which he bore a personal grudge. We supposed it to be a species of curfew-bell; and, deciding that Sunday was over, we caught some beautifully-marked file-fish, and another species, a "perfect love," with regular creamy white stripes on a brilliant scarlet ground.

The people on shore struck us as a shade darker than the Society-Islanders, and some of the women have a slightly Chinese, oblique-eyed expression about them. Spanish, as talked by our Peruvian friend, they do not like. "Like oui-oui" (Frenchman), "talkee plenty too much with fingers." They consider Raritongese to be the first of languages, and after that—some way—the English. They are evidently full of fun, though possibly of a different kind to ours; but, then, who can translate humor?

"Well, good-night, old fellow!"

Monday, October 3d.—About twelve o'clock, a pleasant English-speaking chief came on board, to conduct us to the king, who we supposed was going to present us with the usual complimentary present of bananas and cocoa-nuts. We sauntered along the beach toward his house, taking and giving kindly "Yer hannas" and hand-shakings at each step, till we reached our destination, a long, low, one-storied white-washed building, with a cool and roomy veranda running along its whole front. It was raised, some two or three feet from the ground, on a substantial stone basement, and was embosomed in all kinds of beautiful shrubs, and overshadowed in front by tall cocoa-palms. A straight, white coral sand path led from the door down to the garden-gate, which opened on to the sea-beach. When we arrived, instead of being greeted by enthusiastic crowds, we found the place bare, except of some of the looser sort, who were evidently mere spectators. However, our chief gave us a chair apiece, on each side of the door, and then went his way, leaving us, like a pair of idols, guarding the sacred threshold. Now and then a stray native came up and shyly worshipped us, retiring immediately to squat in the shade, but still gazing reverently, but that was all. And if real idols do not have a livelier time of it than we had, I do not care much for the profession. Still we waited patiently, as beseemed us, not knowing what might happen should we descend from our pride of place.

After a time, there approached us from the right-hand path a marvellous old woman, with hair as white as snow, and leaning on a long staff, bowing low and reverently at every step. P—— descended to greet her, on which she, snatching her straw hat from her white locks, seized his hand, and actually "mumbled" it with delight. I never saw a more darling old lady! She is a woman with a great history, being no less than the very one who placed the first (native) teachers under the historical tree, now to be seen in the mission-garden, and mounted guard over them the livelong night. Even now, wreck as she is, she has a grand granite look about her which makes it easy to believe the tale of her early heroism. After embracing P——, she wagged her head at the younger folk, gave a series of orders which no one regarded, and subsided majestically at the foot of a palm-tree.

There was inflicted on us a sharp, clever, conceited prig of a man (for there are brown prigs as well as white ones, and even *better*) who had spent five years in England, and who was married to a half-caste Corsican, a jovial soul, who had evidently had a glorious figure once, but now fallen into that crummy state so much deplored by Mr. Bailey. Verily, there be strange mixtures in these seas!

To while away the time, we peeped into the house, and found that it consisted of two fair-sized rooms, separated by a passage, opening straight through into the field beyond. The rooms were principally furnished with beautiful mats, and seemed rather reception than living rooms, having but few signs of domesticity about them. Indeed, we fancied that this building plays the part of St. James's to the real Buckingham Palace.

Another thing which helped the time to pass away, was the contemplation of a young girl who, mounting on the boss formed by the aërial roots of a cocoa-palm, had fitted her lithe back and limbs into the curve of the stem in the most graceful manner. We agreed that we had never seen a more lovely study for a sculptor.

After a time appeared a small procession formed by our missionary friends and the king, who was dressed carefully in black; he was attended by his ministers, and there were warm and kindly greetings on all sides.

Gradually the open space under the trees began to fill with natives; the women, to our great comfort, were dressed in pretty white sacques instead of those vile waisted gowns which they sported yesterday. Gradually, also, the veranda began to fill with the aristocracy of the place; among whom were admitted the doubtful Peruvian skipper, a small, sharp, intelligent man, speaking excellent English, and by no means looking the piratical and sea-roverish person he is supposed to be. What he would look like if he were not particularly well pleased I do not know, but I fancy that it would not take much to put a knife-edge on him; as some one observed, "His Peruvian bite might turn out even less wholesome than his Peruvian bark.".

As we sat exchanging greetings, we became aware of the " rub-tub-tubbing " of marvellously slack drums, and, Phemy placed in the post of honor, the meeting was declared open. The gate at the end of the walk being removed from its hinges, there swarmed through its portals a succession of sights stranger than we ever saw before or can ever expect to see again. Had we been short-hand writers, writing the shortest possible hand, we must have left an infinity of quaint and curious things untold. First poured in a mass of men who, though habited reasonably enough after the manner of the "reach-me-downs," chose for some private reason to assume a gorgeous head-dress, compounded apparently of a mixture of the popular idea of the hat of the late Guido Fawkes, the grenadier's cap of the early Georges, with a slight suspicion of the tiara of the Pope of Rome. There seemed to be no masquerade about it, and it might possibly have been the recollection of some native gala-dress of the premissionaristic time.

Yelling yells which would have passed for very tolerable "View-halloos!" in the shires, they advanced up the path, some bearing beautiful mats, and others waving very much less beautiful flags.

In front of them, dressed principally in a white shirt, with a native cloak of many colors, barefooted, and bearing a weapon half spear and half paddle, with great goggle mother-o'-pearl eyes, which he manœuvred like some sort of antediluvian spontoon, advanced the spokesman of the deputation. Advanced?—advance is too mild a term; for he frisked, and bounded, and gambadoed, like a very David before the ark—ay, in more ways than one!

Arrived within good "View-halloo!" distance, the presents of the chiefs were *thrown* down, not leisurely parted with, as with regret, but honestly thrown at you, as if the owners were only too eager to show you honor; and the spokesman, dressed in the old colored cloak of antiquity, began to speak, or rather to bellow like the most Bashantic of bulls. Indeed, some of his utterances really put us in mind of the strange alternate rumblings and squealings of an excited bull. He roared and gasped at P—— furiously and convulsively, gambadoing and cutting strange *entre-châts* all the time, terminating every three words or so with a shrieking yell that went through one like a knife:

"Here are bananas! Yow! yow! yoicks!"

"Here cocoa-nuts! Yoicks! yow! yow!"

Pigs! (as before); mats! (rare and valuable); an awful ankle-twisting gambado! and a yell that made us tremble for his blood-vessels; and so on, till we became accustomed to these terrible civilities. When familiarity brought not contempt but tranquillity, we began to have the dawning of an idea that we had seen our paganesque friend somewhere before; and to our no small astonishment we found that we were gradually constructing out of the features of this hospitable but savage howler the grave and spectacled ones of the *douce* older who had done the bass at service but yesterday—the elder, who had actually held forth to the saints from the platform of Exeter Hall! "Ay, and why not?" thought we to ourselves. "Why not encourage this harmless effervescence and exuberant goodwill as far as possible? Is it worse in any respect than whiskey-and-water and fires, Kentish or otherwise? All honor to you, Monsieur le Missionnaire, for your solid good sense!"

Somewhere about this time natives brought a glorious mat, and spread it over the steps. Also let us remark that the king had at the very beginning of the *fantasia* removed from the veranda, and posted himself under a tree a little distance off; the proof, we thought, of rare good taste and delicacy. He evidently wished it to be supposed that all the homage was offered to P——, and that his presence had nothing to do with the feeling of the people.

Soon afterward the chief of one of the districts and his queen advanced, and shook hands with P——, and immediately the veranda was literally stormed by his whole tribe, men, women, and children. Such laughing and swaying, and squeezing ("I like being squeezed, sir!" said the old lady to the lord-chamberlain), was never seen, even at her Majesty's drawing-room! Every finger was invested instantly, and P—— solved the difficult question of how to shake hands with ten women at once. What made the confusion worse confounded, was the fact that each individual, from the weeist pickaninny to the oldest granny, had brought a present, which they deposited on the mat at the entrance before shaking hands. Some brought a mat, some pretty baskets, a tiny bag of coffee, a sholl, a feather, an ancient stone weapon, or an unfortunate fowl, the latter of which added their discordant "sqnawks" to the general din, as they were trampled on by "the bare feet of laughing (or larking?) girls," struggling in the press. The mass became more and more condensed, till finally, with a convulsive struggle which shook the house, they burst through the narrow passage into the field beyond, and we heard them, chuckling, panting, and clicking, over the grand lark they had just had.

Then in the distance more "rum-tum-tititum" of approaching drums announced another procession from another district. As they came on in a dense cloud, stepping short, and almost marking time, we saw two men dancing and gesticulating in the wildest manner, apparently on the very shoulders of the crowd. As the mass opened out a little, we saw that they were on a rude platform, which formed the dancing-floor. The dance itself was a most weird and strange one, one of the old pagan dances, which were supposed to be extinct thirty years ago. There were certainly some reasons why it should be extinct as it was danced before us, but with a little judicious pruning it might be rendered quite as proper as a polka or a valse. It is certainly infinitely more graceful than either, and the waving motions of the arms were really beautiful. As they advanced, the bearers raised and lowered the platform at intervals, rhythmically, as one might say, accompanying the movement with deep "Hughs!" like those of a pavior at work, though infinitely deeper and louder. Now and again the bearers introduced an impromptu performance, which was neither contemplated nor enjoyed by the dancers, as it threatened to cast them down violently from their pride of place, among the feet of the mob. So they objurgated, and the crowd around roared and yelled louder than ever. This strange myriad-legged beetle—for it resembled that more than any thing else—struggling up the path, was a thing to remember. Strange also it was to see how rapidly the old tarantella-poison spread among the people, and how the young ladies, starting up from beneath the cocoa-trees, betook themselves to the dance in the most *prononcé* fashion. 'Indeed, there was no knowing the lengths to which they might have proceeded, had not our venerable friend, Precentor David (who had not been a whit the better himself twenty minutes before), brought the broad end of his goggle-eyed paddle to bear on the stern of the liveliest young lady with a force which produced a very distinct and decided "smack!"—a smack which required such an amount of energy to be expended in rubbing as to leave none for dancing.

At last the platform approached the steps, and we saw that, besides the dancers above, it was laden with an infinity of pigs, taro, bananas, etc., suspended from its rafters. At a given signal the whole affair was let go by the run, pigs, dancers, and all, to their extreme discomfort and the increased merriment of the mob. Then another storm of hand-shaking and kissing and present-making, till we stood knee-deep in coffee-berries and shrieking chickens.

The next procession was preceded by a company of handsome young fellows, dressed in dark-green uniforms, and armed with wooden muskets, with a slight sprinkling of rusty fowling-pieces here and there. The colonel, who would have passed anywhere as an Italian officer, and a monstrous good-looking one, too, was very well got up indeed. The only drawback was that he had rather spoilt the general effect by attaching a big, unmistakable butcher's steel to the belt where his sword ought to have hung. His second in command, despising pretension, carried a good honest wooden sword, and was not ashamed of it. Any feeling of absurdity which might have been produced by their dress or accoutrements was entirely obviated by the intense expression of gravity and reality which pervaded their countenances. They had no idea of any "make-believe," but had honestly and painfully done their best to please us, showing how they appreciated civilized manners, and wished to imitate them.

Their drill was perfectly wonderful. They formed in single file on each side of the path, smartly enough, and went through the manual and platoon, in a strange manner, which showed most clearly that the greater part of them had been taught the motions without the slightest idea of their meaning. One pretty but not particularly useful manœuvre consisted in the whole party whirling their muskets round their heads, till the line looked like a double row of catherine-wheels.

When the speechifying was over, and P—— had shaken hands with the army, the king's present was brought, a gorgeous piece of seamless tappa over thirty yards long—the one end borne by the talking-man on his shoulders, and the other by the proud woman who had wrought it. This kind of tappa is reserved for chiefs, and, when they wrap themselves up in it, they look like ancient Romans in their togas. This having been presented and rolled up, the king's body-guard, dressed in red shirts and looking rather like marines, formed on each side of the path with the other troops, forming a lane up which the king and the rest of the royal family walked with great grace and dignity; somehow putting us in mind of an old print in which good old King George and his family are doing much the same thing. This was the first time the king and his guests had been together since the commencement of the ceremonies, and with many hand-shakings and "Yer hannas" we waited for the last scene.

The darling old lady, who had mounted guard over the proto-missionaries, was evidently a "grande dame de par le monde," as Brantome would say, for she and she only was permitted to bring her present after the royal one. It was another piece of tappa, quite as long and fine, if not longer and finer than the king's, and was presented much in the same manner, the dear old lady, mother of missionaries, hobbling before on her long staff, chanting strange canticles in her sweet, quavering old voice. One end of the tappa was wound round P——'s neck and the door-post at the same time, while the other end was held up by natives afar off—a pretty way of symbolizing the intimate relationship existing between himself, the house of the king, and the general people.

Then we had a general review of the troops. The chief justice made a pivot-man of himself, and the entire army did some mysterious manœuvres, with him for a centre, which were far too profound for our crude volunteer experience.

The country districts having had their turn, the people of the home settlements began, and the fun grew fast and furious. What happened in the wild confusion I hardly know. A storm of women, infinitely wilder than any that had yet appeared, rushed upon P——, and for a moment I thought that he was going to suffer the fate of Orpheus. They embraced him whenever they could get hold of him; they crowned him with reva-reva crowns; they girded him with strange belts, and clothed him with wild colored mattings, till he looked like a cross between a Roman Catholic priest in full canonicals and the youthful Bacchus. They beat against him as the waves of the Atlantic against the Eddystone, and it was quite a comfort to see him emerge unscathed, now and again, from the *brown* sea-foam. Had he been shorter, I believe they would have kissed the face off him: as it was—

"She who could not kiss his lips
Was fain to kiss his clothes."

After the storm was over, and something like calm produced, the life-guards were, by particular desire, put through their evolutions, and such a drill I fancy was never drilled before. No part of it had the slightest reference to any military necessity, but was a mere *ballet d'action*. If the fellows had to fight in reality, they would strip and take a spear. One manœuvre consisted in porting arms, and nothing else, with a regularity and pertinacity worthy of a better cause. Another still prettier, and equally useful, consisted in their casting away their arms of iron (or wood) altogether, and betaking themselves to their arms of flesh. Counter-marching in double lines, they waved them to and fro, and in and out, with the most marvellous grace and precision, giving the regiment, when seen end on, somewhat the appearance of a gigantic red caterpillar, trying to walk with its legs uppermost, or twisting in mortal agony on its back.

One is heart-broken to think how miserably mean is this description of a most rare and curious scene. Even the white residents had never seen any thing like it. It was a sudden outburst of the old pagan hospitality, so nearly destroyed by modern civilization.

Thoroughly knocked up with the noise and excitement, we went on board the yacht, the queen promising to forward the "tons" of presents; and to follow with her family, in the course of an hour or so.

Soon after luncheon, troops of natives, principally women, began to flock on board, and decks were soon covered and cabins filled. Such nice, kind, cheery souls! There were *acres* of smiles on board. On a portrait of P——'s mother being shown to one, she "clicked" with pleasure, pressed it to her lips, and then put it reverently back again; all done so prettily and gracefully as to be a positive delight. On some compliment being paid, "Yes," quoth the young lady, "I kees it!" All the English she knew, and about the first they learn, I fancy, in these "Paphian bowers."

Then they proposed singing. "They want to sing; they so glad to see the sheep," explained one. And so about twenty of them settled themselves down wherever they could—a perfect bunch of brown tulips bedded in snow—and gave us several pretty melodies in the native fashion; among which we could trace the beloved old "Home, sweet home!" strangely altered, but by no means spoilt.

Soon after arrived the king, queen, and royal suite. Her majesty was got down the narrow companion-way with extreme difficulty, on account of her enormous size and weight; which also gave us the most extreme uneasiness as to how she was to be got on deck again whole.

The spirit of impropriety having entered P——'s

soul, and the missionary being safe on shore, he proposed to have some real native dancing and singing. The merry old king was by no means averse to a lark, and some twenty girls shook themselves down and began.

At first they were, or pretended to be, mighty shy and modest, probably afraid of the authorities; but the king and the chief-justice egging them on with many a queer quip and crank, they gradually became so excited that P—— began to think that he had lighted a fire which it would take some trouble to put out. A song in his honor produced a perfect *furore*, and such a cloud of waving handkerchiefs never was seen, certainly not in the cabin of the Iliad Albatross. Warmer and warmer they grew. Three of the handsomest girls separated themselves from the mass, and danced before P——, waving their handkerchiefs in his face, until at last the very handsomest of them all so far lost her head, or her heart, as to declare her deep and unalterable affection in terms more pointed than proper.

Alas for her young loves! The queen, seeing that P—— looked a little confused at this public declaration, was seized with an attack of the most intense virtue, and, rating the unfortunate victim of the tender passion soundly and sharply, ordered her to sit down, which she did in evident astonishment and confusion. Poor dear! the missionaries had not taught her Latin, or she would have known that—

"Est modus in rebus."

The fire was, however, by no means put out by the extinction of her particular flame, and they performed a really pretty dance—two girls dancing opposite each other, and at certain times crossing each other quickly and kissing as they passed. Then things got more lively than ever; and the young ladies, finding the cabin warm and their garments cumbersome, evinced a strong inclination to assume a garb which Lord Sydney would not have tolerated for a single moment, even at the Alhambra. This was all very well in its way, but *under the circumstances* would hardly do; and so, with deep regret, the extinguisher was reluctantly but firmly put on.

To the philosophical mind this presence and prominence of the handkerchief in these amatory saltations is very curious. In Japan, it is true, where I am given to understand that the art of love-making is carried to the highest perfection, it does not obtain, as the Japanese have not, in the strict sense of the word, any pocket-handkerchiefs to use. But every nation possessing pocket-handkerchiefs bring them into play somehow or another. Does not the sultan—not the soldan of Babeloun, but the sultan of the opera—does he not, like a conceited brute as he is, throw his handkerchief at his favorite sultana? Did not I myself, at the *Baïlo Nacional*, up a flight of wooden steps, right-hand side, called something or other, in the good town of Seville —did not I see Donna Maria Dolores, after a most brilliant fandango, cast her handkerchief into the lap of the staid and astonished Governor of Gibraltar? I am told by experts that the handkerchief plays a very prominent part in those abstruse amusements—"kiss in the ring," and, beloved of white New-Zealanders, the "French-tig." I never played at them myself, though their names sound pleasantly, particularly the first; but I have a hazy recollection of seeing a good deal of business done with nine or less white pocket-handkerchiefs at country fairs, long ago, in some of the dances. Indeed, the old paganesque use of the pocket-handkerchief seems to have been introduced even into religion: why do maid-servants always wrap up their prayer-books? But stop, the subject is expanding too rapidly; let us rejoin the ladies.

The hint to retire being given, our lady-friends packed themselves in the boats as tight as they could sit, leaving hardly room for the delighted sailors to pull a stroke, though I don't think they tried very hard. On the boats grounding in the shallow water, with screams and squalls they tucked up their garments quite as high as necessary, and squatted on shore like a skein of white wild-ducks. Some of them, however, preferred the dignity of being carried, and it was a sight to see Doui, a most diminutive Norseman, strongly suspected of being that sailor's terror, a "Russian Finn," staggering to the shore with a skirling damsel, thrice as big as himself, perched on his shoulders. While he was performing this act of gallantry, the boat, frightened by the row, I suppose, drifted into the deeper water with half a dozen girls in her, who kept the little man trotting about in the water, just paddling out of his reach with their hands and laughing at him. As he always had a very big lump of tobacco in his very small cheek, he could not laugh in return, but one saw his lips strained to cracking.

Then with extreme difficulty, the queen was got up the cabin companion, really, I believe, like a wire, the

longer for the process, so tight was the fit, and placed
in the stern-sheets of our biggest boat, the nose of
which immediately cocked out of the water as if astonished at what had happened. It is rude to talk about
ladies' weight or lightness, but I really believe that
her majesty weighed twenty-five good "stun!" The
princess royal, the Queen of Atia, her niece, was weight
for age—well worthy of her, and would have turned
the scale at fifteen stone easily. She it was who formed
the heaviest billow which had surged against P—— in
the morning, leaving her spray on the top of his head
in the form of a glorious crown of reva-reva. She was
as great a mass of solid good-nature as ever was seen,
but within that monstrous bulk were "feelings."
When P—— gave her his portrait, she kissed it again
and again with the most sentimental devotion, and
pressed it (within a couple of feet) to her beating heart.
An elephant in love was nothing to it!

During our stay at Raritonga a smart Yankee
whaler arrived, on her way to her southern winter fish-
ing-grounds. Her skipper, a charming little fellow,
bright and full of strange experiences, which he told in
a most enviable style, came on board once or twice for
doctoring and gossip. Among other things, he pro-
pounded the strange doctrine that whaling is a safer
employment than carpentering, taking into consideration the barking of shins with adzes, the chopping of
toes with axes, and the mutilation of fingers with
gouges and chisels.

As my friend looks now, he is just the sort of man
I should like to ship with for a cruise, but does he
always look as he does now? Few things are more

curious than the difference one often sees between a skipper on shore, on his good behavior, and on board, possessed of almost absolute power; more particularly when the first mate is in irons for smashing the second mate's skull with a marline-spike; for half-murdering the black cook with a "knuckle-duster;" for throwing a bucket of sludge over the cabin-boy, for shaving the ship's cat's tail! As he is, however, he is very nice, and discourses pleasantly. Whaling seems to be a tremendous science. Sperms, right-whales, hump-backs, sulphur-bottoms, and so on, all being attacked in a different fashion, suited to their different habits and the angle at which the eye is set. If you attack a sulphur-bottom at the angle which would suit a sperm, you would very speedily find yourself in the place where sulphur was a mere drug. The skipper expressed this last sentence much more tersely, but I think that that is what he meant. He tells us that his Fijians are very brave and good harpooners; he brought two or three of them on board, and they looked and spoke as if they and he were on good terms. Again—whaling is quite safe; all you have to do is to keep cool, and mind the whale's eye: that is all! Whales signal danger to each other by turning up one of their "flukes," as natives do their paddles; and each whale passes on the signal to another, and descends into the abyss. When you find your boat resting across the flukes of a whale, you are in a tight place, and had better get out of it. The best thing to do is to jump overboard, and dive as far as you can, and then come up again, and be picked up by the second boat. It is hardly worth while looking for your own, unless you wanted a toothpick. But there is no real danger—oh, dear no! so it seems!

When you go to sea, you must either believe *all* the yarns you hear without unravelling them, or none at all. I prefer the former course myself. Surely there is no great harm in simply believing what may not be strictly true, as long as you do not actually practise on it to your own injury or that of society!

I remember once, in a dead calm, some distance from land, I embarked in the ship's dingy, accompanied by one of the most honest, truth-telling seamen I have ever met with, and, moreover, a man of intellect, and, for his position, considerable cultivation. Our object was to disport ourselves with the shooting of sea-fowl, which we did right joyously, getting fine steady "pots" against the sides of the great rollers, or nipping them neatly as they showed over the tops. Moreover, we enjoyed the sight, at one moment, of the entire of our little schooner, as she showed herself, copper and all, at the top of a water-mountain two or three yards off, and then wished her good-by; as all disappeared but a yard and a half of her top-masts, with their little gilded trucks shining in the sun, as she sunk into the valley on the other side. The freckle of the coming breeze on the leaden-silver sea warned us on board. On exposing our spoil, there was a slight murmur among the men: "Why, them's Mother Carey's chickens!" "Tut!" quoth my friend, "don't you see that these have got two webbed feet, and is it not a known fact that the real Mother Carey has one foot like a cock and the other like a duck?" "'Tis so, no fear!" responded the growler, and peace was restored.

I like the feeling among sailors which prompts them to resent the wanton shooting of sea-fowl from the deck. In a long sea-voyage the smallest Cape pigeon becomes a companion, and gives a sense of life and companionship to the "waste of waters." ("Waste of water," growls an old salt, "it ain't a waste of water! what would navigation do without it?") No one has any right to shoot a sea-bird except for scientific uses or food. They are far too easily killed to give any real *sport*. *Fishing* for albatrosses and Cape pigeons is quite fair; though in the case of the albatross, what is it for a man to set his wit against so foolish a bird? This fishing, though the expression may be slightly Hibernian, is a strictly legitimate sport. You set your intelligence against theirs, and if they lose the game, they have no right to grumble at paying the stakes. Even if you win your game, you can throw it overboard again, not much damaged, and even have a fresh deal. I have seen an albatross caught, thrown overboard, and caught again, in a very few minutes. But shooting the poor brutes is quite another affair; more particularly when, as is generally the case, you have no chance of picking them up. I wonder, by-the-way, whether they hove-to, to pick up the albatross the ancient mariner shot, or whether it fell on the deck? I suspect the former. His crime was, not honestly fishing for his bird; and the rest of the crew got tangled up in it by heaving-to and lowering a boat to pick it up, wishing to make pipe-stems out of its wing-bones, and 'bacco-pouches out of its feet.

Cape-pigeon catching is to albatross-fishing what trouting is to salmon-fishing. The sharp little spotted beauties are cautious, and require fine tackle and delicate handling. Small gut roach-hooks, baited with an infinitesimal morsel of fat, is the best *moyen de parvenir*. Top-baiting with shreds of fat or crumbs of bread is very useful. The albatross cares nothing for the coarseness of the line; but there are rules to be observed even with him, not from his sharpness, but from his clumsiness and stupidity. The common idea of his pouncing on his prey, and even splitting open the head of the man overboard are, as far as I have observed, mere moonshine. I know no bird with less picking up or striking power when on the wing. I never yet saw an albatross which did not sit down, soberly and calmly, to his dinner, and even then he was as likely to miss it as to get it. Bits of fat, small, and floating from the passing ship, or the fragments of squid from the whale's jaw, are what he seems to be in quest of, and very hard work he seems to have to find them. When an eligible morsel appears, there is no lack of convives—pecking, cawing, and barking, while the sharp little Cape pigeon deftly conveys the morsel from under their enormous bills. The life of an ocean-bird in stormy weather must be a hard and poor one. I suppose when in luck they get a great gorge at once, and that lasts them a long time. The albatross rests much more on the water than is generally supposed, and when he alights he is as careful of wetting the soft under-feathers of his wings as a lady is of protecting the hem of her petticoat against the mud of the kennel. To finish this albatrossian screed, let me record that an albatross in a *dead* calm is one of the meanest birds on the wing I have ever seen.

October 4th.—Still with our brains a whirling mass of white muslin, black eyes, glancing teeth, smiles, drills, and dancings, as if we had spent a fortnight, *all* night, in the Mohammedan paradise. For want of something better to do, we overhauled our presents, and here is the account, as made out by Mr. Stevedore Mitchell:

To Presents received.

1. Two rolls of tappa (chiefs' peculiar), each ninety feet by eight.
2. Thirty native mats (choice).
3. Sixteen worked baskets (mixed).
4. Three old native dresses complete, with sea-weed trimmings and reva-reva crowns (very valuable).
5. An ancient sacred staff (the owner having retired from the pagan business and entered the ministry). Unique, alas!
6. Shells (principally of the cowriaginous class). Cocoa-nut cups (as per invoice).
7. Several old stone axe-heads (irreplaceable; very like Danish celts).
8. A sack and a half of raw coffee-berries, about one hundred pounds (and they are also at the bottom of the sea, every berry of them!—

"Deep in the ocean *berried*").

9. Three pigs, one turkey, nine fowls, one bull, or bullet, or little bull.
10. Cocoa-nuts, bananas, yams, etc., etc., *ad libitum ;* which being interpreted means, as much as we can carry.

The schooner was flooded with natives, almost from daybreak. Several chiefs came off, either to bid us good-

by, or to invite us to their houses on the other side of
the island. One brought a boat-load of fruit and fowls,
as a special present to our gallant skipper. It really
seems as if these people could not help giving.

Our bull arrived, and after some trouble was hoisted
on to the deck, about which he skated in the most unpleasant manner, doing occasionally four inside edges
at once, which produced a perfectly new figure of the
"spread-eagle" pattern, out of which he had to be
hoisted by main force. He was, however a kindly bull
of the Raritongian temper, and ate bananas instantly
out of our hands, in whatever position he found himself.
All day long the natives had the full run of the ship—
the cabin full of women, perfectly free and unwatched;
and yet not a thing was taken or even asked for, nor
did they ever for a moment become rude or intrusive.
These people are most certainly nice, gentle, generous,
civil, and easy to please. We showed them maps,
pointing out England, or "Britano" and Raritonga,
which pleased them mightily, evidently proud of being
in the map at all. Then P—— showed them Leech's
sketches in the "Comic History of England," and they
appreciated them immensely, crowding round with their
strange "Um, um, um! click, click, click!" which is
their mode of expressing delight and wonder combined.

When the last batch of visitors had departed, John,
the jolly old pilot, appeared with his native crew, and
we prepared to get under way, with some anxiety, as it
was blowing a fresh breeze right abeam. The only
way to get out was to make sail, point her head straight
for the opening, with a couple of strong warps from
the stem and stern out to windward, and, letting go,

shoot straight through the opening, that is, if she chose to do so. At last all was ready, and ten seconds would decide her fate. "Let go the head warp!" A native, who had been watching this signal, threw up his heels, and, diving like a seal, pulled the slip-knot with which we were made fast to the anchor. "Let go astern!" yelled the pilot, but the skipper would not be hurried, and let her swing off well at first. "Luff! luff!" screamed the pilot. "Mind them traces, or you will be all aback!" "All right!" quoth the skipper, "don't flurry yourself! keep her off now!" Coral and breakers within ten yards on either side of us. "Luff again! Keep her off! Now! All clear!" And we drew the deep breath of satisfaction.

I don't think that you will catch us in *that* "harbor" again, Master John, though it be the safest in the world!"

CHAPTER VIII.

SAMOA.

WHAT a quantity of *old* things there are on this world of ours!—things so old that one reads of them in old, old books, which speak of them as old, even in their time—so old that possibly there is no phase of thought or action which our race has passed through, in its onward progress, which is not represented in some hole or corner of the existing earth. Even in hackneyed old Europe the man who is wise or strong enough to wander on foot, comes continually across bits of human life which carry him back into ages long past away. We are too apt to talk about "antiquities" as connected with dead stone and timber, while, in fact, there are under our very noses live antiquities—men, women, and children, hundreds of years old; thinking the same thoughts, wearing the same garments, and playing at the same games, that their "forbears" did in the misty distance of ages. When one reads an old Coventry "miracle-play," for instance, how infinitely far off the time seems, when such a form of amusement was not only popular but pious! And yet if you go— not to the Ausmeyan affair, which is a new periodical excitement—a "curio," but to Segovia, for instance, you will find the real old thing played night after night, producing full houses and intense interest in the minds of people whose habits of thought are those of the fifteenth century. As for "dress antiquities"—shoe-buckles, knee-breeches, and things of that sort—they may be found in many an out-of-the-way German Dorf. Nay, do not the coachmen even of our own "upper ten" still retain a shadow of the wig which was the glory of the great grandfathers of their masters? Do not the farmers' wives in Wales still wear the tall hat of the women of England in the seventeenth century, under the insane idea that it is a "national" costume, and the correct "Cymraig?" And, again, do not the Highlanders of Scotland, under a still more insane idea, retain the "Iula" of the South-Sea Islander, calling it a "kilt;" though it is no more like the kilt of '45, than a Sunday-coat is like a coatamundi? Do you not find there other antiquities in the shape of broadswords and bagpipes, and 'haggises, which were kicked out of South Britain as useless and intolerable two hundred good years ago? Antiquities indeed! Look at South Britain herself, with her innumerable old paganisms which cunning priests have taught her to look upon as picties, and then "muse," whatever that may be, on the strange way in which some manners and customs are drawn out through the ages, like the threads from which some insects cannot detach themselves. I have seen human beings in Southwestern Australia who were older than Adam himself, at least their dresses were, for they had not even arrived at the art of sewing their wild-beast skins together, which he was taught in para-

dise; being arrayed in a mere dangling mass of foul
poultry, without either stitch or pocket, except possibly
that of the original kangaroo-owner. This sort of thing
is *real* antiquity, though possibly it ought to be called
novelty, as the newest thing on the face of the earth,
we civilized folk being the real ancients by right of age.
A bothering question! • For we know not how long the
Australian has been on the earth; we know not whether
he may not be the last exercise of the creative power,
which formed the earliest races of man, still expanded
into our time, or whether *his* ancestors were the first
men placed on the earth millions upon millions of years
ago.

We are beginning to see that there is a history of
our race to be puzzled out on the surface of the globe.
We are beginning also to see that there is an antiquity far beyond the antiquity of civilization, or what
is ordinarily called history; an antiquity which brings
us dangerously near Darwin and Wallace, and which
whispers darkly that man, after all, may be but an im-
perfectly-developed animal: rising higher and higher,
as the ages roll on, with more perfectly-developed
organs permitting the freer action of a nobler soul, but
still, as far as this world is concerned, an animal—an
integral part of that creation which, as far as our
finite organs can see, had no beginning and can never
have an ending.

New or old, it is worth while to look at the colored
races of mankind as an instructive collection of fossils,
which may be studied by the ethnologist as the others
are by the geologist. There are some very old fossils
of this sort to be found, like the habit of crouching,

not sitting, for instance, which to me always savors rather of the remembrance of tails; or the apey toes, useful as hands, to pick up trifles or to hold the wood to be ignited or drilled; the sharkey grin, no real smile, lighting up the face from within, but the mere removal of the lips from the hideously large and regular teeth; or the brown, opaque eye, bloodshotten like that of a vicious horse, reminding one of a plover's egg with a boiled prune for a yolk, infinitely inferior in expression to that of a well-educated dog. These are the sort of things I should call human fossils, and let us hope that they will be well studied before they disappear, for the destruction of Egyptian monuments and literature by the early Christians of Alexandria is as nothing compared with the effacement of the early records of humanity by South-Sea whalers, Yankee riflemen, and missionaries, who seem to act as so many pieces of moral India-rubber in effacing the old marks and lines of our species. Not that it is of any use complaining. This rubbing out seems to be a part of the great scheme of the world. Who rubbed out the history of Stonehenge? Who smeared out the tale of the American tumuli? *Quien sabe?* Is it that our world is such a small slate that it has to be wiped clean, over and again, in order that new generations may cipher the better on it, not being puzzled by the records of their predecessors' mistakes?

There are fossils and fossils, as there are antiquities and antiquities; some coarse and repulsive, some graceful and pleasing; some mere flint-chippings, others the very perfection of artistic beauty. It is the same with our human fossils. Think of the difference between the "black-fellow" of Australia, and the Kanaka of the Society Islands!

The pleasantest forms of the human fossil we have ever met with have been in the South Seas. India and the East are doubtless highly fossiliferous, and pleasantly so; but the great mass of specimens have been terribly worn, and have lost their real old edging and sharpness by civilization. In the South Seas, spite of the missionary, pure, unpolished specimens may still be found.

The missionary has, however, succeeded in very nearly destroying one fossil, only to cause the introduction of an infinitely more mischievous novelty in its place. He has, wherever he could, destroyed kava, and in consequence has caused the introduction of orange-rum.

The problem of how to get drunk on a piece of dry wood, or rather root—for, though kava *en bloc* looks like the former, it is the latter—seems at first sight rather difficult to solve, but the Kanaka has solved it satisfactorily, at least as far as he himself is concerned. How the occult properties of such a very untempting vegetable ever came to be discovered, one knows as little as in the case of Jesuit's-bark, or in fact of any wild plant; and what makes the case of the kava more curious than usual, is the fact that not only is the root most untempting in aspect, but it requires a peculiar preparation in order to develop its qualities.

How the Kanaka has solved his problem I will tell you by-and-by; what the kava is I will tell you now. It is the root of a plant carefully cultivated by the natives, to whom it serves the purpose of tea—maté, alcohol, coffee, betel, and all that class of stimulants, or "arresters of the decomposition of tissue." The plant itself is, I believe, what the man who names the plants in Kensington Gardens would call a "piperaceous shrub." When nibbled, it tastes like a chemist's shop in general, but has, withal, a certain peppery pungency about it by no means unpleasant.

When I say that the Kanaka has solved the great question of how to get drunk on a piece of dry wood, do not understand me to mean that he necessarily gets drunk every time he drinks kava—far from it! And even if he does exceed, the intoxication produced is very different from the riotous, dangerous drunkenness of beer or spirits. It was from not understanding this that the ignorant and self-conceited men, who were taken from the grocer's counter or the cobbler's stall, to preach their wretched idea of gospel truth, fell into so grave and mischievous a mistake. Kava was utterly tabooed, as pertaining to the fiend, and the consequence was, that the natives invented in its stead the poisonous and maddening orange-rum, which is never drunk without producing an indescribable orgy. Kava, in moderation, is quite as harmless and wholesome as tea or tobacco, and I really believe was tabooed more from that arrogant fondness for forbidding, which was the characteristic of the elder missionaries, and which still lingers in some of the more out-of-the-way islands, than from any real belief in its mischievous qualities. It is hard to believe, but we were told by a missionary, that tobacco-smoking is absolutely prohibited in one of the Cook's group at this present writing, and that under heavy penalties. And these same penalties are not to be trifled with. The chiefs have found that immorality may be made a profitable source of revenue, and so wish for sin to abound, in order that dollars may still more abound—in their own pockets. In fact, as far as I can see, so far from eradicating the old vices of the islanders, these good people have introduced a new one, which was certainly not there before their time; a vice which they possibly brought with them in their clothes or faces — that sneaking, slant-eyed rascal, *Hypocrisy*.

I beg to observe, if you have not already perceived it, that kava is only a thought-peg, and I shall hang as many thoughts upon it as I like. What right have you to drink "kava" after a journey measured by the inches of these pages when I had to go thousands of miles for it?

What was I going to say? Oh! about the abuse of kava—not that anybody abuses it in the proper sense of the word, except the aforesaid missionaries, but the excess of kava. What happens if, in the language of Mr. Richard Swiveller, you "pass the rosy" too often? There is the charm of kava—nothing whatever happens! It is a negative, not a positive intoxication. I never took too much kava myself, not having had an opportunity of doing so; but I have heard, from those weaker or more tempted vessels who have, that it produces a quiet and transient state of "nirwana," a simple annihilation. Like the farmer in church, you "simply puts up your legs and thinks o' nothing." Should your convives, in the transition-stage, be larkily inclined, they will not cork your face or grease your boots, but they will stick pins, fish-spears, stingareestings, wood-splinters, any handy thing with a point, into you, and you will blandly smile on them, unconscious of pain, till you fall asleep. It seems, from all accounts, to be a most marvellous anæsthetic, but then to be anæsthetized you would require a regiment of the strongest-jawed—but this is too precipitate.

You sleep, say, for twelve hours; and then the right thing to do on awakening is to eat a little roasted fa'is, or wild-plaintain—the "soda-water tree," in fact, of these regions—and then go to sleep again for any number of hours you like. I am told that you are none the worse when you wake up finally. The brain does not seem to be exhausted, as from the excitement of alcohol or opium; and, in the vernacular, you rise as "fresh as paint." I am also informed that, if you persist in drinking too much kava, your nose gets red; but, as the European nose in these regions is invariably like the claw of a boiled lobster in color, that does not much matter.

It is doubtless wrong and naughty to waste so much time in doing nothing, but then even if you were not drinking kava you would be equally doing nothing, there being nothing to do; and, if you are asleep for twenty-four hours, you may at least be pretty certain of being out of mischief for that period. Still be it remembered that kava-drinking to this extent is a very exceptionable affair, and that ordinarily it is a mere matter of a cup of tea.

It was at lovely Samoa that I first got initiated into the art and mystery of kava-drinking; an island that would be called the loveliest in the world were there not scores of others equally lovely, gemming that glorious South-Pacific Ocean. We were anchored in the bay of Apia, which forms almost, if not quite, a semicircle, barred from the sea by a coral-reef, stretching from point to point like the string of a bow. And how exquisitely delicious is the curl and flash of the never-ceasing surf on the edge of that same reef! Great rollers, that come straight up to the coral without a break, and then, making a startled leap in the air, fall with a heavy, crashing thump, which subsides into a cooling hiss and swish as it runs up among the bright-hued, branching coral. Apia would not be habitable were it not for the idea of snow and coolness which the foam of the breaking water gives one in the blazing, shimmering heat.

This same reef is rather remarkable as one of the few stations in the world where the polulu fishing, or rather worming, is carried on. These singular creatures —long black and green annelides, from two inches to two feet long, and as thick as a crow-quill—pullulate quite suddenly on the reef, where the water is a foot or two deep, twice a year, and always at a time so certain that the natives turn out with almost unerring accuracy for the fishing. This year the crafty polulu chose Sunday for their first appearance, and, as the greatest rascal on the island told me—"Sunday is a great day in religion," they escaped a whole day. The swarm only lasts two days, and only then for an hour or two before sunrise. Polulu-fishing is one of the great larks of Apia. You turn out in an outrigger-canoe at four in the morning, and find yourself in the dark among a cloud of others, filled with men, women, and children—laughing, squalling, skirling, and flirting, the noise almost overcoming the incantations of some of the old women, who sing either to the sea or some sea-goddess to pullulate. Polulus eat plentifully and prodigiously, all waiting for the first tinge of light to guide them to their prey. Your fishing apparatus consists of any thing you can get, from a bit of matting up to a magnificent net made out of a piece of window-curtain stretched on a bent stick, like a battledoor.

As the light increases you become aware of the fact that the water is alive with myriads of wriggling worms: you have but to dip and you bring up lumps of writhing stuff, which puts one in mind of the confused mass of battle-stars' legs which you bring up sometimes in the dredge. This you empty into your bucket or calabash, and dip again. There is no law on the water on these occasions. If you see Moó in a good place, you are perfectly justified in twisting her canoe round by the outrigger and taking it yourself. If Toó is flirting instead of attending to her polulu, you have a perfect right to reach over and empty her bucket into yours; and if she splashes you with her paddle you splash her with yours—you won't spoil her clothes—and so the fun goes on. The dawn gradually gets clearer and clearer, bringing out the splendid statuesque figures fishing for big fish, on the outer edge of the reef, with long bamboos, in the most artistic manner, casting their bait of squid into the very surf itself; until at last—

"Nor dim, nor red, like God's own head,
   The glorious sun uprist!"

and sends his level rays gleaming through the blue-water walls of the surf. Then instantly all the sport ceased. The polulu vanished, not to reappear for six months more; and skylarking, racing, and splashing, we all sped homeward. On examining my share of the spoil, I found that I had got a quart or more of the aforesaid worms; and certainly any thing which looked more hopelessly uneatable I never saw. I had got my white elephant, but what to do with him I knew not. But instructed by the charming Coé—(I put an accent on the *e* to prevent scandal)—I learned that they should be wrapped in a piece of banana-leaf and baked; moreover, that they would keep for a long time if they were occasionally rebaked, so as to keep them dry. When cooked I found that I had by no means a disagreeable mess before me, more like a lump of dark spinach than any thing else. In taste it was like a mixture of spinach, laver, and crab; and with oil, vinegar, and cayenne, was by no means to be despised. On toast, like caviare, it was also very good. Almost the only objection to it was a slight suspicion of that very disagreeable coral-smell which always puts me in mind of phosphorus.

To show how accurate are the calculations of the natives, let me mention that we all turned out the next morning (Tuesday), and did not collect a tablespoonful of polulu among the whole fleet. The crafty brutes had taken advantage of the sabbatarianism of the natives, and swarmed on Sunday.

If I remember right, it was on this day that I first tasted that suave and delectable liquor "Monongahela whiskey;" but what liquor would not have been ambrosial, presented by the rosy-brown finger-tips of Coé herself, as a consolation for our disappointment!

To say that Apia is in the South Seas, is almost to

say that the shore is fringed with a noble belt of cocoa-palms (I spell it *coco*, but I am by no means sure that it should not be *koker*). Around the feet of these are masses of hibiscus-bushes, all ablaze with crimson-and-yellow flowers; other plants there are which we cannot distinguish by the eye, but every light waft of air from the land bears with it Sabean odors, which fully realize one's old fancies about the spice-islands: indeed, lovely Apia, to the best of my recollection, is the only place where the sweet scent of land-flowers is distinctly perceptible at sea. Scattered about beneath the trees are the bright white houses of the European settlers; and kindly, pleasant, and hospitable houses they are—English, American, and German, vying with each other to make the stranger at home in a strange land. Beside them nestle more modestly the brown huts of the natives, built generally of cunningly-interwoven palm-leaves, a real brown hamlet. This native town is just now in a somewhat dilapidated condition, in consequence of a prolonged "war of succession," caused by the too evenly-balanced state of the different parties. There is a truce for the moment patched up, I think mistakenly, by the missionaries. It will prove but a hollow one if all I hear is true.[1]

Behind the cocoa-fringe, the land sweeps up into lovely wooded hills some four thousand feet high, not so abruptly picturesque, perhaps, as the general tone of the Society Islands, but marked with beautiful curves and long, graceful sweeps of vivid green. Here and there, valleys permit one to see far away up into the

[1] This has since proved to be correct. If they had been allowed to fight it out at once, it would have been much better.

mysterious heart of the hills, where many a strange
and weird thing may be enacting at this moment in
the gloom of the forest. Far away is the gleam and glitter of an enormous water-fall, marking the green with
a silver bar, which it takes a whole long day's walking
to reach. The timber, generally, is finer than that of
the Society Islands, and the varied richness of the coloring infinitely superior. Much of the beauty of the
Society Islands has been injured by the guava-shrub,
which has overrun large tracts, and gives an unpleasant
monotone to the landscape.

The land generally has an older look than the
islands to the northeast. Every thing is rounder and less
abrupt; there are fewer buttresses of trap, standing
out like black, ruined castles from the green hill-sides;
and the lines seem washed down to their present angle
by the gentle hand of Time, instead of being decided
by the mad dice-throw of the volcano. When we pen-
etrate into the interior, indeed, we find ravines, sharp
and abrupt enough to be highly picturesque in the true
sense of the word, though even there the grimmest of
crags has almost invariably decked his bald pate with
the loveliest greenery. Oh, the heat of those breath-
less ravines! the black rocks seem to pulsate and throb
under its intensity—heat too great, even, for the native
birds, who sit silent and gasping on the branches, longing for evening—a dead silence, broken only by the
occasional solemn boom of a pigeon dreaming of love
in his doze. One odd thing connected with these ravines is the fact that the higher you go the more water
you find. You toil up over gigantic lava-bowlders, polished as glass, and slip off them up to your ankles into

dry and dusty volcanic sand, till your soul is parched within you, and a ghastly terror takes possession of you that, as there is no water where there is generally most, there will be none where there is generally least. It is not so, however. Unlike the Thames, which begins, I believe, in half a mile of dusty land, and expands in its brimming breadth as it approaches the sea, a Samoan stream begins in bubbling plenty and ends in utter drought a mile or two from the salt-water. Gradually as you ascend you become more and more hopeful; moist patches of sand appear here and there, then tiny pools that a fallen leaf might cover, then larger ones, with little, thread-like runs of water between them; larger and larger, till at last you reach some hard ledge of trap, over which a glorious stream gurgles and splashes into a pool ample enough for the bath of an elephant, and you cast yourself down and plunge in your face to the ears. There are fishes in these pools—brisk, bright little fellows, shaped exactly like small dace, with bright-yellow tails and fins, cruising about in wee shoals, and rising at the tiny flies in the most sportive manner. Wait a little quietly, and from under the stones will come a purple-and-red crawfish, of no small size, who will winkle and twinkle at you with that strange expression of mystery and concealed wisdom, which is after his kind. Here in the cooler part of the ravine come the birds to drink toward the afternoon. Splashing and dipping within a yard of you, and looking up ever and anon, as if to ask you to appreciate their enjoyment. Lovely little black-and-crimson honey-birds, and jolly, little impudent "ripiduras" (pardon the word; if you do not like it I must give you a still harder Maori one), who flirt, and chirrup, and coquet with you within reach of your hand: singing, I heard none—but the boom of the pigeon is wondrous pleasant and drowsyfying, and suiteth well with tobacco.

Before the ruthless missionary came there was a pleasant idyllic sort of sport in these valleys—now, I fear, vanished forever. The sport in itself was utterly harmless, but was tabooed (horrid word!) as leading to possible harm. It was a species of pigeon-fancying. The great delight of the natives was to build a bower of branches green, just large enough to cover them securely, and then, placing a tame pigeon outside, to ensconce themselves within, waiting until his or her blandishments tempted down a wild bird to indulge in a little flirting; then slowly and cautiously emerged the brown paw of the concealed Samoan, and the wild bird was wild no more. This was not for the base purpose of eating the beauty, but merely that the cocoa-leaf hut should have a pet the more.

"I have found out a gift for my love,
 I have found where the wood-pigeons breed"—

sort of business. How could harm spring from this? But it did, or was supposed to do so; which to the nose of your true "Smelfungus" is the same thing. It happened in this wise: It was not absolutely necessary to go alone to the mountain to enjoy the sport; indeed, on the contrary, the long hours of waiting, day or night, rather made a companion desirable, and so they went in pairs, and, as Pistol would have said—

"Conclusions past their careires."

"Smelfungus" not being inclined to superintend

the pigeon-fancying portion of his flock personally, an act which would necessitate some active physical exertion, put a stop to the whole affair, and so there is no more Strephon-and-Chloe-ing on the ridges of Samoa. Is it not strange that on both sides of the equator those innocent little birds, the pigeons, should, as Rob the Grinder pathetically complains, lead to so much mischief?

Dr. Gräfe, a naturalist working this glorious island, told me that one day he was as nearly as possible committing Samoacide in one of these valleys. Seeing a pigeon fluttering about in a curious way, he stalked it, and was just on the point of firing, when a gray pate and brown face popped up through a hole in a heap of leaves and demanded quarter.

By-the-way, these islands are rather famous for their pigeons, though I saw nothing to equal the lovely little green, mauve, and yellow gems we used to get in the Isle of Pines and New Caledonia. One of the most remarkable here is a reddish-brown bird, rejoicing, I believe, in the euphonious name of didunculus, which is confined to these islands. Even in Samoa it is so rare as to have been supposed to be nearly extinct, until the present war drove skirmishing-parties into out-of-the-way places, where they discovered rookeries (all breeding-places of birds or seals are rookeries in the South Seas), and we were fortunate enough to procure a pair. Its great peculiarity is that it seems to be doing its best to grow into a parrot, its bill being thickened and notched in a most un-pigeonesque fashion— a fact dear to Darwinians. May I state, as one of the few Europeans who have ever tasted it, that its flesh is brown and delicious! There is another pigeon, much petted, which is called, in Samoan, tu cimeo, or something like it; which, being interpreted, means "the pigeon which is sulky with its food," which seems a great deal to be contained in so small a word. It seems that the natives after eating have a custom of washing their mouths and hands, and casting the water outside, leaving a moist splash at the entrance of the hut. The tame pigeon, coming to share the family meal, feels hurt at his friends not having waited dinner for him, and flies away to a tree to sulk with injured dignity. Knowing this peculiarity of temper, evil boys splash the ground outside the hut before dinner has commenced, with the certainty of hurting the feelings of the fowl.

These Samoans are wonderful bird-tamers, which I think arises from their slow and gentle movements; nothing abrupt, brusque, or startling—all calm and quiet. He who wishes to make a friend of a cat must follow their example.

Coming down from our ravine, we pass through a wilderness of imported plants and shrubs, flourishing in wild luxuriancy. That red-and-brown flower, which makes such pretty wreaths for the girls' heads, and the down from whose pods is so dangerous to the eyes, is an importation, Heaven knows how, from America; and not only is it an importation, but it has imported its own butterfly with it, that splendid yellow-and-brown fellow who looks as if he had got half his color from his natal flower. Here we push through a bush of indigo, then through one of bright, glittering green coffee, through which shoots the green pillar of the quaint, prim, but pretty papaw—here used only for feeding fowls, the natives being ignorant of its tenderizing effect on beefsteaks, had they any beefsteaks to tenderize. Even nutmeg-trees are here, but I am given to understand that they are not the real Banda species.

As we pass along we hear a skirling and a splashing, and come plump upon a bevy of island beauties, disporting themselves in a pool of muddy water, having first filled their calabashes, which stand in order on the bank. The water is so muddy as fully to act the part of garments, more particularly as it is much the color of their skins, and they joyously splash and shriek, and ask for tobacco. Asking for tobacco seems here to mean little more than a form of kindly greeting. They begin to beg a little here; from Tahiti to Samoa we were never asked for a single thing; and even here the begging is of the very mildest possible form, particularly to those hardened by the perpetual "backshish" of the East. Indeed, among many of these people, not only is begging or asking for a thing unknown, but they have no word to express thanks or gratitude. If they want a thing (among themselves) they take it, expecting their neighbors to do the same by them. There are no thanks, because it is a right, not an obligation, and there is nothing to be thankful for: to a certain extent the Sam Wellerian form of philosophy, "If I wanted a thing I took it, for fear I might be led to do something wrong for want of it."

As we emerge from the thicket on to the bright white beach of coral-sand, the sun's rays are beginning to slant, and the natives to wake up from their siesta. As we pass along, however, we may still see some of them enjoying their nap, sheeted from head to foot in white tappa, and the back of the neck reposing on a bamboo rest, to save the treasured head-dress; they have rather a ghastly look, and a stranger might easily mistake them for "streekit corpses."

The cause of this wrapping up is those most infernal flies. Apia is certainly the very headquarters of Beelzebub, where "each man walks with his head in a cloud of poisonous flies" by day, and where by night

"Most undelightful is the ceaseless hum"

of that most hateful of created beings, the mosquito. There is no sound in Nature expressive of such venomous, acrid spite, as the "ping" of a mosquito; and though they rarely bite me, the mere wickedness of the expression keeps me awake many a hot and weary hour. The only sound I know at all to be compared with it, is a peculiar way women have of saying "my dear" to each other.

This superabundance of winged life has been the origin of one characteristic of Samoa—the fly-flap, which every one with the slightest pretension to respectability carries as invariably as we do an umbrella. These fly-flaps are made of delicately-plaited cocoa-nut fibres, attached to a prettily-carved handle about a foot long, and when not in use are carried gracefully over the right shoulder. When in council, the sages, leaning on a long staff, whisk it solemnly to and fro, and seem to consult it as a Japanese does his fan, or a Levantine his string of amber beads.

As we saunter along, we find our course impeded by a broad, bubbling brook, and we pause for a moment to decide whether we will pull off our shoes and stockings, or walk through with them on; a problem I always, somehow or another, find it difficult to solve. Indeed, it is not as easy as it looks. If you walk through with them on, you are bored to death by that abominable squelching which proceeds from shoes full of water; and if without them, you are perfectly certain to tread on some infernal thing or another, which sends you hopping and "cussing" for half an hour after. I know few things more difficult to do than taking a splinter out of the sole of your foot while standing on one leg, particularly in a strongish stream.

We, however, are saved the trouble of deciding, by half a dozen strapping young fellows offering their backs, with every sign of good-nature and civility. If you want to get the tone of our bearers without going round the world, remember Velasquez's Borrncios at Madrid; they are wonderfully South-Sea.

The opposite side of the stream brings us face to face with the horrors of war—desolate taro-patches, ashes of burnt huts, and the stumps of charred cocoa-trees. Was it not the French in Egypt who conceived the brilliant idea of injuring the enemy by killing the male palms? See what science can do in the way of labor-saving! Here the savage burns down all his enemies' palms indiscriminately.

Soon we reach the settlement, built since the peace, and showing, by the flimsiness of the workmanship of the huts, that there is no very strong belief in its continuance. They are generally simple, low-eaved affairs—some not more than four or five feet high, some six or seven, oval, and from ten to twenty and even thirty feet long—a mere ridge-roof of interwoven palm-leaves supported by posts. The low eaves make them dark and cool inside, and they are always clean and neat; the bright matting which covers the floor making the most perfect of carpets for a hot climate.

What small cooking they require is generally done outside, but I have not unfrequently seen a small, square fireplace inside the huts, more for lighting cigars, I fancy, than for roasting bread-fruit or plantains.

Bending low, we enter the hut of the chief, at an undignified angle of forty-five degrees, which produces a sense of shyness. It is not pleasant to present yourself to a society of grave and reverend seigniors in the attitude of a telescope, and one slinks shyly to the place pointed out to one. There is etiquette here; you must sit cross-legged, or at least with one leg doubled under you; to sit with both legs extended is an unpardonable impropriety. It is bad to lean against the wall of the hut, as the chances are that it gives way unexpectedly, and leaves you on the broad of your back gazing upward into the faces of the astonished outsiders. Put your back against one of the supporting posts, where, if not comfortable, you are safe. The great drawback to this position is the fact that these posts seem as "arm-racks," and around them are arranged the chief's stock of "fire-irons," from the old brass-bound Tower musket to the smart new match-Enfield, with its platinum-lined back-sight. Round the hut are seated the principal chiefs, glimmering with palm-oil, and dressed for the most part in the simple "tappa," "sulu," or kilt. By-the-way, is this word "tappa" derived from the rap-tap-tapping noise produced in its manufacture?

The chiefs and great men who sit around us are all men of mark, though there is but little to distinguish them from the profane vulgar, as far as dress goes. Among the most remarkable of them is a fine young fellow, who has lately fought his way to high eminence, by storming, almost single-handed, one of the enemy's fortifications; and, not content with that, using it, Nelson-like, as a bridge to storm others: and be it remembered that these fortifications are something serious—good wall-and-ditch work.

The sulu in which the men were dressed permitted us to see their glorious forms in full perfection, and there are few finer races in the world than these Samoans—a little heavy and provincial, perhaps, and wanting somewhat of the delicate grace of their cousins to the southeast, but still magnificent men. We fancied that they had more decided and aquiline noses than the Society-Islanders. Time was when I used to think that no sculptor of the "nude" could ever be worth his salt, unless he had spent a year or two in Africa. Now, I should most certainly send him to the Society Islands, where he will see his fellow-men as they ought to be—not cramped from infancy by strange ligatures and straps and shoes, but with every life-bearing artery and vein unconfined, permitting the perfect development of every part. No sacrifice of one to the other as with us, but a true harmonious balance of the whole. We are apt to boast, and not without some reason, that we are not as other nations are, as regards the early physical education of the more fortunate, of our children, but we are as far behind these islanders, in some of the mysteries of early infant training, as we are before the Flathead Indians.

My brown friend on my left is not a Flathead Indian, though his head looks as if it had gone through some queer squeezing process early in life, which makes him look very different from the rest of the society. So odd was his look, that I could not help studying him, and he seemed flattered with my attention. His forehead ran up to a peak—not a Shakespearian peak, but a sharp point, something in the style the profane used to draw poor old Louis Philippe, in the days of the great pear-joke. There the resemblance ended, for instead of the heavy masses of skin which hung over the eyes, and the heavy jowl of "Le Roi Poire," the eyes are as clear set as a diamond *au jour*, and the lips and jaw sharp and cleanly cut; the lips thin, not as to the inverted part, but from without inward—so thin, as to make one fancy that one could see the markings of the teeth through them—mobile and in constant action, as if the very muscles thought, or at least, answered every thought; and so the muscles of the mouth do till weaned out of the practice by civilization and society. I will wager that Touchstone had many such a queer buccal twist—not a grin, but rather a bottling in, as it were, of the half-developed whimsicalities. This sort of mouth is by no means rare in Italy. There was something in my neighbor's eye, too, which struck me—an eye which did not like to be found out; not from conscious rascality, but from the perception of some hidden absurdity which would not do for the general public—an eye capable of giving very quiet and solemn winks to itself—a Touchstone eye again.

How it fell out I know not; whether we winked at each other, and found a similarity of souls in that simple action, or that the mysterious ether of Tomfooldom, emanating from each of us, intermingling, caused a mutual recognition, must forever remain a question. But the fact is, that the recognition took place. Neglecting the great ones of the earth—chiefs, consuls, and earls—he attached himself to me alone, and, taking the palm-leaf fly-flap from my hand, he fanned me with an expression of the most intense interest and affection. He was the court fool.

Being late, we found that our friends were weary of waiting, and had already prepared their five-o'clock kava, which was being strained by an ordinary native woman, by means of a handful of vegetable fibre. This was evidently a nice operation; I don't mean what Prescott Hewett would call "a nice operation," but one requiring considerable care. A general clapping of hands indicated, either that they were glad they were going to have their kava, or were impatient of further delay—I rather believe the former; and a pleasant-looking slip of a lad presenting half a cocoa-nut shell to the woman, she squeezed about half a tumblerful of the gruelly fluid into it. Then the talking-man of the chief chanted out the name of the man to whom it was to be delivered, adding a string of compliments, a sort of Samoan, "for he's a jolly good fellow" business. The proper thing is, to clap your hands gently when you hear your name mentioned, to show that you appreciate the compliment, but are not proud.

You should also look a little the other way in a deprecating manner, as though to say "Oh, dear! you're very kind, *but—*" You take the bowl, drain it, and cast it with a graceful skim on to the mat-covered floor. A slight grunt, something like the throat-clearing "Hum'm!" of the old Puritans, thrown in here, does well, and indicates a genteel satisfaction. The first drink is given to the greatest chief, the next to the highest talking-man, then another chief, then another talking-man, and so on. I thought this a very graceful recognition of the nobility of intellect, among a race so aristocratically inclined as to have two distinct dialects, a court and a plebeian one. I was most glad to see that my friend Touchstone was by no means the last man to have his drink served out to him. I would have given a deal to know what he said, for he is looked upon as the sayer of infinite good things; but who could translate his winks, let alone his words?

About this time a performance took place which disturbed the local color, and somehow put me in mind of Baker Street—a place I hate. The chief's wife, a good and genial soul, with her hair cut short to her poll, and a sore hand, but such a pretty one! had a tray of tumblers before her—vile glass grog-tumblers, filled with cocoa-nut water (it is *not* milk, or any thing like it), specially prepared for us slaves of civilization. I would none of it, as disturbing to the proper kava frame of mind.

After the bowl of kava was finished there was a pause—a pause of contentment and satisfaction—and, looking out of the corner of my eye into the glorious golden sunshine, I saw that something great was in preparation outside. What I saw I cannot describe in words. Titian might have sketched it in a happy moment, or Velasquez have made a painted poem of it; but my poor pen and ink are utterly unable to produce the slightest outline worthy the original. Let me merely hint that it was as though brown angels were undressing and dressing themselves, or rather *vice versa*, for, when I think on't, they put on a great deal less than they took off. The "tiring-room" was a small hut of cocoa-leaves, and branches of small bush —the bare stumps of the bushes which had furnished their quota standing thickly about it, to the no small danger of the bare toes of the rank and fashion assembled around, evidently brimful of expectation. They were utterly without rudeness, and infinitely better mannered and behaved than the surging mass of snobbism which thrusts its snub nose into the carriages of ladies going to a drawing-room at home.

At last, from under the leaves of the tiring-room appeared a figure of strange loveliness, which fairly took my breath away. Shimmering in the golden setting sunlight, like a gun-metal (not bronze) statue, stood a live princess—*the* princess, the greatest beauty and richest match in all Samoa. A really beautiful creature, in all her half-developed early girlhood. Self-possessed, gentle, and modest, every movement and gesture showed the true lady. Her face was a face one could dream of as that of the reigning beauty of the court of an early Tothmes. Her only dress was a most beautiful mat, soft and lissom as the most *ondoyant* satin, wound round her hips with exquisite grace, the fringe below hardly hiding her dainty little

feet, that—(No! I won't quote Suckling this time. I
wonder how many of those who do ever read the original ballad?) Her charming head was—it pains me to
say so—shaved, but still so shaved as by no means to
detract from the general effect; on the contrary, to an
eye accustomed to the weird head-dressings of European women, it was rather pretty than otherwise. The
forehead alone was shaved, and down her pretty shoulders hung a long and ample lock of straight brown
hair. Whatever unartistic there might have been
about this was relieved by a glorious wreath of intensely crimson hibiscus-flowers, which would have
utterly "put out" any European face, but which
lighted hers up like—well! like r—ge. Round her
neck she wore a double row of crimson berries, as large
as small walnuts, and altogether a daintier darling, or
a more graceful, eyes have seldom seen. With her
was another girl, stout and handsome and more fully
developed, but utterly without her grace and delicacy.
This was her maid of honor. She was dressed in a kilt
of white tappa, particularly high kilted; also, she wore
a wreath of hibiscus-flowers, but, as showing the necessity of her inferior beauty being heightened by ad-
ventitious ornament, or as a hint of her wealth rather
than her breeding, she wore diamonds, that is, the
representatives of diamonds in these parts—a necklace
of sperm-whales' teeth scraped down so fine as to look
like the claws of some gigantic tiger—a necklace of
utterly incalculable value!

 The two girls seated themselves gracefully on
beautiful mats spread in the sunshine outside, and the
great kava-bowl was placed before them with mighty

care and reverence. It was hewn out of a single block of dark wood, oval in shape, some two or three feet long, by half as much broad; very shallow, and supported on elephantine legs. I am told that your kava-bowl should be old; it is not good to put new kava into new bowls; something in the sap of the wood, I suppose, acts on the kava at first; the test of excellence is, that the interior and lips are of a fine golden bronzy tint, like that on good old Japan-ware.

The princess *looked* to her maid of honor "Am I all right?" and the maid of honor looked back "Lovely!"—and so they sat and were admired of all.

Then the point of interest changed to the interior of the hut in which we were sitting. A great officer handed a lump of kava-root, about the size of half a cottage loaf (the bigger the root the better the kava) to the great chief, who, casting it gracefully at P——'s feet, said, "Let this be a sign of friendship between us." Upon which P——, being properly instructed, cast it gracefully back again to him, and answered, "Let it be prepared for our mutual gratification." (*Mem.*—I am not responsible for these translations; I suspect the last word ought to be "jollification.") The lump of dried root was then handed to the high official, who, bearing it to where the girls were sitting, chopped small, thin slices off it with a wild-looking billhook, and laid them before them. After carefully rinsing their mouths with a cocoa-nutful of fresh water, each beauty took a bit and commenced the process of —chewing? Pah!—Mastication? Bah! let us say rumination; steadily, quietly, and nicely, as the daintiest Alderney in her grace's fancy dairy. This may sound strange, and possibly even disagreeable to some, but I declare that there was a grace and dainty delicacy about the whole thing, even to the way they picked up the chips of kava with their slender fingertips—that had its charm. I should as soon have thought of quarrelling with a "Cordon-bleu" for dipping his forefinger into the sauce to test its quality, as feeling offended by any part of the process. The young ladies did not ruminate entirely alone; near them sat a stalwart young fellow, who, turning half away from them and us, quietly took up a piece, and, judging from the action of his jaws, ruminated too. This is the thing to do—the delicate thing—the nice thing!—the real, quiet, unobtrusive way of showing your nascent affection! You help *her* to ruminate kava. I am not, I trust, more than properly envious of other men's good parts, or social accomplishments; but I confess that I should have liked to ruminate for her better than he did! But, after all, it might have been that he ruminated only for the maid of honor. I thought I saw the faintest twinkle of a wink hover for a moment in the corner of her eye—if so, well! If not, may he come a cropper the next time he carries the missionary over the bowlder-encumbered stream—and then, my word!

After about ten minutes or a quarter of an hour, three balls of vegetable matter, each the size of a largish walnut, were placed in the bowl. The young ladies then filled it with fair water, stirred all up slightly, and then entered the hut in which we were sitting, seating themselves at the end opposite to us. The bowl was then brought in and placed before them, and the second act of the mystery began. Taking a large handful of the white inner-bark fibres of the hibiscus, the princess dipped it into the bowl, and then, with many a graceful twist and twirl of her dainty hands, wrung out the fluid part of the mess; repeating this again and again, the gruelly fluid became clearer and clearer, the fibres of the bark retaining the vegetable *débris* of the kava-root within its interstices. This was really a pretty business from the great grace and delicacy with which H. R. H. managed her hands and arms. Sir Joshua would have made a glorious picture of her as "La Belle Blanchisseuse," portrait of her grace the Duchess of Washington washing her own lace. "But Lord!" as Pepys would say, "to see the care her maid of honor had of her, though brown, and how she guarded her mat against the drippings."

A shy, coquettish smile told the company that the kava was ready, and we clapped our hands as gracefully as we could: taking a carefully-shredded handful of hibiscus-fibres in her dainty fingers, she dipped it into the bowl, and squeezed it into the cocoa-nut, which went merrily round till all was done.

I was really surprised to find how utterly free from all unpleasant associations the process was; that is, if you did not look *too* closely, and I drained my first bowl of kava without hesitation, whatever my secret fears of the consequences might have been. It struck me as tasting like thin gruel, into which the slightest suspicion of white pepper and rhubarb had been cast; and, though possibly not particularly pleasant, it left a warm, stimulating flavor on the palate, which I can well believe might become, through use, exceedingly refreshing and agreeable in this exhausting climate. I waited patiently for all sorts of effects, mental and physical, but none came; I might as well have drunk half a bottle of flat ginger-beer, for that matter.

When we had finished the bowl, the young ladies giggled and flirted among themselves for a time, either making personal remarks upon us, or remarking the effect their own personalities had upon us. Then entered men bearing mighty baked fishes in woven baskets, which they laid at our feet. One of them was an enormous file-fish, eight or ten pounds' weight, with his great jagged dorsal spine sticking out of his back like a boat's mast. We needed no warning to eat none of him, his own recommendation preceded him from afar, and a morsel for politeness' sake was enough; he was, however, borne solemnly to the yacht, whence he was, on our arrival on board, most promptly returned to his native element.

A little smoking and a little conversation served as a screen to the proceedings of our young lady-friends at the other end of the hut, who were evidently in a state of preparation for something or another, having been joined by two others apparently of like mind to themselves. As for their hair-dressing, they were much like the princess and her maid of honor; but as to their ornaments they were different: instead of flowers they wore coronals, made of the last pearly whorl of the nautilus-shell, sewn on a bandeau of some material, a really pretty head-dress. Let me remark, while these preparations are going on, that these hair-dressings and head-dressings are serious things among the young ladies of Samoa—that is to say, among the unregenerate. When a young lady joins the church or forms a connection, matrimonial or otherwise, with a white man, she lets her hair grow, and all the mystery and poetry of the thing is gone. Among the unconverted, however, there are certain capillary signals understood by the initiated. For example, the lock or tail of hair worn by my princess is a sign of great goodness, like the old Scottish snood, rather a rare article nowadays. If the whole head is shaven, it is a bad sign, and betokens fastness, not to say looseness, and many such delicate devices. Again, if a girl should have, as sometimes happens, a head of golden-brown hair, it is "lapued" by some great chief, and not a hair of it must be cut till it is in its full harvest of gold. Then comes the great chief, bringing with him rare and soft mats instead of money (no jokes about matrimony!) and casts them down at the feet of the bearer of the golden fleece, which he shears off to weave into his own elaborate wig. If this sort of thing did not happen every day in Europe, particularly among the golden-haired girls of Brittany, what savages we should think these Samoans!

It is wondrous strange that hair-fashions should just at present be the same at London and Samoa. The blond fashion at the latter place reigns supreme, and, oddly enough, is served on both sides of the equator by much the same means. The taste for reddish hair in good Queen Bess's time found means of expression by the use of a lye of wood-ashes; in good Queen Victoria's time it is managed by much the same thing—strong alkaline washes; your Samoan uses coral-lime for the same purpose, but he or she has the decency to say that it is done more for the destruction of animalcules than from any feeling of personal vanity. At any rate, the custom has an odd effect as far as the men are concerned. Imagine a brown London footman seized with raving madness just at the moment he has finished powdering his hair, tearing off his garments and swaggering up Pall Mall with nothing on but a dinner-napkin, and you have a good idea of a Samoan swell. In full fighting-fig, a Samoan is magnificent in a gigantic bush of hair standing out two or three feet from his head like the nimbus of a saint. The care required to keep this glory intact produces, as in the case of the full-bottomed periwig, a stately and gorgeous gait, which was never sketched properly except by Thackeray, who has caught the careful pose of the advanced leg marvellously. I really think there is something fine in the fashion—I know the wearers do. A brother of one of the chiefs sits for hours in the cabin merely to be looked at; indeed, I rather suspect that his brother brings him as a show, which has to be paid for in handfuls of broken biscuit, and really he is worth it. His beard and mustache are also always very carefully trimmed, and, though his entire garment may be only a fathom or two of tappa wound round his loins, the Samoan gives one the idea of a dressy man, who takes considerable interest in his personal appearance. By-the-way, any theologian who wants to understand the real meaning of Solomon's "oil which maketh man to be of a cheerful countenance," should come out here. I know not why, but certainly a good rub of cocoa-nut oil over a brown face lights it up like a smile.

The young ladies, having completed their arrangements, favored us with a little singing and dancing. The songs were very strange and wild. The very quick time to which they were sung, the slapping of the hands on the thighs, and the drumming of their knees against the ground, had a wonderfully exciting effect. It would hardly do to describe the dancing very particularly; it was certainly pretty in its way, and of that style which I think Mr. Murray mentions in his "Hand-book for Spain," as having obtained among the "improba Gaditana," which I suppose may be translated "the improper Cadiziennes." It is the same dance all over the world; from the gypsies of Granada to the gawazee of Egypt; from the gawazee of Egypt to the nautch-girls of India; from the nautch-girls of India, all musk and patchouli, and silk, and gems, to the dirty little gin, of Western Australia, with her stinking bundle of possum-skins, it is all the same; nay, even in the jig of Ireland and the almost pious reel of Scotland, "Smelfungus" can detect the lingering relics of pagan impropriety.

In this case, however, the young ladies danced neatly and properly, and the most severe guard-municipal would not have interfered. One little *ballet d'action* was prettier to see than to describe, and had a *mignon* gŕace about it that delighted me, and made one think of Theocritus. The kid (the princess) has lost her mother, and, gently and fondly bleating, she advances in little jumps, first in one direction and then in another, pausing between each, with her head coquettishly on one side, and her eyes fixed intently to listen for the response. The chorus answer her with a gradually-increasing bleat, till at last she finds her mother, in this case represented by P——, whose paternity she acknowledged by a pretty tap on the chin with her forefinger, and then fled back to her fellow-maidens covered with brown blushes as with a garment. Another pretty dance they have which is called the "pigeon-dance." The girls while dancing keep up a soft and mewling "*r-r-r-r!*" like the call of the female pigeon, which is answered at regular intervals by the sturdy "*boom!*" of the admiring circles of males—really a graceful and pretty thing.

Oh! why did I not leave well alone? Why did I not depart from Samoa with my heart aglowing with the soft and timid purity of my princess? What devil was it tempted me to wander along the white coral-strand under the feathery cocoas, in the soft moonlight, and be induced by the rascally chief who had the brother, to get up a *fantasia* by the light of blazing cocoa-leaf baskets? There was my princess with five others, each infinitely worse than any one of them, frisking and gambadoing in the most *fearful* manner! dressed in a garment which would not have been tolerated at Highbury Barn, dancing dances that ought never to have been danced, singing songs which would have blenched the cheek of Terese, winking winks that ought never to have been wunk, even in dreams! making the very cocoa-trees above our heads bristle with horror! Oh, you naughty, naughty girl!

CHAPTER IX.

SHIPWRECK.

There are three great classes of fools in this world: first, the wise fool, who knows he is an ass, but considers the fact a secret to be kept between himself and his Maker; secondly, the happy fool, who considers himself rather a genius than otherwise; thirdly, the fool of fools, who consciously and defiantly proclaims his asininity to the world in general.

I belong to the latter class, the consequence of which is, that I am now sitting down to compile the history of our shipwreck. It is copied nearly *verbatim* from the log that I kept all the time, and is truer to life in nothing more than in its malignant dulness. If, when this is published, any respectable person could come to me and conscientiously state that the perusal of the account had bored him as much as the real shipwreck had bored me, I should rest happily, feeling that my work had been a success.

It is not tragical; it is not humorous. How can one do any fine writing, sitting on a brandy-case, with the rain coming down in long, perpendicular rods, not drops, which break on one's head and trickle down one's nose on to the paper; stopping every fifteen seconds to take a revenge on a dozen or so of mosquitoes that are grazing coolly on one's hands; whereby one spills the ink, drops the book, and loses the pen, which is discovered some time after planted two inches deep in the mud like a young tree: one can't even grumble fluently under such circumstances.

Most people who have written shipwreck and Robinson-Crusoe stories have invented them out of their fertile brains, and those who have actually described what they have seen and been through in that time, have put their adventures on paper, after they had been sifted in their memoirs till little more than the tragic or romantic sides of them remain. Or, if their accounts have been actually committed to paper at the time, they have been polished afterward, and little dabs of romance, sentiment, or tragedy, stuck in to please the gushing and sensation-loving public.

This is the fault of such stories, and partly out of obstinacy, and still more out of laziness, I intend to avoid it.

Besides this, I consider originality is a thing to be striven after, especially when it is to be acquired at the cheap price of relating bare facts.

Robinson Crusoe is a delusion and a snare; even in the credulous days of infancy I was always slightly skeptical on the subject of the "Swiss Family Robinson;" their inventions were so wonderfully ingenious, and Nature seemed to fit in with their wishes and wants with a readiness that seemed scarcely real. I never pinned my faith on "Foul Play" for the same reason. Did the heroes or heroines of those books happen to want a hip-bath, a balloon, an umbrella, a pet animal, or any such small thing necessary to a person living on a desolate island, the ingenious author would immediately provide materials and the way to use them. A hip-bath? One of those large water-gourds cut in half, scooped out, and stuck upon legs, and the thing was done—(here would follow a long and learned dissertation from the well-informed member of the shipwrecked party—there always is an abominable prig of this sort to act as chorus in such books—on the subject of the large water-gourds of the South-Sea Islands, cribbed out of an encyclopædia or some book of travels). A balloon? Of course there were India-rubber trees on the island—I don't know exactly how they would set to work, but give the author of such stories the trees, some flat stones, a fire, some scientific treatise on the action of heat, and perhaps an old frying-pan, saved from the wreck, and he would rig them out a balloon in no time.

An umbrella? The plaited leaves of the pandarius or screw-palm was just the thing!

A pet animal? A seal will do capitally; there ain't any in that part of the world, but that don't matter. And so on, *ad libitum;* indeed, I really don't know why a man with plenty of books to refer to and a ready imagination should be shy of building a cathedral on a coral-reef.

"Masterman Ready," that most delightful of books, has got the stamp of reality about it, but the romance of the life is kept uppermost, while its unutterable boredom and countless petty miseries show too faintly.

I suppose I say this because I am not a hero.

I don't like being turned out of my warm bed at

night into the cold and wet of a fierce gale to be shipwrecked and perhaps drowned.

I don't like being chucked from one side of the cabin to the other like a sack of potatoes, barking my shins and nearly breaking my ribs.

I don't like being banged and crashed on a coral-reef all night, expecting instant death by the sea or future extinction by cannibalism.

I don't like landing on a beastly little island without water, except pouring rain, and living there.

I don't like sleeping night after night with the rain trickling into my ears, with a swollen face and a toothache.

I don't like starting up in my sleep at every little noise, expecting to be tomahawked.

I don't like wearing wet clothes for a fortnight on land.

I don't like being cramped up for thirty hours in a little overladen open boat, in an unknown and dangerous sea, alternately soused with salt-water and burnt by a tropical sun.

Heroes like such things, I believe; I don't, though I can put up with them if necessary, without much grumbling. And, though the greater part of our shipwrecked company were as brave as men could be, they weren't a bit like the heroes one finds in some books. When the spray was flying over the doomed vessel, and the pitiless coral was crushing her groaning sides, etc., etc., they were *not* filled with a joyous exultation in defying the raging elements—not a bit. They thought the wet and the danger and fatigue confoundedly disagreeable, and were as cool and prompt and cheerful as they could be under the circumstances.

I believe those ideal heroes who delight in every thing uncomfortable, exist chiefly in novels and lunatic asylums: I hope so, I am sure, for I shouldn't like to have to live with one.

We had had a most charming three-months' cruise from Tahiti to the Samoas, visiting all the Society Islands and Raritonga on the way. Everywhere we had been treated like princes, and our cabin was lumbered with all kinds of curious presents—besides a large collection of bird-skins, some very rare and valuable.

We left Samoa the morning of October 18, 1870, intending to look in at Levuka, the chief port of the Fiji Islands, and thence to sail to New Zealand. On leaving Apia, the chief port of the island of Apolo, we coasted along, and ran between it and Savai, the largest island of the group; the coast of the latter in this passage is a mass of lava, so honeycombed by the action of the sea, as to produce innumerable spouts of water, rising, I should think, a good hundred feet, like great jets of steam.

October 19th.—Light fair wind.

October 20th.—Cloudy, murky weather. Passed Proby's Island (known by half a dozen other names), lately the scene of a terrible eruption. In the evening it came on to blow.

October 21st.—At about half-past three this morning I was aroused by a crash overhead that woke us all up, and we scampered on deck, thinking the foretop-mast had gone; but it was only the old fish-ing (one of the boats) that had got into trouble. A sea just slapping her underneath had neatly unhooked the tackle of the fore-davit; the boom to which she was lashed had snapped with the sudden weight, and she was hanging by the stern, with her bows dragging through the water. They seized her in the main rigging, and, by means of the throat-halyards and another tackle from the foretop, got her on board again not much damaged.

It blew fresh all day, while the weather grew thicker and darker, which made us rather anxious and uncomfortable, as we were approaching the dangerous and intricate Fiji Archipelago. After several false alarms we made land ahead, which we concluded to be Explorer's Island, to the south of the Narinku Passage, by which we intended entering the group. The wind was now about east by south, and blowing a gale, so we wore and reached out under what canvas we could carry, as it would have been madness to have run in among the numerous reefs and islands in the dark with such weather; the vessel headed about northeast, and, though we could not make much headway in such a sea, we were confident of weathering all the groups to the north of the passage, according to the chart about forty miles dead to leeward of us.

The wind grew stronger and stronger all the evening, bursting down in fierce, rainy squalls, and the sea very heavy. It was as dark as pitch, but thinking ourselves to windward of all dangers, and being confident in the sea-going qualities of the Albatross, we cared nothing for it all. At about nine o'clock the life-boat was got on board, and, being rather drowsy, I turned in.

At about ten o'clock, as I was dozing off, I felt a sudden shock, a terrible lurch, and a long, trembling grind. The doctor shouted to me that we had struck, but it needed not that nor the cries on deck to tell me what had happened. I rushed out of my cabin to get on deck, when a heavier lurch and crash sent me slithering right across the saloon under the table. I scrambled up again and made for the companion, Mitchell appearing from his cabin with a hurried "What's the matter?"

"You may say your prayers now," replied I, with a ghastly grin, "for the game's up with us." We climbed on deck and found ourselves in about as awe-inspiring a position as could well be imagined : the vessel lying almost on her beam-ends, the foam flying over her in a white cloud, every sea lifting her up and bringing her down again with a sickening crash, that made the cabin-floor heave like an earthquake, and her whole frame tremble, the scream of the wind sounding even above the roar of the surf, and all these horrors magnified by an intense darkness. The doctor and I said "Good-by!" Indeed, at that moment I don't think anybody but the skipper expected to live ten minutes.

Nor should we if the vessel had been deep laden, in which case she would have been crushed against the edge of the reef and sunk in deep water. As it was, every sea drove us farther and farther on to the coral.

The courage and steadiness shown by all hands was very striking. Braund (the master) behaved as he always does in times of danger, his cheery voice ringing out above the infernal din, and his honest face lit up by a quiet smile whenever it became visible in the glare of the skylight. Tim Bougard (the mate) backed him up in a cool, smart way, and the men did all that men could do. There was no confusion or unnecessary shouting; the boats were all got over to the lee-side and made ready to be cut away at a moment's notice, a work of no small difficulty when the angle of the slippery decks and the perpetual jerks and plunges of the vessel are considered.

As far as my own feelings were concerned, I could not help being amused by noting that with all the awe of death, and wonder about what was to come, was mixed a kind of sulky irritation at being turned out of my warm bed into the cold water, and a feeling of unutterable disgust at the destruction of all my knick-knacks and curiosities.

And when I succeeded in realizing the end that I thought was coming so soon, a host of old familiar faces from all parts of the world flitted swiftly before my mind, never so vividly remembered, and never perhaps better loved than at that moment, striking me with a sharp pang of sadness.

The skipper came up to us, and kindly and gently advised us to go below and get dry clothes while there was yet time. So down we went and sat talking at the foot of the companion, cheerfully enough all things considered, Mitchell and Warden (the steward) bustling about, to the imminent danger of their bones, to collect a few provisions and necessaries before everything was spoilt by the water that was fast filling the vessel.

Then an alarm came that we were being driven over the reef, and should sink on the other side, so we went on deck again, and waited, ready to take to the boats. Soon it was discovered that the water was quite shallow to leeward, so there was no fear of that particular danger. We went below again, it being determined to stick to the vessel till daylight if possible, and felt quite cheery at the reprieve. It is wonderful how soon men *get accustomed* to being in danger. Whether it is unconscious fatalism, or merely the natural carelessness of human nature, I don't know. The saloon was now getting full of water, so we were obliged to cram ourselves into Mitchell's little cabin up to windward, where we passed rather a terrible night, though we laughed and joked as much as we could to keep our spirits up.

Our prospects certainly were not pleasant; the ship could not hold together long, and we might have to go many miles in the strength of the gale in open boats before we could reach an island; and, if we did happen to hit upon an inhabited one, we should be nearly certain to be killed and eaten by the inhabitants.[1]

It was a sad thing to hear the crashing and straining of the old ship, and the mournful toll of her bell overhead, and to see the decks opening and the bulkheads breaking up inside her, with the chairs, books, clothes, mats, and a hundred odds and ends, floating

[1] We found afterward that our apprehensions on the score of cannibalism were needlessly great; but I have decided to give them as they were felt and written down at the time. Our sole informant and authority on the subject was the "South Pacific Directory," which described the Fijians, and the Ringgold-Islanders particularly, as the most ferocious cannibals.

about the cabin. But every thing pathetic or tragical has a comical side to it, and I could not help laughing to see the steward scrambling about collecting various articles for preservation, and continually slipping up when a heavy jar came, and almost disappearing in the dirty water to leeward. To make it better, he had my matches and their appurtenances, my pipes and tobacco, in his pockets; their appearance when produced was rather "mixed."

Occasionally the skipper came down to report the state of affairs, or advise what should be provided, and, though I know he was terribly cut up, he talked coolly and cheerily, and was very gentle and considerate.

He told us that he was on deck when she struck, looking out amidships. Louey was doing the same forward, and old Nelson (the second mate) was on the quarter-deck, but it was so dark that none saw the breakers until she struck the coral and was dashed upon it broadside on. The night seemed to pass away slowly; about every ten seconds came an awful jar and crash that woke me whenever I began to doze, and made us wonder how long she would hold together. Collecting provisions and necessaries, and longing for light, the weary hours passed away.

October 22*d*.—At last the day broke, gloomy, wild, and wet, and we went on deck to find out our situation. About a mile to leeward of us on the same reef appeared a small island, and about half a mile from that a rather larger one; the vessel was lying about fifty yards inside the first break of the reef in about three feet of water.

The very heaviness of the sea had been our salvation, hurling us right up on to the coral-ledge into comparative safety.

Then one by one the boats were sent off, laden with compasses, quadrants, guns, ammunition, provisions, blankets, etc. Joining company again clear of the breakers, we made for the little island, thirteen men in all, and all ready to fight if necessary.

It was a little coral-sandy place about one hundred and fifty yards long, by one hundred wide, with a steep beach, and a second step or terrace about thirty yards back, as if there had been a recent elevation.

We landed, and emptied the boats of their soddened and sloppy contents, and then, by way of making things more thoroughly miserable, the rain came down in a black, hopeless, tropical torrent.

Depressed and exhausted as we were, it was certainly most wretched; we made a kind of shed out of the sail of a life-boat, and at last succeeded by means of a dead log and some tarred twine in making a fire, which improved matters a little; then every one except the doctor, Warden, Little Taff (cook's mate), and I, went off to the wreck to fetch the live-stock, and save what they could. Meanwhile the doctor went exploring for water, which he didn't find, while I amused myself by trying to dry the blankets and clothes as they came ashore—rather a futile occupation. Taff got us some bacon and tea, which we ate ravenously.

As I lay down, I seemed to feel the ground shaking and heaving under me. I thought it was an earthquake at first, so did the doctor, but we found it was nothing but imagination, produced by the continued jarring and shaking we had had all night.

I could also hear the voices of the men shouting above the roar of the surf, and several times the illusion was so strong that I went down to the beach, fancying the boats had come back from the wreck. At last they all returned, very tired, having brought ashore the live-stock, sails, preserved meats, pots and pans, mattresses, meats, etc. After they had had some food, they rigged up two capital tents, a big one with the vessel's square-sail, and a smaller one for the doctor and me, out of the topsail.

Louey, an ingenious little Norseman, chopped himself some sticks, and made a splendacious bedstead to sling his mat to.

I have succeeded in saving my manuscripts, though they are rather damaged. "Whatever anybody may say of your poems, none can call them *dry*," remarked the doctor, with a grin.

Close to our camp is an old native "marai," or place of sacrifice, formed of big flat coral-stones. A kind of rough line, about three feet wide, runs down the middle of it toward the sea, terminating in a *cul-de-sac*. The height of the chained posts on each side of it tells very plainly what has been hung to cook there. A most villanous-looking hole! . And a nice place for a lot of shipwrecked mariners to have within twenty yards of their camp—something like the skulls and bones that the old hermits used to keep about them, to remind them of their end.

We can make out two islands in a west-by-south direction; one a low clump of trees, like the one we are on, and the other a high mountain, some thirty miles off.

Though we do not know yet exactly where we are, as no place in the chart answers exactly to the bearing of this island, there is no doubt that we are somewhere in the Ringgold Islands, the most cannibalistic part of the Pacific. So we may think ourselves very lucky to have hit on an uninhabited place.

Great reefs stretch away in several directions as far as we can see; more dangerous waters for navigation cannot be imagined.

It came on to pour again, but the skipper and his men rigged mats and boat-sails round the bottom of our tent, and made us pretty snug. Nothing could be kinder and nicer than they all have been, and we are more grateful than we can say.

Made a capital dinner on chicken-slop, and soon turned in. Rained hard all night.

October 23d.—All discovered this morning that they were very much bruised and knocked about, a fact that they were quite unconscious of yesterday.

At low water most of the party went off again to the wreck, and brought off more things.

The skipper tried to get an observation, but was put out at the critical moment by a bird settling on his head. The only reef resembling this on the chart is a place called Nukumbasanga, in the extreme northeast of the Ringgold Islands.

The poor old ship is breaking up, her lee-side being raised two feet or more, and all the butts open enough to put your hand between.

Our plan at present is to wait for fine weather,

determine our position, and run right away in the
boats for Sevulsa, some one hundred and fifty miles;
for, if we are compelled to stop anywhere, we shall have
to fight to avoid being eaten. We have got five guns,
two axes, two revolvers, and five tomahawks, and I
think all of us intend to take "utu" as the Maories call
it, for ourselves, before knocking under.

The life-boat will tow the dingy, and by means of
lights the fish-fag will be able to keep close to us.

It is rather provoking to think that we are within
sixty miles of islands flowing with milk and honey,
and yet daren't go near them. If we had been lucky
enough to get wrecked in the Society's, Cook's Islands,
or Samoas, we should have been half-killed with kindness, and made little gods of; whereas now we pray
fervently that no one may see the wreck and find us
out.

I don't approve of this kind of thing. If ever I
am shipwrecked again, I prefer doing it in the regular
magazine-story style—a dismasted vessel—a lee-shore
—half an hour's agony—life or death—a rocket—a
life-boat—a gallant preserver—a lovely female (with
or without a sweet infant, according to the taste of the
author)—and then a watery grave, or warm dry blankets and hot brandy-and-water! Warm dry blankets!
I can hardly bear to think of such luxuries.

There are a few cocoa-nut trees on this island, but
the chief vegetation consists of small India-rubber
trees, with big, broad leaves, on which certain curious
crabs perch, and run about like birds. There is
another kind of crab here that runs so fast that one
mistakes it at first glance for a small bird skimming

along the shore—the more so as he takes occasionally the most extraordinary flying leaps.

There are quantities of pretty little terns, their breeding-place being close to our camp; the eggs are just laid on the sand, and the young ones hidden under the large black stones.

By-the-way, these black rocks that cover the beach on one side of the island are very curious: they are quite hard and solid, but they have been boiled in such a hurry as to have great shells embedded in them.

There are also man-of-war birds, curlews, rats, pigeons, mosquitoes, flying-foxes, and lizards. Any amount of beautiful shells are scattered about the beach.

After a good dinner we went and sat under the life-boat sail by the cooking-fire, and had some pleasant talk about past adventures. Every one hopeful and cheery, though this weather would give Joe Miller the blues.

Rained hard in the night, and my bedding getting drenched, I had rather an unpleasant time of it. Besides this, I had a fearful nightmare: dreamt that we were attacked by savages, and woke finding that I had got hold of the doctor, who had stumbled over me trying to get out of the tent.

October 24th.—It cleared a little in the morning, and the camp soon presented the appearance of a great washing establishment, every wettable article being hung out to dry. I went to get a dip in the sea, when I met old Nelson, rushing violently through the bush in pursuit of an imaginary turkey (we have turned all our live-stock loose on the island). Mitchell afterward went out on the same quest, armed with a gun, wounded the turkey, and a pig in the nose, who disappeared squeaking, whereupon Mitchell came back disgusted.

His appearance is rather wild; he has been working like a brick for the last three days, and has worn his knees sore with the friction of his wet breeches. So he sports a pair of "pajamas" which he tucks up above his knees, and which, combined with a flannel shirt and a pair of Davy's boots unlaced, and about three sizes too large, give him an appearance of a cross between Robinson Crusoe and a brigand in a play.

Tim went off in the dingy and saved some more miscellaneous articles.

The captain got an observation to-day that makes him pretty sure we are on the Nukumbasanga reef, though it is quite misplaced on the chart.

Most of the company are rigged in my socks, which I should think would want tying up at the toes to make them fit.

In the afternoon a regular hunt after live-stock, the skipper managing to shoot a pig. Killing the fowls for dinner is great fun: we go after them through the bush with long sticks, driving them toward each other, and making long sweeps at them whenever we get a chance, but the trees generally get in the way of the stick and the fowl scuttles away into the bush triumphantly, till at last some one makes a lucky shot and bowls him over.

At four o'clock it came on to pour heavily again. This is miserable weather.

After dinner we went down to the big tent and had a talk. It would have made a splendid sketch in the flickering candle-light—the two long rows of men on each side, lying on their mats or bedding in every kind of position; some dozing, some smoking, talking, or reading old scraps of newspapers that had been saved by some chance, while in the centre were heaped up cases, guns, clothes, and all kinds of odds and ends.

There we turned in for the night; the skipper, who could not take more care of us if we were his own children, looking in to see that we were all right.

October 25th.—Went out of the tent with bare feet and trod in an ant's-nest. I understand now why the sluggard is to go to the ant. It will make him lively if any thing will.

No change in the weather, except that it is blowing harder—very depressing. The dingy went off again to the wreck: no amount of knocking about seems to injure that little boat, whereas both the others have suffered a good deal.

Mitchell has painted a placard, and nailed it to a tree: "Albatross—wrecked. October 27, 1870. Start for Leonka the first fine day."

All pretty cheerful in spite of the weather. Old Nelson trots about the sea-shore like a school-boy pursuing crabs, and studying natural history generally. He is afflicted with cramps, and dreams of savages at night, that cause him to awake with unmelodious yells, and clasp his neighbors by the throat, much to their disgust.

The doctor goes fishing daily, but seldom seems to catch any thing definite, except wet clothes. As he says himself, "If he was being ferried over the Styx he would stop Charon to let him have half an hour's fishing." Mitchell, the skipper, the doctor, and I, played cards in the evening.

October 26*th.*—I find that sleeping on the top of an aneroid, two revolvers, a pair of boots, and a cigar-box, is not the most comfortable way of passing the night. The fact is, my bed got so swampy that I was obliged to turn off the mattress.

Gloomy and wet as ever. The captain went off to the wreck and got us some books, a great godsend. The vessel has been driven in nearly another length, and is slewed head on to the shore.

"D—— the rain!" said I, heartily. "Damming's just what it wants," replied the doctor, "but unfortunately there is no way of doing it." However, to-day the sun shone nearly ten minutes, and quite dazzled us.

The doctor caught some fish for dinner, after which we went and played cards in the big tent.

October 27*th.*—I woke before daybreak, drenched with rain, with a toothache, a slight cold, and half a stiff neck.

Rained hard half the day, and then drizzled. All hands employed in rigging bedsteads to keep them out of the wet as much as possible. Jim and Mitchell made us two splendid four-posters. If it had not been for the porous nature of the coralline soil, we should have been all knocked up before this.

Harry (the cook) tried to catch a pig to kill it; whereupon a certain old sow ran at him, and made hostile demonstrations till he was obliged to let go. The captain caught a big crawfish.

We should sleep better if it were not for the perpetual alarms of savages. Last night, as I was rolling about on my mattress, I heard the doctor cry, "Qui vive!" My hand was on my revolver in a moment. "What's up?" I whispered. "Something has been moving between me and the mouth of the tent for the last minute. Why, it's your head!" At which we both laughed, and went to sleep again.

Jim told me that for the first two nights he could scarcely sleep at all, and even now the slightest noise wakes him. And the skipper told me that he woke the other night all of a tremble, fancying that he heard the doctor crying for help.

Half an hour's clear weather would enable the savages in the neighboring islands to see the wreck, and bring them down on us *en masse*.

A pleasant position truly for a lot of harmless innocents like us!

No change in the weather. Some of the party visited the other island, where they found some wonderful eels (murena), shells, and "curios" generally. This would be a wonderful place for a naturalist, but unfortunately our sojourn here is a miniature type of life: we can carry nothing away with us—so it's no use collecting.

I cannot help groaning occasionally over the tremendous loss of utterly irreplaceable things, all pleasant to look upon, for the sake of the generous people who gave them.

"O Moé! where are the mats you gave me, and the pretty little arrowroot hats, and the reva-reva prepared by your own little brown fingers? O Tampoa

Wabine! where are the native dresses you sent to your most obedient? O maidens of the Society Islands! where are the crowns you worked with such care, and threw down before my unworthy feet? O Te Mitiki, commonly called Mitchell! where are those sixty precious bird-skins you prepared with such care? O chiefs and chieftainesses of Raritonga! where is your tapa? where are your mats? where your sacred staffs? where the precious garments with which you decorated me? Oh, bother! that's flat." This is the lament of Te Pemlinke, Rangatira of the Kaibuhe Albatross. Oh, that I might eat the man who surveyed these islands!

However, the mats and live-stock have proved invaluable in our adversity.

This is an awful place for sores; the slightest cut or scratch refuses to heal. Every one is longing ardently for clear weather and a start. Rained in the night.

October 29th.—" Look what I've found!" said the skipper, as I came out of our tent in the morning; "a cross between a crab and a turtle." It certainly looked very like it, being a great white crab, like an inverted saucer, the legs and claws fitting in underneath it when drawn up, giving the idea of some ingenious portable invention. Weather a little finer, but the sky not yet washed and painted blue.

Harry killed one of the pigs, Tim and Taff warding off the attack of the old sow with a stick. I don't much believe in that old sow. She is a philanthropist —I mean a "philporcist," a regular Mrs. Jellyby of a sow. She neglects her own children in the most careless manner; but if any one touches one of the other pigs that are no connection of hers, and, indeed, come from a different island, she manages to work herself up into a state of most vicious (she would say generous) excitement. If ever her soul transmigrates into a human body, it will either get up a flannel waistcoat and moral pocket-handkerchief society for infant blacks, and make virulent speeches at Exeter Hall, or else it will go in for the opposition business, become a "religious," desert its family, and fuss up and down in a blue dress, with a great starched napkin on its head, and a large quantity of rope and rosary dangling about it.

They got an observation to-day, and decided we were on Nukumbagansa, which is considerably misplaced on the chart. How we ever got so far to the westward is a problem. .There must have been some extraordinary current springing up with the gale, for we were swept thirty miles nearly dead to leeward in less than five hours.

The noise of the rollers on the reef when we were wrecked was very like the falling of great trees. Often since, when I have been in a brown study, and the men have been chopping down trees for firewood, the crash of the falling branches has made me start, and half expect to feel the shock of the sea.

The doctor, the skipper, and Mitchell, went off to the wreck, which is gradually breaking up.

I feel as if I had been months in this place, and, strange to say, am getting quite contented with the life. I get up at daybreak, and bathe; then, if it is not raining hard, pick up shells and so on till breakfast. After that, smoke pipes, read Shelley, write up my log, help to hang up the clothes to dry, and take them in again drenched half an hour after; then luncheon; then more pipes, and a stroll round the beach to study the habits of terns, or throw stones at them; then dinner, and cards or a chat in the big tent. When I want exercise I go and chop down a tree. But where's the romance of this kind of thing? unless you call it romantic to hear the terns screaming on the other side of the island in the middle of a dark, wet night, and to creep through the bush toward the place where they are crying, expecting to find a canoe full of hungry, murderous savages, just landed, with the head chief serving out sherry and bitters to give them an appetite for supper.

Well, there is a certain grim pleasure, doubtless, on such occasions, in grasping a tomahawk or a revolver, and thinking of the life you will take as payment before you give up your own. But that is a selfish, avaricious feeling, not worthy of the name of romance.

It strikes me more and more forcibly, every day, how strangely cool and fearless men get when they have been placed for a little while in a desperate situation. We all of us know, I suppose, what we have got to go through in making our escape—fatigue, exposure, misery, and danger, for thirty or forty hours on end at the shortest, and an indefinite time if the wind comes ahead, besides the prospect of certain death if it comes on to blow hard. And yet no one seems funky, and we are all longing to make the attempt. The main reason for this is the almost superstitious confidence we have got in the courage and resources of the skipper, who is one of those men created especially to lead others. We all feel that he will bring us safe through if it is possible, and if not, we can but die once.

This morning we found the tracks of a turtle on the sand, that had visited the island in the night; but it had laid no eggs. Probably she had been suddenly confronted by an inquisitive pig, and gone away in a sulk.

Polished up the guns and revolvers to-day. The camp is beginning to stink of decaying animal matter. If we are not off soon, we shall have dysentery.

October 30*th*.—Hurrah! fine weather! or rather, the best imitation of it they can get up in this blessed island. The skipper at once determined to start to-morrow; so the sheep were hunted down and slain, the fowls had their necks broken, after being knocked down with sticks, and Harry set to work to cook every thing he could lay hands on. Now we *must* go, or we shall be starved. Our fleet consisted of a small life-boat, by White of Cowes, eighteen feet long, sharp at both ends; the fish-fag, a rough, serviceable boat, about the same size and shape, but much less deep; the dingy, a wonderful little craft, fifteen feet long, like a whale-boat with ten feet taken out amidships. They were all more or less damaged by the bumping they got at the time of the shipwreck, but were good sea-boats, and fair sailors.

The doctor, the captain, Harry, the cook, big Taff and I, man the life-boat; old Nelson, little Taff, and Loucy, the dingy; Jim, Mitchell, Warden, Tom, and Davy, the fish-fag; which consequently will have the strongest crew, as is necessary. If the dingy turns out too slow, she will be towed by one of the others.

We shall be forty-eight hours at least, I should think; and, with calms or head-winds, any time. Unpleasant, but can't be helped. If it comes on to blow, with our deep-laden boats, God help us!

I believe the proper platitude to use on such occasions is "trust in Providence;" but it seems to me that people who do so are as likely as not to be disappointed. I mean no irreverence, and am quite ready to trust in Providence, in the wider sense of the expression, but I don't believe He changes the wind and weather, or any thing else in this world, for the benefit of particular individuals. The men on whom the tower of Siloam fell were no worse than any one else in the town. Two sparrows do not fall to the ground without God knowing it, *but the sparrows fall all the same.* We shall either be providentially drowned or providentially saved.

11 A. M.—We have changed our plan, and start as soon as the meat is cooked, as every hour of calm weather is of vital importance. Now for the pinch!

There are two kinds of mosquitoes here, a small black one, and a big spotted one. Both bite only in the daytime.

By three o'clock the boats were all loaded and ready for a start. The men very naturally wanted to save all their things; the consequence of which was, that the fish-fag and life-boat were filled with lumber even above the thwarts, and, with their crew of five men each, were almost down to the water's edge at every little lurch, by no means a proper trim to go one hundred and fifty miles through open sea, tide-rips, and perhaps breakers.

However, we didn't like to throw away any thing till it was absolutely necessary; so as soon as the dingy, that had been used to bring off the cargoes of the other boats from the shore, was ready, the sails were set, anchors weighed, and, with the life-boat as commodore leading the way, we crossed the reef and bade farewell to Nukumbasanga.

We had three courses open to us: either to run to leeward of all the Ringgold Islands, and then haul up for the Somo Somo Passage; or to keep to windward, and try and weather all the reefs and islands till we got into the Naruku Channel, some twenty miles distant; or else, if we could not succeed in weathering them, to lay on our oars for the night, and run between them next morning. We determined to take one of the last two, and stood away close-hauled about south by east, the life-boat taking the dingy in tow.

But our troubles began early. Though the weather was fine and there was no great sea, the boats were so deep and dead that they made very little way; and the fish-fag and life-boat could only pull one oar with any effect under sail on account of the lumber. We kept at it as hard as we could till sundown, but there were still no signs of the Naruku reef, which we judged to be right ahead or on the weather-bow, while the long chain of smaller reefs were somewhere close to leeward of us.

Just before dark we perceived the crew of the fish-fag, that had dropped astern and to leeward of the other boats, making signals to us, and we bore down to them to see what was the matter.

We found them in a very uncomfortable state of mind. She was as dead as a log, they said, and they could scarcely keep her free by baling: if she wasn't lightened, she would sink under them. We could not help them by taking any of their load, being in much the same predicament ourselves, the water slopping in on all sides; but we shifted Warden into the dingy, (which was much more buoyant than either of the others), and told them to chuck the things overboard if necessary, as we should have to do in our boat.

The fish-fag's painter was then made fast to the dingy, and the three boats went on their course attached to each other. But in the dark our position became far more exciting than pleasant; we knew we were close on to the reefs, and every breaking sea was the cause of an alarm.

"There it is to windward!" "I see it to leeward!" "Breakers right ahead!" Very trying to the nerves of me, the steerer, being the only one who could not look out ahead.

After about half an hour of this work, the skipper decided to down sail and lay on the oars till daybreak. We were disappointed, but there was no help for it, as we should have been among the breakers before we had time to turn in the dark. The order was passed to the other boats, the painters were cast off, and the masts were unshipped. At this critical moment, when the boat was lying helpless in the trough of the sea, "big Taff," who was unrigging the boat, looked over his shoulder and yelled out: "There it is, sir; close on the lee-bow!" and letting go the mast made a snatch at an oar, and nearly tumbled overboard. The skipper promptly got a paddle over the stern and slewed the boat round, but it turned out to be another false alarm.

Then the boats closed up and were kept head on to the sea. Sometimes as one of them forged up alongside, emerging out of the darkness like a white ghost, a small attempt at chaff or a joke would be made, but it died a natural death; every one was too tired and wretched.

An awful night it was!—hour after hour pulling and baling in a rough, broken sea, wet to the skin and tired to death; listening nervously to the roar of the surf, watching the black masses of water as they charged our bows and shut out the dim horizon, and gazing up anxiously at each cloud as it rose and hid the stars.

"What a precious scrape we are in!" I kept thinking. "I wonder if we shall be still living two days hence? I always used to complain that I never met with any adventures in my travels, but this business will set me up in that line for some time if I get out of it alive." And then again a ghostly procession of old faces and places passed before me, with an intense vividness and reality in their perfect love and happiness, that seemed like some bitter, devilish mockery.

A feeling of want of sympathy is the mainspring of human misery. In joy and in sorrow the stars twinkle, the wind blows, and the sea moans alike. And then from the depths of a man's soul rises the cry that has been the origin of so many great religions: "O God! give me a sign that I may know that I am not utterly lonely and forsaken."

Few men *trust God enough* to be rationalists. Few men have humility, faith, and courage, to say: "There is a great Power that made the illimitable universe, and all that is in it: I know not why it was made, nor the purpose of all the pain and misery that I see round me; I know nothing except that I am placed here with certain instincts of right and wrong; God is omniscient and my understanding is limited; I must learn what I can of His laws, and fearlessly trust the rest to Him that made me."

For most minds this is not sufficient; there is a natural longing for something tangible and sympathetic to cling to. There is something so terribly dreary, lonely, and forsaken, in that confession—that the misery of life, and the purpose of the universe, can never be known or explained by man.

Who can look up at the stars without some such feelings? Where is the end of that dark, mysterious space overhead? What is happening in those countless worlds that we are gazing on? Perhaps souls higher than we can conceive, and natures to which ours is as a rough sketch by the side of a finished masterpiece, are doing their work there to some great end. How many millions lie beyond our view? Perhaps the universe is illimitable! Who shall say? It is as easy to comprehend that, as the past eternity which must have been. Where was the beginning? where will be the end? and what is the purpose of it all? Go mad, man—go mad! for the wisest sanity is but infinite ignorance.

You cannot tell me why that moth that has just flown into the candle was made to suffer those agonies.

Pious people say it is because Eve ate apples, but that seems precious hard lines on the moth. Go mad, I tell you! But you won't, you man; you are but an animal yourself—you eat, drink, sleep, die, marry, and are sold in marriage, and are only superior to the other animals in that you can wonder occasionally what it all means.

I remember when I was a little child the awe with which these things used to fill me. They used to seize me like some magic spell as I lay awake at night. I could not escape from them; but would try hour after hour to realize in my baby-mind the idea of past time without a beginning (that was always more awful and strange to me than the endless eternity), until I was half-mad with terror and bewilderment, and with a gasp, like a drowning man rising to the surface of the water, struggle back to my animal life again.

I don't think these terrors of childhood are things to be laughed at and despised; they are the first dawnings of the infinite mysteries of creation and life on the young soul.

As men grow older the vividness of their wondrous reality grows faint by their constant presence, but to the child they are new and terrible in their sublime immensity.

Every thing is so strange and vast that nothing seems tangible or comprehensible. Well I remember the awful agonies of prayer and despair that used to seize me—the desperate longing for some absolute and comforting revelation to believe and trust in implicitly.

Bang! splash! and a bucketful or so of cold saltwater souses me all over, and completely puts an end to my prosing reverie.

At last the day began to break, and as soon as it was light we got the other boats alongside, and served out their biscuits, brandy, and water. Such a pale, woe-begone set of wretches as we looked in the morning light I never saw. Fashionable young ladies after a heavy ball at the end of the season were nothing to it. I believe we would all have sold our birthrights for a cup of hot tea.

We found that we were literally on the reefs, the water being quite shallow, but it did not break anywhere as far as we could see; this accounted for the nasty short sea we had noticed all night.

Budd's Island lay about west by north of us; close to that were Holmes and Maury Island; while to the southwest we could dimly see the peaks of Lauthala and Kamia, for which we steered as soon as the sails were set. There was a fine fresh breeze aft of the beam, but, finding that we were rather dropping the dingy, we waited for her and helped her by a tow-line; when the fish-fag took the lead.

The little boat made capital weather of it, and the fish-fag did pretty well; but the life-boat was so heavily loaded that she could scarcely rise to the sea, and took it first over the weather-quarter and then over the lee-gunwale, in a most unpleasant style.

The doctor, who had had his spell at the oar, went fast asleep, in spite of the continual sluices of cold water, which were scarcely enough to keep me awake, as I was steering, though I had done no pulling in the night.

We passed right over the long chain of reefs, there being no actual break on them that we could see, but soon after got into a nasty tide-rip that we were very glad to get out of again, with the boats in such a trim.

In about five hours we had run pretty close to Kamai, and then, being assured of our position, we made all sail before the wind for the north point of Tavinni, whose great, heavy-clouded mountains began to grow distinct. There we managed to get something to eat and drink, and, though the chicken was strongly flavored by the various articles it was jammed against in the locker, and the biscuits were steamy and inhabited by cockroaches, we felt much more lively after it.

It was a pretty sight to see the three little boats bowling along together before the crisp, fresh breeze under their main-sails and square-sails.

No one but the steerer appeared to be awake in the fish-fag, and we were much in the same condition.

On reaching Tavinni we ran close along the shore, and to our surprise saw unmistakable traces of white inhabitants, but we determined, if possible, to get to Goat's Island before night, and didn't land.

The shore here was covered with splendid trees right up the steep slopes and gorges, with great masses of pendent creepers rising to and hanging from the very tops of them—a grand bit of hill-side.

In one of the bays was a small schooner standing off and on the shore, and, running toward her, we tried to speak with her; but apparently she did not like the white ensign that the life-boat carried, and made all sail away for the Somo Somo Straits.

On this the life-boat ran inshore toward a house that had a missionaryish look about it, while the other boats kept their course. But seeing nothing human fairer than mahogany, we stood out again in the track of our companions.

At last we rounded a point and were fairly in the strait. The wind here died quite away. Tired and "played out" as we were, we could not help being struck with the strange beauty of the scene. On one side the beautiful Tavinni, the garden of the Fijis, as it is well called, with its splendid vegetation stretching from the shore up the sides of its precipitous mountains and wild, dark gorges, mysteriously half-hidden in dense masses of cloud; before us a glassy sheet of water, calm and smooth, yet gloomy and dreary, only broken by the wooded rocks of the Little Goat Island, that seemed like a bubble on its surface; while on the other side the peaks of Vanna Levu rose one above the other till they were lost in the dim distance.

Soon we observed the other boats stop and wait for us, and on coming up they cried to us that they thought they saw a ship lying at anchor in the distance.

We looked, but were not certain, as it was a long way off, so we determined to pull for Goat's Island, try fairly with a telescope, and then make for the ship, if ship it was.

The masts and sails were stowed, a modest go of liquor served out to put a little life into us, and away we went.

The life-boat had forged some way ahead of the others, when it occurred to us to ask questions of our suspicious friend the schooner, that was lying becalmed not far off. As we drew up to her we perceived a lot of natives on board, but only one white man. We pulled under her stern, and asked, "What vessel is that lying at anchor?"

"The Duke of Edinburgh, bound for Levulara to-morrow" (spontaneous relief, joy, and excitement in all our countenances). "Do you belong to a man-of-war?" said he.

"No; a yacht, wrecked in the Ringgold Islands. Are you an Englishman?"

"No; I'm a Swede."

Whereon the doctor became inspired, and spoke to him in German. What a weight seemed taken off our minds!

When the dingy came up, we gave them the welcome news, and then the weary fish-fags.

Another sip of brandy, to give us a gallop for the land, for our troubles were nearly over. And then away we went, and a precious pull we had: the tide was against us strong, and the deep-laden boats seemed as heavy as lead to our weary muscles. When, at last, we got alongside, and found ourselves on the deck of the vessel, I could scarcely stand from cramp and fatigue. The passengers looked curiously over the bulwarks at the strange boat-procession, each laden with such an extraordinary cargo of nations. And well they might stare, for we certainly were not pretty to look at.

Our clothes had been dirty and drenched with salt and fresh water for nine days on end; our arms and faces were of the color of a boiled lobster, with the skin peeling off them—my nose, in particular, being literally raw—our eyes fearfully bloodshot, our lips cracked and bleeding—altogether, an imaginative man might have taken us for a gang of overworked firemen, from the infernal regions, coming up to get fresh air. However, they were all very obliging and kind, one old gentleman in particular, who provided us with blankets, etc., to sleep on.

The sun was just setting as we reached the vessel, and we soon sat down to a capital tea, with butter and real bread! My word!—as they say in the colonies. Oh, the pleasure I experienced that night in hearing the pouring rain, and knowing it could not get at me!

And so this unpleasant adventure came to a happy conclusion. It is nice to look back upon now, and if I were to rewrite this article I could make quite a romantic story of it, without much alteration or exaggeration. But I vowed a vow to use no *rouge* or pencils, and, with the exception of that dreary reverie in the boats, only admitted on the strength of its extreme prosiness, I have kept my oath.

I had another small turn at the shipwreck business about a month afterward—the steamer bound for Leonka to Auckland running into a coral-reef in Gavo Harbor. But it was a very kid-glovey kind of shipwreck, the vessel being got off in twenty-four hours without the smallest damage; indeed, its only redeeming feature was the extreme terror of a selfish, cantankerous old parson, who was so concerned for the safety of his soul, or, perhaps, its vile earthly tenement, that D—— had to be sent for to soothe and comfort him. He had been making himself obnoxious to many of us, and we gloated over his misery. I was even wicked enough to say, mysteriously and solemnly, to a friend in his hearing, "If we don't get off this tide, and a breeze should spring up, the vessel will break her back and sink suddenly, to a moral certainty." It was brutal, but I have no mercy on a cowardly parson; a selfish fear of death being a direct contradiction, in practice, to all his preaching.

I hate cowards, but, since I have learned what danger and discomfort really are, the ideal story-book hero has become my pet detestation.

It used to puzzle me why so many people, represented as villains of the deepest dye, were always trying vainly to knock him on the head, shoot him, stab him, poison him, or get rid of him somehow. I understand it now, and sympathize deeply with those villains; the fact is, he was simply unbearable to ordinary mortals. We were a good-natured, tolerant, peace-loving set of Christians on the whole; yet, I am certain that if we had had one of these danger-and-discomfort-loving heroes among our shipwrecked party we could not have borne him for more than three days. His perverse lunacy would by that time have become intolerable, and after a solemn meeting and deliberation we should have attempted to cut his throat. I say attempted, because we should never have succeeded in doing it; he would have made his escape on the back of an alligator, or something of that kind; or else, after successfully sticking him, and suffering agonies of remorse for five years, he would turn up again, and we would discover that we had not murdered him but some one else, who was our long-lost brother, second cousin twice removed; or, better still, the chief instigator of the dire attempt. You can't *kill* these people until they have married some equally uncomfortable heroine, when, I suppose, the spell becomes broken, and they finally die a natural death, surrounded by a rising generation of young idiots, like themselves. If it wasn't for this law, the breed could never be kept up.

If it should ever be the destiny of any reader of this work to be shipwrecked, let me advise him to do it in a dry climate, at a fine season of the year: wet weather adds to the misery of the thing a thousand-fold. Rain is a detestable invention, and it really makes me quite sad to think that, since the creation, no better way of fertilizing the earth has been found out and adopted. In the innocent days of childhood I used to fancy that it came from some tap in the sky which was turned on whenever the sun parched up the earth too much; this might seem an awkward and imperfect method, but it was at least comprehensible as regards its utility. But as I grew older I was obliged to discard my poetical ideas of angels with big watering-pots, being informed that rain came not originally from the sky but from the earth itself. Why on earth they can't leave the water where it is, instead of first sucking it up and then sluicing it all down again, it is difficult to conceive. Perhaps they use it to wash the cherubs with, or clean their teeth: they have got teeth, according to the pictures, though what they want them for I don't know, as they can't eat any thing with only a head and wings. But this is getting too glaring a copy of the style of St. Thomas Aquinas, who used to calculate the exact number of angels that could dance at once on the point of a needle, and debate seriously as to whether certain things existed and were used in heaven that are not ordinarily mentioned in the gilded saloons of duchesses. He was a saint and an early father, and so might write what he pleased; I am not a saint, nor even an early father, so I mustn't.

Metaphysical theology is to me much as Charles I. was to poor Mr. Dick in his memorial. If I had to write an article on ladies' chignons, clock-making, the Court of Chancery, or any thing you please, I am quite sure I should find myself analyzing the theory of the fall of man, or the foundation of belief in miracles, before I had got half through my paper.

I wrote my chapter on missionaries first, in the hope of working off this tendency for the time, but I find that my case is hopeless: I feel the fit coming on me strong at this moment, and lest I convict myself irretrievably I shall bring this story to a close.

Read this chapter carefully and dispassionately.

CHAPTER X.

MISSIONARIES.

Is Christianity the only true and useful religion in the world, without which none can be saved?

Is religion an end, and not merely a means to an end?

The majority of Christians would, I believe, answer these questions with a dogmatic and rather indignant affirmative; but there seems to be a small but steadily-increasing body of educated men who, if they do not at once deny such propositions, at least hesitate before giving their unqualified assent to them.

Is it not a bold thing to state that the religious belief of one portion only of humanity is a direct revelation of truths from God, while those of the rest of mankind are mere inventions of man, or of that humanly invented bogy the devil?

As I pass from one race or religion to another, from the Christian to the Moslem, from the Moslem to the Buddhist, and from the Buddhist to the Hindoo, and see each faith, contradictory or imperfect as it may be, doing more or less good to the morals or mental development of the people who hold it, I had almost said—I cannot help feeling a conviction—that each is a step in the Almighty's great plan of improvement leading to some great end, which as yet we can scarcely guess at; and that every religious system in the world is a ray of light more or less indistinct and imperfect from the same great luminary.

Such a doctrine might seem at first sight to tend to a dangerous quietism, checking or sneering down that enthusiasm of belief which has caused the most extended creeds of the world to spring up and spread with such marvellous quickness and vitality. But this is not the case if it is more profoundly examined, for it teaches us how, step by step, God has allowed His laws and ways to become revealed, however slowly, to the different human races; and it teaches, above all things, a belief in the continual progress, however gradual, of the mind of man. A religion or a nation comes forward, does its work, and dies of old age and inability to keep up with the onward march—a higher development of race being possibly necessary to appreciate a higher religion; another steps into its place, and the universe moves steadily on to that destination, known only to its great Leader and Creator. This kind of belief naturally inclines me to judge of a tree solely by the fruit it produces. If I were a believer in the doctrine that there was no salvation out of the pale of my own particular creed, I should be the first to worship, help, and encourage the man, who, humanly speaking, wastes his life, talents, energies, his own and other people's money, for the sake of making a few very doubtful Christians out of the same number of tolerably respectable Mohammedans or Hindoos. But, looking at the case from such a mental position as the one I have just sketched, I am naturally inclined to say that it is a pity and a mistake, much as I may admire the individual who gives up any thing for what he believes right.

Wherever I see old and evil customs, such as cannibalism, human sacrifice (though the idea of the latter lingers in the most respectable religion), or any such little weaknesses of ultra-savage life, suppressed by the incoming of a higher religion, I hold that it has done good (though there is good reason to believe that the mere intercourse with higher races would have abolished them without the necessity of any distinct *religious* teaching); but when, on the other hand, I see the general customs, morals, and character of the people, very little if at all altered for the better by their change of faith, I am inclined to look on it as a sheer waste of time, talent, and money, squandered on an attempt to teach people a religion that is utterly unsuited to their temperament and understanding — a tithe of which, expended at home, would have produced results of incalculable value. Some such idea as this seems to have been used by the Hindoos, to the slight botheration of the Baptists in India. One of the brethren complained piteously that the Hindoos do not think it right to "win souls." "According to their system, all religions are right, all are but so many different ways to one blissful end. Provided every one has faith in the religion of his own peculiar country and nation, he will be saved at last. Religion is a *national* thing all the world over; and for an Englishman to disown Christ, or for a Mohammedan to disown Mohammed, is, in either case, the most grievous sin a soul can commit."[1] The brother does not give his answer to this argument, which puts one in mind of the old rhyme:

> "Many a one
> Owes to his country his religion,
> And in another would as strongly grow,
> Had but his nurse or mother taught him so."

My personal acquaintance with individual missionaries is perhaps not very extensive, but the species is such a large and prominent feature in South-Sea society that it is impossible to help hearing a good deal about them, whether from their fellow-workers, traders, white residents, or natives. In a very short time one seems to know half the reverend gentlemen of the South Pacific by name, and to have a general sketch of each one's character and method of working.

The missionary, especially on the smaller and less-frequented islands, is a public character, or great chief, on whose character and policy depends, to a great degree, the success of the trader, be he beach-man[2] or merchant-skipper.

It is a disputed point whether the Roman Catholic or the Protestant missionary is the most powerful, not to say tyrannous over his dusky flock. It depends very much on the form and strength of the native government. If that be central and strong, I should think the Protestant would have the advantage if he

[1] Seventy-eighth Report, Baptist Mission, p. 51.
[2] Beach-man, or "beach-coomer," is a slang name for the white men who have settled down among the natives. They are generally ex-whalers, men-of-war's men, or merchant-sailors who have "run" their ships, and not unfrequently are to be found "gentlemen," who think it unadvisable to revisit civilized communities.

made himself useful to the reigning chief; in the other case, I should think the Papist would have what in these seas would be called the "pull." Their men are more highly educated and cultivated than the greater part of those sent out by the various Dissenting bodies. They are also more successful in keeping other religions at a distance, and by no means particular as to the means they use to gain their end, and which they carry out in blank opposition to all human rights as at present understood. Not that I have any reason to believe that the Wesleyans are much better at heart on that point—they only want the power, not the will. This, for want of that iniquitous and horrible power the priests gain over their flock through the confessional, they cannot get; though I believe that some sort of monthly catechising and ticket system answers somewhat the same purpose.

Whatever good the Wesleyans may do "spiritually," the mischief they work "commercially," whenever they have a chance, is beyond counting, and the common name of their missionary schooner, the Palm-Oil Trader, is, according to their own account, well deserved. If the Wesleyan Society had not published the facts themselves, I should have hesitated to state them. Can it be believed that out of the kindly credulous Tonga-Islanders, just struggling into civilization, and whose every dollar, hardly earned, should and would be spent on the improvement of their country, were it not for these canting sharks, they get "the noble and astonishing sum of £4,489 16s. 2d., which, with £1,550 received as class and oil money, makes a total of £6,000, being £3,500 above the current expenses of the mission for the year, to assist in sending the glorious Gospel of Christ to regions beyond!"[1] Beyond where? To those who know the generous, excitable natures of the South-Sea Islanders, this must be looked upon as sheer pillage.

However, as I don't want to be impertinent or to hurt any one's feelings, as Daniel O'Connell said when he called the Speaker an idiotic old fool, I must carefully distinguish mere hearsay information from that which I know from personal experience or have learned from the missionaries themselves.

I will begin by a bit, not of hearsay, but of printed and published information, which bears on my statement anent the Roman Catholics and the Wesleyans; and I am the more induced to do so, as the authority is of the highest, though the publication is not easily attainable:

Dr. Gräfe, an eminent naturalist, who thoroughly knows the Kanakas and their ways, tells us that the inhabitants of the beautiful island of Uvea have already had severe combats with the Tongans in order to maintain their independence. The last took place in 1832, when an army of Tongans, with their chief, sailed from Keppel's Island for Uvea, on board a whaler, under the pretence of spreading the Christian religion among the then heathen Uveans. This they proceeded to do somewhat after the good old fashion of "Olave the *Saint.*" They descended on the little island of Nukatea, which did not belong to them, and founded what they called a Christian colony, from which they were to extend their "privilege" to their neighbors. Not

[1] Wesleyan Methodist Missionary Report, April, 1870.

finding the *suaviter in modo* do much good, they tried the *fortiter in re*, by threatening an influential man called "Sohni" with destruction in this world if he declined any longer to insure himself from worse in the next, at their office. He, however, resisted [resolute in deed], and his people rose against the religious invaders. These had come provided with plenty of arguments in the shape of muskets and ammunition, and when the Uveans attacked them many were killed; this slaughter, however, only nerved the heathens to greater efforts, and, with nothing but spears and slings, they won the blockhouse on Nukatea, and put to death all they found there. So far so bad. Now comes the second part of the story. About twenty years ago the Uveans were "converted" by the French Catholic Marists, and thereupon conceived a vast dislike to the Protestant or Wesleyan religion, on account of the old attempt to convert them, and they expelled all the Protestant converts and the missionaries. King George of Tonga, upon whose island these suffering ones landed, was naturally anxious to get rid of them, not only for their sakes, but his own, and determined that they should be sent back, even with force of arms if necessary [gentle in].

"How far the Wesleyan missionaries in Tonga spirited up the king to this action is unknown; but it is worth observing that it is stated that the captain of an English man-of-war, the Brisk, which visited Uvea in 1867 (?), insisted on landing Wesleyan missionaries on a Roman Catholic island, and, to stop all remonstrance, pointed to the guns of H. M. S. as a part of his argument, which there was no gainsaying. If this be true (and it is published in Dr. Gräfe's "Reisen nach verschiedenen Inseln der Sud-See, 23 and 24 of ' Ausland,' 1868 "—*Gotta of Augsburg*), it is only another proof of the astounding liberties taken by sentimento-religious captains of men-of-war. Whims are always dangerous, be they religious or laical; but when a man backs his opinions with Queen Victoria's powder and shot, the thing becomes very serious. But it is of no use appealing to common or any other sense on this subject. Those who do these things are so encased in a rhinoceros-hide of self-conceit and self-laudation—believing that they and they only, are doing the " work of the Lord," that the ruin and misery they inflict pass them by as things of no import, and if at any moment some twinge of conscience hints to them that all is not quite right, half an hour on the sacred platform of Exeter Hall acts as an effectual anodyne, and soon stills the remembrances of the men they have ruined, and the nations they have insulted, to say nothing of the flag they have dragged in the mud in the prosecution of their own miserable little narrow-minded "beliefs." Of all the reckless mischief-makers in the world, commend me to a captain of a man-of-war attached to a "strong religious persuasion!" Would they were all knocked on the head like that worthy who received his quietus "introducing the gospel," with "the sword in one hand and the Bible in the other," as if her Majesty's navy was instituted for the propagation of "Dissenterdom!"

In order to prevent any confusion arising from the vague terms "Kanaka," or South-Sea Islander, which may be construed to mean either a hideous little squat Solomon-Island negro, or a great, perfectly-formed, yellow Marquesan, I will lay down a set of definitions which may serve to prevent mistakes, however erroneous they may be from a scientific stand-point:

1. Polynesians, inhabiting the Society, Sandwich, Marquesas, Low Archipelago (Pomotu!), Cook's, Hervey Islands, etc., etc.
2. The Western Polynesians, inhabiting the Navigation, Tongas, etc., who are slightly touched with black blood.
3. Lenmelanesians, such as the Fijians (N. Z. Maories?), etc.
4. Melanesians, i. e., the New-Caledonians, Solomon-Islanders, New-Hebrideans, etc., etc.

Thus, having cleared our way, let us go back to our missionaries. The greatest schools I have come across are the Roman Catholics (of various "denominations," if I may be permitted the word), the Wesleyans, the emissaries—mostly "Congregationalist"—of the London Missionary Society, and those of the Church of England. The "Baptists," for reasons of their own, which I do not pretend to fathom, do not "work" the South Seas, sticking more particularly to the East and West Indies; in which, particularly the former, their success seems hardly to be worth the money expended, except to their missionaries, in spite of their quotation of Sir J. P. Grant, which, read by the light of the unregenerate, is any thing but complimentary to them.

The Roman Catholic missionaries, of various denominations or sects, are widely scattered over the islands of the South Seas, more particularly in those wherein there has been some sort of civilization already effected by another mission, which is very notable in the disgraceful affair (more to England than France) of Tahiti. They play the part of jackal to the old English missionary lion, not leading him to his prey, but coming in to steal as much of the carcass as they can after the struggle is over, going noisily about with a few miserable bones in their mouths, to make all foolish animals believe that they killed the savage monster themselves. The success of any missionary efforts, so far as "religion" is concerned, is more than doubtful; but considering the early start of the Catholics in America (shall we say?), and its consequences, they have no right to crow over Protestants in the way they do. Moreover, they do not play fair. The other day some of theirs—all most honorable gentlemen—at Tahiti, distributed pictures among the natives, representing the Crucifixion, and informed them that the figures standing round and mocking the Saviour were Protestant missionaries of all the different sects represented in the South Seas! The natives only laughed at them; and the Protestants, with a good sense that was hardly to be expected, contemptuously declined to take any notice of such an attack. Apart from Tahiti, which the weakness of England permitted them to occupy, their principal and special fields of labor are —New Caledonia (where they don't labor at all); the Isle of Pines, where they labor a great deal too much, to the great annoyance of the government of the former island, the Marquesas, and the Gambier Islands. In the Marquesas, I was informed by Admiral Cloué, they had not made a single convert, had given up proselytizing as hopeless, and taken to cotton-planting, "for the good of the Church," of course. One missionary was found there so completely nativized as to have forgotten his own language. In the Isle of Pines the Roman Catholics carry on as brisk an oil-trade as the Wesleyans in Tonga.

In the Gambier Islands their work has certainly been very remarkable. They have converted the natives with a vengeance, and they bring them into the paths of virtue in a style which reminds one forcibly of Tom Hood's butcher, in the "Ode to Rae Wilson," "conciliating" a sheep to make it go in the one direction he wanted. They rule the natives with a rod of iron. They allow no woman to oil or decorate her hair, shut lots of them up in convents (shade of Captain Cook! imagine a Polynesian nun), and have in fact bullied them into such an unnatural state of virtue, that the unfortunate people, who certainly do not seem to have been created by Providence with an "ascetic" (? acetic or vinegary) tendency, have taken to make their escape in canoes, preferring the chance of being drowned and going to Hades, to having their souls saved by such very disagreeable processes. They are even reported, by the French, to have enlisted the dogs of the island in the cause of virtue, but the manner in which this is done would be difficult to describe in print. A stranger landing there is watched the whole time he is on shore, sent off forcibly if necessary to his ship at sunset, and on the slightest infringement of the missionary laws is imprisoned, and even flogged. This last they did to a Frenchman, who published a pamphlet at Tahiti, exposing the severity of this fatherly priestly rule. It was answered in the usual fashion by the Roman Catholic bishop. If any one wants to know

MISSIONARIES.

more of this extraordinary resuscitation of the sacerdotal tyranny of the middle ages in the Pacific, I cannot do better than advise him to get these two little books, and draw his own conclusions. One fact—if it be one —regarding the Roman Catholic missionaries all over the world, is worth mentioning—a fact which peculiarly regards the French missionaries. They are, if not from the beginning political, invariably followed by political movements. That most shameful Cochin-Chinese invasion (to say nothing of the equally shameful Tahitian one) was introduced by the French missionaries. And had it not been for the Franco-German War, France would have attacked China in defence of a class of men who set themselves against all settled authority.

Here I must make rather a lengthy digression about the Polynesian character, in order to air my views on this kind of treatment by whatever sect of missionaries it may be used.

He is brave, and, I have good reason to know, honest, generous, and good-natured to a fault, and possesses the most perfect manners I have met with in the world—natural, unostentatious, with an ever-present kindly tact, and quiet, generous consideration, that make it impossible to associate with Polynesian men or women without feeling and acknowledging that nearly every one, from the highest to the lowest, is a gentleman or a lady. There is no such thing as a native snob, east of the Navigator and Friendlies (Tongas), where, strange to say, the slight difference of race seems to produce a large quantity of most intolerable specimens of the great snob family (a Tongan, in par-

ticular, being almost as insufferable and conceited a
cad as a Jamaica negro). Yet these most charming
and delightful people, who in many ways come nearer
the early Christian ideal of what men and women
should be than any race in the world, have not the
smallest idea of chastity whatever.

This fact presents at first glance a curious puzzle to
a man accustomed only to civilized races. He naturally associates the idea of unchastity with degradation
of character, and such qualities as courage, gentleness,
courtesy, and honesty, with at least a tolerably high
standard of female virtue. He must remember that
"with the law came sin." Among civilized people
want of chastity is a sin, a fall, a degradation, bringing with it a shame and a depravity of character that
tends to destroy or annul whatever other virtues the
sinner may possess. But where there is no pain or
shame connected with unchastity or illegitimacy, there
is no fall and no degradation, and therefore little or no
injury to the other good points of the natural character.

The great question to be considered is, whether
"sin" is a term to apply equally to the same action all
over the world, or whether it is something relative to
surrounding circumstances.

There are, I believe, two great schools of philosophers: one, that declares ability or necessity to be the
source of all virtue; and another, that holds to a
moral sense or original instinct of right and wrong in
the mind of man. Is it not possible that both are
partly right?—that our earliest ancestors had little or
no natural instinct of virtue; but that, finding certain

things necessary for the good of themselves and the community, they gradually developed certain social or religious laws to enforce them; which laws, carried through many generations, gradually caused an instinct or moral sense to arise on the subject of right and wrong? In much the same way as the original dogs who were trained to point game have transmitted the accomplishment as an instinct to their successors. Possibly in some such way what we call conscience would spring up, rude and imperfect enough in its birth, but developing and improving, as it does I believe to this day, with the march of civilization and advancement.

Do we not see different stages and developments of the moral sense in nearly all the races in the world, and is it not possible to trace the effects of natural circumstances and positions in the different ideas of the quality of virtue that they hold?

Supposing this theory of the origin of what we call sin, conscience, or right and wrong, had any foundation in truth, the character of the Polynesian is easy to understand. He has plenty of food, and no regular work is required to preserve life. Except when an occasional pinch comes, half a dozen mouths more or less make no very serious tax on the family purse. Moreover, his life is essentially a lazy one, partly from his natural disposition, and partly from the peculiar circumstances in which he is placed; he has no strong incentive to grow rich, and no profession or special occupation on which to concentrate his energies. In his case certainly it would seem that natural circumstances do not force him to develop a moral sense on the subject of chastity. If you tell him, "You shall do no murder," or, "You shall not steal," his sense of right and wrong makes him agree instinctively with the justice of the commandment; but when you tell him that unchastity is a sin, he asks, "Why? it amuses me, and hurts nobody!" There is no sense of degradation or sin on either side, and he follows it as he would any other appetite.

We should always remember, in meddling with native customs, that many of them, though almost repulsive to us, are of very great value in relation to the physical well-being of the native. Many of our most ordinary domestic habits are looked upon by the Fijian with far greater horror than I think we have a right to express against the almost necessary custom of polygamy. No one howls against the customs of the chosen people in the Old Testament.

Among civilized people, of course, unchastity is a sin, and a most grave one, because, from the very fact of their advanced civilization, and the laws which it has produced, it brings sorrow and misery, and, being a sin, degrades and vitiates to a greater or less degree the whole natures of those who are concerned in it.

Upon such grounds I venture to find fault with the tyrannical and terrifying mode of spiritual government when applied to these people by any sect. Many men use it, I am afraid (possibly unconsciously), from that intense love of power which is so often the failing of the priestly mind. Others, simply because they believe that what is a deadly sin in one state of society must necessarily be a deadly one in another, and that without exception such things are followed by eternal damnation. I do not hesitate to say that, if I believed what they do, I should act in the same way, and should not hesitate to make the poor Polynesians miserable in this life if I was sure that I was saving them from eternal misery in the next; but I do not, and I take the liberty to question the right of any set of men to tyrannize over others because their opinions do not agree —more particularly in the smaller affairs of dress and similar matters.

It is common enough to hear the persecutors of the middle ages, men who ruthlessly condemned hundreds of fellow-creatures to death, spoken of as brutal and extraordinary monsters; but we should remember that it was their creed which made them what they were, and curse the creed rather than its simple believer. If I had lived in those days, and been a good churchman, steadfastly believing that the Almighty and Omniscient God would devote to a horrible and eternal punishment beings that He had created because they did not believe in the doctrines preached by a particular set of men; and, moreover, if I had been brought up on the unnatural and detestable system of celibacy, my reason would have told me (however much my *feelings* may have revolted against it) that to extirpate heresy in the most awe-inspiring manner, was but a common duty to humanity. The doctrine of exclusive salvation still remains among a large proportion of Christians, but the hearts of most of them are better than their heads, and they acknowledge instinctively that persecution is a wicked thing, without troubling themselves to see how far it is warranted by the dogmas they profess to hold. Whether the "religious," particularly the "professional religious," would not roast each other to-morrow were it not for a lay police, is another matter. I rather think they would—joyfully!

If these races can be taught to appreciate the superior beauty of Christianity for its own sake, a nobler purpose for a man to devote his life to, can scarcely be conceived; if not, are the enormous sums taken from the relief of our terrible home necessities, wisely expended? and are the "missionaries" to be looked upon as working in their proper sphere?

I have never come in contact, personally, with any members of the Wesleyan mission, and therefore I am bound to state that any thing I may say about them must be taken *cum grano salis*. I have *heard* a great deal about them from white residents—from the white residents in Samoa and the Fijis, and the evidence on the whole is decidedly unfavorable. I have *heard* them described as ignorant, fanatical, and extremely inimical to all white men but themselves; but this last is not a peculiarity of their sect, and is neither an uncommon nor unnatural feeling among the island missionaries generally. The missionary of one island (not a Wesleyan) proposed to the king some years ago to pass a law expelling every white man from his dominions. "Very well," said the king, "but you must go too"—which was a sell for the missionary.

The cause of this dislike between the missionary and the "white man" is simple enough. The beachman or white trader is in a great many cases of a class with which the missionary can hardly be "hail fellow, well met" with, or of a moral character which it would be possible for him to countenance if he wished to improve that of the people. The beach-man is announced as "that missionary feller, givin' himself such high and mighty airs," while the richer trader turns up his nose at him as idle, luxurious, and useless. The most degraded runaway sailor can pay off his grudge by sneering down the preacher among his parishioners, or at least by setting them an example of how little a white man cares for his pastors and masters. And I have no doubt but that the missionary does give himself airs occasionally, and it is rather hard lines for the unfortunate beach-man, to be treated *de haut en bas* by a man originally intended for a small grocer in a country town. The fact is, that, although there are plenty of clever, liberal-minded, and tolerably well-educated men among them, there are not usually many of what the lower classes call gentlemen "born and bred," and the aforesaid lower classes are as quick as any one at finding out the fact. But there are exceptions to the rule, as at Raiatea in the Society Islands, where the Congregationalist minister, Mr. Vivian, spoke well of the whole men on the island, and they with great respect of him. The Wesleyans, as I said before, are not much liked in the Fijis. And the native teachers, who come trooping through Lavaka of a morning, with clean white shirts and mighty Bibles under their arms, still less so. It is curious to notice how many of these men have acquired the expression of the lowest and most fanatical class of missionary, the real priest-look, which by no means enhances their originally very doubtful beauty. I heard a story of a well-known and influential Fijian planter and merchant who was continually bothered by a lot of these gentlemen, who used to come and steal his yams (there is no legal method of doing any thing in Fiji, and I suppose this was their way of collecting tithes or church-rates). Not being anxious to quarrel personally with the mission, he went for a constitutional, and dropped a hint to his Solomon-Island laborers that if they *did* happen to find any one stealing yams they might break his or their heads, and no questions asked. The "native preachers" *did* come, but it was for the last time!

I had the misfortune once to find myself on board a vessel that ran into a coral-reef in Euva Harbor, in the Fijis. It was of the greatest importance to get her off at the first high tide, before any wind or sea arose; but one of these dusky missionaries actually dissuaded his native flock from assisting to do it, because it was Sunday. Dear me, in Fiji or in Scotland I thought to myself that, if I found that ass in a pit, I shouldn't care to help him out even on a week-day.

As I have already said, the Wesleyans seem to be rather inclined to force Christianity on natives generally, whether they will or not. Mr. Baker, who was eaten in the Fijis, and whose death must have been an immense advantage to the society (how many martyrs can it furnish?) met with his fate through sheer fanatical obstinacy. In spite of the remonstrances of the native chiefs, he insisted in penetrating into "tapud" ground for the purpose of spreading his doctrines among the "Devils," as the inhabitants of the sea-coast politely designate those dwelling in the interior; but he would go, and not even alone, but attended by "native assistants." Good-natured "Devils" came and warned him that, if he would not let them alone, they should be obliged to knock him on the head; and, after that, by way of utilizing him, eat him.

But he would not listen to them, and so they did eat him; and one of those who partook of him, told an acquaintance of mine, in Fiji, that he was very good— better than usual; for there is an idea among cannibals in these seas that white men "eat" abominably salt, which fancy probably arises from the fact that they usually get hold of well "marinated" salt-junk eating sailors. Now, this is very dreadful; but suppose I trespassed on "tapud" lands in England, should I not be—not "devoured" actually—but very smartly dealt with? And should I go to the Church of the "Virgen del Pilar" at Saragossa, and cast that well-petticoated doll to the ground, should I not be certain to be as full of knives in five minutes as Mr. Rogers's shop?—and would any English paper, except possibly the *Record*, deny that it served me perfectly right? This murder, or whatever you like to call it, was not done on "religious" grounds. The "Devils" have a well-founded belief that the presence of a white missionary is too often followed by loss of land, either to the white settlers, or to the chiefs who protect them on the coast; and so they do their best to hold their own. They have not learned the wisdom of the Japanese, who have, or had, a French priest insulting their religion in every possible way, in order to gain admission into the noble army of martyrs. "No," quoth the wise Japanese; "suppose we cut your head off, plenty too much French man-of-war come;" and so he will have to go to heaven by the ordinary route.

While the Wesleyans range principally over the

Friendly, Samoa, Fijis, and some Melanesian groups, the London Missionary Society extends its wings over the Society Islands, Cook's group, Loyalty Island, Samoa, etc. And certainly it has the very *crême de la crême* of missionary position in that part of the world. It is true that the climate of many of the islands is very enervating, particularly for European women, and the children should be sent to another climate, say New Zealand, between the ages of six and twelve; but these are no greater hardships than those suffered willingly in India for one-half the comfort and position possessed by the missionary, and the question of "self-sacrifice" is reduced to a minimum. From what I have seen and have been told, the London Society seems to be of a very liberal nature. It seems to care more for "results" than for doctrines, and sends out its emissaries with a free permission to teach almost any form of Christianity best suited to themselves or their natives. This very "easiness" tends to keep men of very extreme or narrow ideas out of their ranks, and is one great reason why they get on so much better than most other sects. The Society seems to launch its young missionaries much like a puppy that is chucked into the water to teach it to swim. It takes the young gentleman (figuratively) by the slack of his reverend breeches, and pitches him all alone into an island, saying unto him something of this kind: "Learn the language, get up a school, improve the people how you best can; teach them any form of Christianity that is likely to suit them; keep clear of native politics. God bless you!" They say that they learn the language and people quicker this way than if they were apprenticed to an older hand. Occasionally, however, they are found to be quite useless, and have to be sent home again. Mr. Saville, the minister at Huahine, told me that, on his second Sunday, he was able to preach his first sermon in the native language.

I think that all the missionaries of this Society that I met with were "Congregationalists," and, though of course there are exceptions, they struck me as being wonderfully good, intelligent, liberal, practical men; not wilfully blinding their eyes to any imperfection in the success of their labors, or fanatically trying to force the natives all at once into their own groove, but patiently trying to make them peaceful and happy, and to instil into their minds a sense of the nobility and beauty of Christian morality, rather than any abstract and disputed dogmas.

"The young missionaries," said one of them to me, "have a new work to do. The old ones who first introduced Christianity captivated the minds of the natives by their superior accomplishments. 'These men,' cried they, 'can build ships without outriggers, make leaves speak' (write), 'and many other wonderful things; let us believe all they tell us, and we shall be able to do the same.' But after this first rush, there comes a reaction when they find that they do not gain all the advantages they expected; and we young missionaries will have to try and plant a *real* religious feeling in their hearts."

One of the best aids the Protestant missionary has is his wife, whose example of fidelity and real affection must do more good than fifty sermons. In this he has an enormous advantage over the Roman Catholic priest,

whose example is simply ridiculous in the eyes of his
flock, if even they believe his celibacy is as real as he
wishes it to be understood, which I take the liberty of
doubting most exceedingly. I am not sure that marriage is positively required by the London Society, but
it is encouraged at least, for I never knew or heard of a
member of this mission who had not a European "help-
mate"—and invariably one most worthy of that honest
old English term. I must not mention names, or I
would gladly publish that of a "kindly Scottess" who,
with rare good sense, abolished, as far as she could, all
the detestable European "go-to-meeting" dresses worn
by the women, and induced them, yea, even by example, to return to the modest, peaceful, and most becoming muslin "sacque"—the prettiest dress, when its
wearer rightly understands its mysteries, that a pretty
woman can wear. Talking of marriage, in some of the
islands the native chiefs have kept to themselves unlimited power of divorce, which is good for themselves
but bad for their subjects, as it becomes a mere matter of dollars, and makes the marriage-tie a decidedly
loose one. One missionary told me that when a couple
came to be married, he always said to the ardent
bridegroom, "By-the-by, where's your other wife?
what has become of her?" or to the woman, "What
have you done with your late husband?" He only
asked on spec., but he said that it generally turned out
that they had stray partners, either divorced or "somewhere about." At the same island I knew a man who
was pointed out to me by the minister as an exempla-
ry character, rather a pillar of the church than otherwise. He had run through seven helps-*meet* for him,

and was about to go in for the eighth. He must have had rather a curious experience; but, as Touchstone says, " O sweet Audrey," etc., etc.

I cannot help admiring these missionaries for the honesty with which they disdain to conceal such little weaknesses in Polynesian Christianity, and the large-minded, practical way in which they refrain from fanatical declamations against what to the natives is but a natural mode of life, and which, in their hearts, they regard much as Lieutenant Lismayhago's Indians did, in that memorable attempt at conversion narrated in "Humphrey Clinker." I am myself by no means sure, though I scarcely expect that any of them would agree with me in this, that this easiness of divorce is not without its virtues in the present state of the Polynesian character, for it acts as a safety-valve to their almost incorrigible immorality; it is not much, it is true, but it is something more than they ever had before.

They begin their amourettes as soon as Nature permits them, and, like their cousins in New Zealand, sin, unreproved by their elders. Chastity is, in fact, unknown eastward of Samoa, where a chief's daughter, when heavily "tabooed," is supposed to be virtuous, until she is found to be otherwise. In one island I visited, the power of divorce, as well as that of marriage, was in the hands of the missionary. He was a young man, just arrived, and unable to speak the language; and the repeated applications for legal separations were perpetually placing him in fresh dilemmas. If he granted their requests, he felt that he was weakening the marriage-tie; if he did not, the injured and

disappointed applicants would go and break the seventh
commandment all over the parish. Some of the missionaries
have told me that they think the general immorality
of the people arises from their habit of sleeping
all in one room, and that any other race would be
just as bad under the same circumstances. I am inclined
to think that there may be some truth in this,
at least as far as the immoral precociousness of the
boys and girls are concerned; but, on the other hand,
the Irish, who "pig" together literally, are remarkable
for their "personal" chastity. Also, some missionaries
regard these common sleeping-rooms as rather
good things than otherwise, as acquiring publicity and
close relationship among the sleepers.

But, in fact, this question of personal chastity cannot
for certain be referred entirely either to the religion
or the domestic habits of a race. One of the greatest
causes of South-Sea immorality is, I believe, the universal
system of "adoption," or of "birth-parents,"
and "feeding-parents," the origin of which I have been
unable to find out. A very large proportion of Polynesian
children have nothing to do with their real
parents from the time they are weaned, being taken
care of and brought up by some one else, who often bespeaks
them even before they are born! Such a system
must necessarily tend to weaken one of the
strongest ties of matrimonial affection.

The Society Islands were never disgraced by cannibalism;
but their old religion was a very bloody
one, and had something very ghastly about its method
of performing human sacrifices. I have stood on the
old "marais," a long, rampart-like place, formed of

two rows of great upright slabs, filled in with smaller stones and coral, so as to form a kind of oblong stage or platform, and felt a strong shudder as I thought on all the terrible stories they could tell. What made it more fearful was the fact that the victim was always a member of certain families set apart for that purpose for generation after generation: how this caste originated I do not know. Many of them used to put to sea secretly in canoes, preferring the almost certainty of drowning to the horrible fate which was always hanging over their heads.

A man would come to the priests and demand some heavenly or rather infernal favor; and they occasionally, from whim, superstition, or malice, would tell him that the god required a human sacrifice, and, naming the victim, would present the supplicant with the deadly "death-stone" as a warrant. This he hid somewhere about him, and, collecting some companions, sought out the doomed wretch. At last, perhaps, they found him sitting with his family under a tree or mending his canoe, and, gathering around him, would start a conversation in the most indifferent and peaceful manner. Presently comes a pause; a hand is opened, and the death-stone discovered: a short, furious struggle, and the wretched victim is overpowered and led away to the merciless priest. In some cases the victims have succeeded in escaping from their captors and have fled to the mountains, where they have lived and died undiscovered. Who can say that the men who have changed such things for a mild though lax form of Christianity have not done some good?

I am afraid that the South-Sea natives are apt to

live two lives—a church and a natural one—and naturally the missionary reports the church one. I was much struck with this in one island, where I attended divine service, and saw all the chief ladies of the land dressed out to the nines, taking notes of the sermon with big pencils on foolscap paper, and looking as if butter would not melt in their pretty lips. I gazed sadly on them, thinking what much better fun I should have had if I had visited the island fifty years sooner; but I was comforted the next day when I saw the identical saintly creatures madly executing the most improper gambados, all as wild, savage, and amorous as they were in the days of Captain Cook.

But I must not tell tales out of school; and, after all, might not the same story be told of some much nearer home? I once travelled on a steamboat with a young lady, who used to lay in a tremendous stock of piety every morning at prayers, worked it off gradually all through the day, and at about 11 p. m. ran short of it altogether on the "fo'castle;" she always laid in a fresh stock next morning, so I suppose the balance was about even.

The natives, to use one of their pastor's own words, "won't let the missionaries know too much!" They keep their orange-rum drinkings, with the attendant highly-improper dancings, and the other little diversions that accompany them, tolerably private. At one island, not long ago, a native drum was introduced from "abroad;" and, at the very first finger-taps, the little children of ten and twelve years old began instantly to dance the very naughty dances which were supposed to have been extinct for thirty years, showing clearly that there was a very efficient *maître de danse* somewhere *in petto*. — → in reserve.

I hardly like to say that the older missionaries were guilty of deliberate lies when they reported that all the old native superstitions, lascivious dances, and other improper excitements, were entirely suppressed and forgotten: the wish was father to the thought, both in them and those they reported to. But such exaggerations, whoever started them, have placed the new generation of missionaries in a very awkward and painful position. As we said before, when the young missionary comes out, and honestly reports the real state of the case, they either entirely disbelieve him at home, or tell him that it is his own fault.

I heard from another missionary much the same story which I have already recorded. "The old missionary, who was looked on as a kind of god by the natives, because he was surrounded by the superior inventions and appliances of civilization, which they had never seen before, and could scarcely understand, could alter, or at least keep down, any thing he disapproved of." Now that the reaction has come, and the natives have discovered that the priest is only a man, and a person not more ingenious and wonderful in invention than a layman, but rather the contrary, the missionary has lost most of his power, and is puzzled how to act. In fact, the native wants to improve his body, which he cares a great deal about, and the missionary to save his soul, which he cares nothing about, even if he believes he has one. The missionary sees clearly enough that the old root-and-branch method will scare more birds than he can catch, and at the best is of very temporary advantage; but, if he honestly declares in favor of a liberal, gradual, moral influence and example, he is apt to fall into disgrace with—not only the "hellfire" fanatics at home, but, still worse, with those who make decent earnings out of the "mission platform." Every man is willing to pick holes in his coat from one side or another. If he goes on the old principle, every white man on the island is ready to cry out about his tyranny over the natives; if on the new and more liberal one, they sneer at him for living a comfortable life (which he most certainly does), and doing little or nothing to earn it, not to speak of the abuse he gets from the Exeter Hall-ites, for not supplying them with sufficient "flap-doodle." If some of them get disheartened by such a hopeless state of things, and let things slide, who can wonder at it?

The crude truth is, that nine-tenths of foreign missions are not got up for the benefit of the heathen abroad, but for the good of the sect at home.

I only know one island of the London Society where the minister has both the power and the will to keep up the old puritanical tyranny over the luckless natives subject to him—subject to him by what right, except that of blatant impudence?

This worthy allows no tobacco to be used on the island, regulates the dress, habits, and manners of his parishioners after his own sour-headed fancies; and on one occasion, when he had been away for a short time, and the women had taken the opportunity to buy some pretty prints, he preached a furious sermon against them the first Sunday after his return, and made the women destroy them all before him. It is perhaps needless to say that these gay and godless garments were purchased from a worthless whaler, and not from the store sanctified by the spirit of Wesley.

This kind of extraordinary missionary power, though it may make the people very good as long as it lasts, can only exist in spots which are but little frequented, and, when it is undermined by intercourse with the outer world, it leaves few good effects of a permanent duration. The more isolated and unfrequented the island, the greater the power of the missionary; and when there are no more unfrequented islands, we shall have no more missionaries of the old ruling type—they will be improved off the face of the earth, like their flocks. The so-called demoralization of the Polynesian by the white trader, really means the demoralization of the missionary, and nothing more.

No amount of intercourse with white men could possibly make the Kanaka less virtuous than he was before—on the contrary, he has learned a new virtue —honesty, because he found out that it paid: as for disease, they had worse than we introduced before we found them; and the diseases we introduced are infinitely milder than they are among ourselves. The only real mischief they have received is from the change of clothing, the forbidding of bathing, and the substitution of orange-rum (thanks to the missionaries) instead of the wholesome kava.

The people who do the most mischief to missionary labor are the missionaries themselves. When one sect intrudes upon the field of another, the improvement of the native character comes to an immediate stand-still, as in the case of the Maories. The temptation to run down each other's faith, works, and power to the natives is usually too strong for the priestly mind to resist. Tahiti, Samoa, and New Zealand (though in the latter place there were other causes), testify to this melancholy truth. Birds of a feather may flock together, but when they do they usually fight over the carcass. In one island two different sects of so-called Christians did actually levy war on each other, but I believe such a case is not quite unknown in Europe.

These meetings of different sects on the same ground should be avoided by mutual consent, if the conversion or improvement of the natives is the great object to be obtained; and, in the matter of some islands, an agreement took place, if I remember right, between the London Mission and the Wesleyans. Of course, the missionaries who belong to that most dogmatic and conceited of religions, Roman Catholicism, will agree to no such compromise; and I will back half a dozen enthusiastic Jesuits or Marists, going the round of Polynesia, to do more to demoralize the people, and to shake what small hold Christianity has upon them, than five hundred of the most dissolute sailors.

If you want real mischief done, place your cause in the hands of a few "earnest" and "well-meaning" men.

The London Mission has certainly had great success. At the Society, Cook's Island, etc., the islanders are, for the most part, nominal Christians, and, although their sexual morality be very lax, their honesty, bravery, and general good feeling, would compare very favorably with many European races. They are lazy—but why should they not be? They are very well off with-

out working, and wise enough to be contented. When
one mixes with such generous, kind-hearted people,
gentle without cowardice—gentle, but not fearful,
courteous without humbug—it is difficult to imagine
that so few years ago they could have been disgraced—
some by human sacrifice, others by actual cannibalism;
and remarks how infinitely the virtue of common honesty has progressed since Cook's time, let us pay all
honor to the missionaries, if they have wrought the
change. But when any one who knows any thing about
the real nature and morals of the Polynesians, hears a
report of them at a missionary meeting at home, he
very naturally puts the resident missionaries down as
a set of lying, or at least disingenuous humbugs.
When he hears, for instance, how, in twenty years, the
saving grace of Christ has descended on the souls of the
heathen of Raritonga—how dutifully they attend the
churches and schools—how decently they dress—how
they have entirely given up all their heathen customs,
and lascivious dances—and a like quantity of half
truths, he feels inclined to insult the first missionary
he meets. But the fault lies chiefly with the people at
home, who snub the young resident teachers whenever
they expose the opposite side of the picture, and oblige
them to hold their tongues altogether, or to cook their
accounts as prettily as they can. They have only to
confine themselves to the meeting-going side of the native character—to omit all about the systematic orange-
rum meetings, with their accompanying orgies, and the
incorrigible immorality and laziness—and to dilate
upon the wonderful good temper, generosity, kindness,
and bravery of the race (natural characteristics little

influenced by the change of religion, if the early voyagers are to be believed)—to make as pretty a report as need be.

To put it coarsely, the homo parsons must have a good strong bait to catch their gold-fish with. If they were to state, as they might do with truth, that three women out of four, from the island queen downward, had not the smallest notion of chastity, shame, or common decency; that the people were in the constant habit of going off in groups of fifty or sixty for the purpose of drinking themselves mad on orange-rum, and committing the most fearful bestialities; that their old lascivious dances were as well known as ever, and that five-minutes' excitement turned church-members into frantic savages—there might be a slight falling-off in the subscriptions. It is not fair to show only one-half of the picture, though it may be very convenient occasionally. Of course, in some cases a little actual lying is required to make things sound nice, but I have only been referring to the better specimens of Polynesian Christianity. It seems somewhat strange, at first sight, that the work of "conversion" should succeed so rapidly and effectually in some places, and should fail so completely in others, where the races are nearly identical. One great reason for this is, the varying form of government. In places like the Society Islands, where there were hereditary kings and queens, with nearly absolute power, the missionaries who then, as I said, could easily acquire great influence, had only to convert him or her, and steadily use that influence, to gain over the great mass of the people, who naturally followed their leader.

In an essentially republican country like New Zealand there was no such short cut to success; the people being subdivided into numerous tribes, and absolute kingly power being, except in war-time, nearly unknown. There was, in fact, no government strong enough to draw up a code in a copy-book, and fine its subjects smartly for their peccadilloes, as in the Fijis, for instance, where I have seen the luckless savage squeezed of his last dollar, the "native missionary" assisting in the operation with a sharky grin which would have done honor to a Jesuit at a death-bedside.

Christianity in New Zealand has also met with that hopeless death-blow, the contact of different sects of missionaries, which invariably inspires the sharp Maori with a distrust of all of them.

But the most important reason of the utter collapse of the "faith" among the Maories lies in the peculiarly low and practical view they take of all religion. Like many of the Old Testament Jews, the Maori of thirty years ago looked on the divine power as a mere convenient aid to the great end of whacking his enemies. Where the white men appeared he naturally argued, from their superiority in murderous weapons, that their religion was "stronger" than his own, so he turned Christian. When he found out his mistake, and saw that the heathen could fight nearly as well as a Christian, and that in spite of his Christianity he was gradually going to the wall, he said, "Bother Christianity!" and used the leaves of his New Testament for cartridges; and invented a most blood-thirsty and abominable religion out of the *old* one—a book which, by its combination of the beautiful moral laws of

Christianity with the sanguinary superstitions of Judaism, with its degraded, limited, and human idea of the Creator, has been and will be the undoing of many an earnest Christian.

This new form of Judaism, Hau-Hau-ism, is not unlike the Taeping religion in China, and took its origin in the same way—the missionary determination to force very old wine into very new bottles. The Maori, moreover, in spite of his Christianity, seems to possess all the vices of both the western and eastern Polynesians without any of their virtues, except their bravery. He is as idle, immoral, and useless as a Tahitian, without his perfect manners, unselfish generosity, and general kindliness. As snobbish, untruthful, and avaricious as a Tongan, without his constructive and inventive power, he is a savage to the backbone, liking fighting better than any other occupation, and living a much better life when he is fighting than at any other time. In fact, I believe that Christianity is slipping off the Maories like water off a duck's back, in spite of the assertion in high quarters that New Zealand presents the most marvellous proof of the success of missionary work that the world has ever seen. The reports of the different men, employed to represent the real state of things to the New-Zealand Government, are almost unanimous in declaring that Christianity is fast losing its hold on the people; and a Maori missionary stated, in a public lecture given at Otago in 1870, that he found a wide-spread hatred of the Gospel, with which the natives associate the many evils which afflict them, and which threaten their extinction. I have myself seen in a native church, raised at no small cost, an immense heap of Maori bibles, prayer-books, and hymn-books, piled in the centre, crowned by two or three human skulls as a sign of desecration.

A traveller in the South Seas is often puzzled to define what "civilization" really consists in. It is difficult for him to avoid looking upon the courteous Society-Islander, with his refined but natural manner, as a civilized man; but when he meets the Fijian, who is superior to him in constructive and inventive power, and has a far higher notion of female fidelity, he acknowledges instinctively that the man is a savage, and that the still more ingenious and subtle Tongan is a most absurdly vain and insufferable barbarian snob. "Tongans first," say they, "then white men, and then all the rest of the world!" They hold that Wellington and Napoleon the First were both Tongans, having drifted away in canoes to Europe. If a white man laughs at this, they say, "They were great men, weren't they?" "Certainly." "Then they *must* have been Tongans! How stupid you are!"

The other day the Tonga Parliament held a debate on the question of annexing the Fijis. One member made a grand speech, in which he said: "Tonga is a great power: so was the Roman Empire; but she extended her conquests too far, and so fell. Let us beware lest the same fate should befall Tonga!"

They were much disappointed that Prince Alfred did not visit them; but their absurd conceit would hardly let them own it. They said the queen would not let him come, because the Tongese ladies were so notoriously beautiful that he would be sure to marry one of them. And they also wished that if her Majesty did intend sending a son to visit King George she would send the Prince of Wales, not a mere royal duke. On the declaration of war between France and Germany, King George expressed his intention of preserving a strict neutrality.

I am inclined to think that the custom of making native parsons ought to be very restricted, though no doubt but that there are many good and useful men among them. Those in Fiji have a very bad name; and, though Raritonga, a cannibal island, was certainly first converted by brown preachers (I remember making the acquaintance of the old lady who pluckily protected them on their first arrival), they rather marred the beauty of their work by intriguing with the wives of the principal chiefs. In New Zealand they are looked on with little favor. One bright and shining light went to England to be made a fuss over and shown at meetings: he employed his leisure hours in learning how to make gunpowder to shoot white colonists with; but I am happy to say that he blew himself up on his return to New Zealand while prosecuting his scientific researches.

I was at first rather puzzled to understand why the Roman Catholic missionaries gained ground so slowly in Tahiti, when they have so many advantages over the others, and the hold of any missionaries over the natives is only skin-deep, and requires much "wheedling" to exist at all. Their faith, at first sight, seems to be so much better suited to the easy-going, festival-loving, demonstrative Society-Islander, than the simple, quiet form of the London Mission. One reason is, because they hate every thing French, and like every thing English. Another reason is, that a Society-Islander has a very strong sense of humor; and, though he is demonstrative, is seldom inclined to exaggeration in general behavior. I have more than once heard them sneer and make fun of Frenchmen and Spaniards, "for talking plenty too much with their fingers." The secret of the Kanaka's wonderful good manners is his real extreme *good-nature;* not in that unnatural affectation of it which so often makes the civility of an Italian, Frenchman, Spaniard, or Hindoo, so repulsive to English feelings. This simplicity, combined with his sense of humor, inclines him to the belief that any hocus-pocus, or affectation in dress or manner, particularly in religion, is out of place, and to be despised.

Of the English missionaries in Melanesia I know very little. I understand that they have met with but little success among the mass of the people, who are mostly of a savage and ferocious disposition. Bishop Pattison has gradually collected about a hundred boys, whom he is educating at Norfolk Island, to serve as Christian teachers. Whether these boys will keep up, and spread their Christianity on their return home, remains to be proved. In New Caledonia and the Isle of Pines, the missionaries were mostly Roman Catholics, and were by no means popular either with the French officials or the settlers; the first declaring that they supplied the natives with arms and ammunition, and the second declaring that they "tapud" the pigs and cocoa-nut oil for their own benefit. This "tapu" is performed by cutting a cross on the stem of a tree; and the sailor-boy, who acted as my boatman in those parts, invariably chose a tree marked with this sign to steal cocoa-nuts from; and if they proved bad, he solemnly cursed the tree, saying that "the parsons had tried blessing it, and that didn't seem no good, so he'd try t'other tack."

And now I must bring this article to a close. I have tried to give an impartial account of all that I have seen and heard concerning South-Sea missionaries, and I have refrained from telling more than one anecdote against them, for fear it might be an invention or an exaggeration; but if I have trod unnecessarily on anybody's toes, I beg most sincerely to apologize.

NOTE.

The Maori notion of prayer reaches no higher than the thing we call an incantation. One day I was talking to an old Pakeha-Maori (i. e., a white man who lives among the Maories) on the subject of missionary labor. At last he said: "I'll tell you a story that will establish your name forever at Exeter Hall, only you mustn't tell it quite the same way that I do. I was here at the time when both the Protestant and Roman Catholic missionaries were first beginning to make their way in the country; and the Maories of my tribe used to come to me and ask me which had the greatest 'mana' (i. e., fortune, prestige, power, strength)—the Protestant God or the Romanist one. I was always a good Churchman, and used to tell them that the Protestant God could lick the other into fits. There was an old Irish sailor about five miles from me who used to back up the Roman Catholic God, but I had a long start of him, and moreover *was the best fighting-man* of the two, which went a long way. In a short time I had about two hundred of the most muscular, blood-thirsty, hard-fighting Protestants you could wish to see.

"Well, it so happened that one day we had a little difference with some of our neighbors, and were drawn up on one side of a gully all ready to charge. I liked the fun of fighting in those days, and was rigged out in nothing but a cartridge-box and belt, with a plume of feathers in my hair, and a young woman to carry my ammunition for me; moreover, I had been put in command of the desperate young bloods of the tribe, and burned to distinguish myself, feeling the commander of the old Guard at Waterloo quite an insignificant person in regard to myself in point of responsibility and honor.

"Lying down in the fern, we waited impatiently for the signal to charge; had not we, on the last occasion worth speaking of, outrun our elders, and been nearly decimated in consequence? 'Shall it not be different now? See! there is the great war-chief, the commander of the "Taua" coming this way!' (he was a real 'toa' of the old stamp, too seldom found among the degenerate Maories of the present day). Little cared he for the new faith that had sprung up in the last generation; his skill with the spear, and the incantations of his 'Tohungas' (i. e., priests or magicians) had kept him safe through many a bitter tussle; his 'mana' was great. Straight to me he came and addressed me thus: 'Look here, young fellow! I've done the incantations and made it all square with my God; but you say that you've got a God stronger than mine, and a lot of our young fellows go with you: there's nothing like having two Gods on our side, so you fellows do the proper business with him, and then we'll fight.' Could any thing have been more practical and business-like than this? But I was quite stuck up; for though I could have repeated a prayer from the liturgy myself, my worthy converts, who philosophically and rightly looked upon religion merely as a means to an end (i. e., killing the greatest possible quantity of enemies), were unable to produce a line of Scripture among them.

"There was an awkward pause—our commander was

furious. Suddenly one discovers that he has a hymn-book in his pocket. General exultation! 'Now!' cries the old chief, foaming at the mouth with excitement, 'go down upon your knees (I know that's the custom with your God), and repeat the charm after him. Mind you don't make a mistake, now, for if one word is wrong, the whole thing will be turned topsy-turvy and we shall be thrashed!'

"And then, having repeated one hymn word for word on our knees, I and my converts charged, and walked into the Amorites no end; but whether it was the hymn or the fighting that did it is of course an open question to this day."

THE END.

www.ingramcontent.com/pod-product-compliance
Lightning Source LLC
Chambersburg PA
CBHW032048230426
43672CB00009B/1522